The American History Series

SERIES EDITORS
John Hope Franklin, *Duke University*
Abraham S. Eisenstadt, *Brooklyn College*

Arthur S. Link
Princeton University
GENERAL EDITOR FOR HISTORY

Philip Weeks
KENT STATE UNIVERSITY

Farewell, My Nation

The American Indian and the United States 1820–1890

HARLAN DAVIDSON, INC.
ARLINGTON HEIGHTS, ILLINOIS 60004

Library of Congress Cataloging-in-Publication Data

Weeks, Philip.
    Farewell, my nation.

    (American history series)
    Includes bibliographical references.
       1. Indians of North America—Government relations.
2. Indians of North America—History—18th century.
3. Indians of North America—Removal. I. Title.
II. Series: American history series (Arlington Heights, Ill.)
E93.W39   1990   973'.0497   89-25793
ISBN 0-88295-860-7

Cover design: Roger Eggers. Cover photo: Three Blackfoot (or Piegan Chiefs)—Four Horns, Small Leggings, and Mountain Chief—on the upland prairies of Montana. Courtesy National Anthropological Archives, Smithsonian Institution.

Manufactured in the United States of America
93 92 91 90 89 EB 1 2 3 4 5

FOREWORD

Every generation writes its own history, for the reason that it sees the past in the foreshortened perspective of its own experience. This has certainly been true of the writing of American history. The practical aim of our historiography is to offer us a more certain sense of where we are going by helping us understand the road we took in getting where we are. If the substance and nature of our historical writing is changing, it is precisely because our own generation is redefining its direction, much as the generation that preceded us redefined theirs. We are seeking a newer direction, because we are facing new problems, changing our values and premises, and shaping new institutions to meet new needs. Thus, the vitality of the present inspires the vitality of our writing about our past. Today's scholars are hard at work reconsidering every major field of our history: its politics, diplomacy, economy, society, mores, values, sexuality, and status, ethnic, and race relations. No less significantly, our scholars are using newer modes of investigation to probe the ever-expanding domain of the American past.

Our aim, in this American History Series, is to offer the reader a survey of what scholars are saying about the central themes and issues of American history. To present these themes and issues, we have invited scholars who have made notable contributions to the respective fields in which they are writing.

Each volume offers the reader a sufficient factual and narrative account for perceiving the larger dimensions of its particular subject. Addressing their respective themes, our authors have undertaken, moreover, to present the conclusions derived by the principal writers on these themes. Beyond that, the authors present their own conclusions about those aspects of their respective subjects that have been matters of difference and controversy. In effect, they have written not only about where the subject stands in today's historiography but also about where they stand on their subject. Each volume closes with an extensive critical essay on the writings of the major authorities on its particular theme.

The books in this series are designed for use in both basic and advanced courses in American history. Such a series has a particular utility in times such as these, when the traditional format of our American history courses is being altered to accommodate a greater diversity of texts and reading materials. The series offers a number of distinct advantages. It extends and deepens the dimensions of course work in American history. In proceeding beyond the confines of the traditional textbook, it makes clear that the study of our past is, more than the student might otherwise infer, at once complex, sophisticated, and profound. It presents American history as a subject of continuing vitality and fresh investigation. The work of experts in their respective fields, it opens up to the student the rich findings of historical inquiry. It invites the student to join, in major fields of research, the many groups of scholars who are pondering anew the central themes and problems of our past. It challenges the student to participate actively in exploring American history and to collaborate in the creative and rigorous adventure of seeking out its wider reaches.

John Hope Franklin
Abraham S. Eisenstadt

CONTENTS

VIII   CONTENTS

MAPS

ACKNOWLEDGMENTS

Among the persons who lent assistance while I worked on this project, I am especially grateful to these scholars who perused this work in draft and generously shared their ideas and expertise with me: David Wallace Adams, Donald J. Berthrong, Blue Clark, Donald L. Fixico, the late Arrell Morgan Gibson, Park Dixon Goist, Michael Grossberg, William T. Hagan, Morrell Heald, and George W. Knepper.

Likewise, it is a pleasure to acknowledge the following individuals associated with Harlan Davidson, Inc. for various considerations: John Hope Franklin, a thoughtful, sympathetic, and encouraging mentor, who with Abraham S. Eisenstadt invited me to contribute a volume to the American History Series; Arthur S. Link who first suggested this project to me over breakfast in a hotel restaurant in Akron, Ohio; and vice-president and editor-in-chief Maureen Hewitt for her many efforts on behalf of my work.

I owe a special debt of thanks to my parents Dick and Helen Weeks, whose examples taught me from a young age the joy of learning and inquiry. I am pleased to have this space to express deepest gratitude to Jeanette Weeks, my wife and my best friend, for countless contributions she has made to my life, including generous assistance as a fastidious "in house" editor. And, I would be greatly remiss if I failed to acknowledge our son Michael, the source of his mother's and my greatest joy. His gentle insistence that his father join him at baseball, basketball, or in his favorite pastimes, rather than working continuously (so it must have seemed to him) on this project, served as an important reminder of what in life truly creates the greatest happiness. For the host of treasured memories you have provided, I am forever grateful Michael.

Philip Weeks

Dedicated with deepest affection and appreciation
to Jeanette and Michael Weeks,
Maxine C. Wright,
Dick and Helen Weeks,
And Shannon: "Blithe spirit and simple trust; . . .
Strong in Life, bravest at Death's door."

The sun rose dim on us in the morning, and at night it sunk in a dark cloud, and looked like a ball of fire. That was the last sun that shone on Black Hawk. His heart is dead, and no longer beats quick in his bosom. He is now a prisoner to the white men; they will do with him as they wish. . . . Farewell, my nation! Black Hawk tried to save you, and avenge your wrongs. . . . He can do no more. He is near his end. His sun is setting, and he will rise no more.

BLACK HAWK, SAC AND FOX

CHAPTER ONE

The United States Turns to a Policy of Separation

Dead Dreams

They could now get on with the task of burying the dead. For the previous three days, the last three of the old year, a ferocious winter storm had pummelled the upper plains. By the morning of New Year's Day, 1891, the blizzard had blown itself out and the sun began to break through the grey clouds. As the sky cleared, a train of wagons accompanied by individuals on horseback set out from Pine Ridge agency, situated near the southwestern corner of the Sioux's Pine Ridge reservation in South Dakota. The party's destination was the valley of Wounded Knee Creek some twenty miles to the east. There, Sioux and troops of the U.S. Seventh Cavalry had battled on December 29, 1890, leaving twenty-five soldiers dead, thirty-nine wounded, and hundreds of Sioux either killed or severely wounded.

The Sioux who fell at Wounded Knee were followers of the Paiute mystic Wovoka, whose message combining Indian mysticism and Christian millennialism had found a substantial following among western tribes in the late 1880s. All Indians, Wovoka preached, must adopt a pacific life-style. They must put violence behind them and purge themselves of enmity toward the whites. If they obeyed, Wovoka reported, God promised to return the earth to the Indians—the living as well as the dead—and give them back the buffalo.* In short, the nearly four-century Euro-American epoch in the New World would end as the meek inherited the earth. To hasten that day and the return of the dead, Indians must learn a special dance and perform it regularly. The more often it was danced, the sooner God would vanquish the whites and return the earth to the Indians. Whites called it the Ghost Dance because of its promise to awaken the dead.

Kindled by despair and privation in the aftermath of the Plains Wars, Wovoka's doctrine spread quickly throughout the system of western reservations in the late 1880s, where it was accepted with great rejoicing by the hungering tribes. Fervidly many Indians performed the Ghost Dance, believing that God would soon destroy the whites and return the world to the Indians. What warfare had failed to accomplish, faith would. In March 1890, eleven messengers brought word of Wovoka and his joyful, wondrous tidings to the Sioux at their five South Dakota reservations. They were impressed sufficiently to convene a council and select representatives to journey to the mystic's home to evaluate and learn his teachings. After a week's stay with Wovoka in Mason Valley, Nevada, the delegation returned, trained in the beliefs and movements of the Ghost Dance. The Sioux eagerly accepted Wovoka's revelations as divine inspiration, and many on the Sioux reservations converted to the new faith. Overnight their abject depression changed to overpowering expectation.

---

*the American bison, commonly referred to as *buffalo*.

The dance went on throughout the fall of 1890. The Sioux prepared themselves for the return of the buffalo, their dead friends and relatives, their former lands, their old way of life, and for the vanquishing of the white man. Their problems seemed small in the face of their people's imminent rebirth. As Wovoka's message spread among the Sioux, however, it dramatically altered, deviating greatly from the original doctrine. The time-honored cultural values of a warrior people were superimposed upon Wovoka's vision of peace and harmony. Christ-like meekness was replaced by strident activism. The Sioux transformed the Ghost Dance from an instrument of regeneration into a symbol of resistance and insurgency. Dancers soon wore special Ghost Dance shirts, which, they believed, could miraculously repel an enemy's bullet.

Alarmed by the mounting frenzy among the Sioux, federal authorities ordered the Ghost Dance halted. Most Sioux acquiesced. A few hundred refused and tried to flee to the Dakota Badlands. They were intercepted by troops of the Seventh Cavalry and taken as prisoners to the small settlement of Wounded Knee. On the morning following their capture, the soldiers moved to disarm the Sioux. A shaman, reminding them of the protection offered by their Ghost Dance shirts, harangued the men to resist. One pulled a rifle from under his blanket and fired into the massed soldiers. The Seventh Cavalry responded with a volley of rifle, pistol, and artillery fire. The Sioux and the soldiers then clashed in hand-to-hand combat. Women and children, terrified and hysterical, fled to escape the melee. Many of them became casualties. Later that day a blizzard swept over the Dakotas, freezing the bodies of the Sioux into the positions of their violent deaths. The task of burial was delayed three days until the storm passed.

Among the seventy-five Sioux departing Pine Ridge on New Year's Day, 1891, were thirty local whites. Their leader, Paddy Starr, had secured a contract from the army to bury the dead Indians at two dollars a body. The men anticipated this task would earn them a sizeable sum. At least 150 Sioux, lying dead on the battlefield since December 29, would need interment. Another one hundred corpses could be found scattered about the surrounding countryside. A contingent of soldiers accompanied the group to provide protection. The Sioux, led by Dr. Charles A. Eastman, a Santee Sioux and the agency's physician, journeyed toward the battlefield in a state of great emotional agitation, hoping to discover which of their relatives did not survive the confrontation.

They reached their destination shortly past noon. Robert M. Utley, in *The Last Days of the Sioux*, the most satisfying account of this affair, described the ghastly scene that riveted the attention of all in the party, as they looked in stunned silence upon the Wounded Knee battlefield: "Strips of shredded canvas and piles of splintered lodgepoles littered the campsite, together with wrecked wagons and twisted pots, kettles, and domestic utensils. Here and there the skeletons of a tepee rose starkly from the wreckage, bits of charred canvas clinging to the poles. Snow-covered mounds cluttered the ground from one end of the camp to the other; beneath them lay the shattered bodies of the victims of the battle. Other mounds dotted the floor and sides of a deep ravine along the edge of the campsite; and beyond ... the mounds lay thick and numerous. ... Each mound hid a human form, torn by shrapnel and carbine bullets, caked with blood, frozen hard in the contortions of violent death. They were of all ages and both sexes. The storm of shot and shell had spared none."

Yet, incredibly, a handful of people had survived the melee. Dr. Eastman searched frantically among the bodies, looking for signs of life, while all around him the pitiful wails of the Sioux he had accompanied split the cold winter air. "It took all of my nerve to keep my composure in the face of this spectacle," he remembered, "and of the excitement and grief of my Indian companions." To his horror, he found many of the dead women with their shawls pulled up over their faces, as if this last act might somehow shield them from the soldiers who stood above them with weapons raised. Amidst the piles of people frozen into hideous postures, Eastman discovered a four-month-old girl, wounded twice by soldiers' bullets, but alive. Lying next to her dead mother, still bundled tenderly in a shawl and wearing a cap embroidered in beadwork with a flag of the United States, the infant had miraculously survived her wounds, the blizzard, and three days of freezing temperatures. The searchers rescued two more children, a little girl and a little boy, as well as five adults.* The survivors were placed aboard wagons and removed to Pine Ridge agency.

The doctor recalled the anguish of that day in his autobiography, *From Deep Woods to Civilization*: "All of this was a severe ordeal for one who had so lately put all his faith in the Christian love and lofty ideals of the white man."

The white workers likewise combed the macabre, snow-covered mounds, collecting the bodies of the dead Sioux from whom they stripped clothing and other items for souvenirs. After being gathered into a huge pile, the corpses were cast without ceremony into a mass grave dug on a hill overlooking the battlefield. Four days earlier, artillery pieces raked the Sioux from this hill. "It was a thing to melt the heart of a man, if it was of stone," remembered one observer of the burial scene, "to see those little children, with their bodies shot to pieces, thrown naked into the pit." Before dirt was shoveled atop the bodies, the workers posed around the grave for a group photograph, apparently collecting another memento of the occasion.

Wounded Knee was the last battle between the Indians and the United States Army, although no one knew it at the time. War Department annual reports throughout the 1890s indicated that the military anticipated other outbreaks of trouble. The full significance of Wounded Knee emerged in time: It was the conclusion of a struggle that had embroiled the United States since its inception over one hundred years ear-

---

* All three children were later adopted. The baby wrapped in the shawl found a home with Brigadier General L.W. Colby, who renamed her Marguerite Colby. Some Siouan women preferred to call her Ikicize-Wanti-Cinca, that is, "Child of the Battlefield." The other two orphans likewise found foster homes. The little girl was taken in by Captain George Sword, head of the Pine Ridge Indian Police; the little boy by Lucy Arnold, a local schoolteacher.

lier, and, before that, the European imperial powers for almost three hundred years. It epitomized two overriding realities of the Indian-white experience: the recalcitrance of many Indians to accept the unalterable reality of white hegemony over the continent, much less their own lives and destinies; and the long-standing incapacity of federal Indian policy to define a workable and mutually acceptable solution to what whites commonly called the "Indian question." And finally, it has become an historical allegory that is, at the same time, artificial and accurate. For many, Wounded Knee symbolizes the passing of "Indian America," although most tribes had experienced their own "Wounded Knee," their own culminating episode, years, decades, or centuries before. "I shall not be there. I shall rise and pass. Bury my heart at Wounded Knee," wrote Stephen Vincent Benét in his poem "American Names," providing an appellation for those who viewed Wounded Knee as a microcosm of Indian history in the post-Columbian period, characterized by victimization and cultural imperialism, futile resistance and absolute defeat. This theme gained a wide popular audience with Dee Brown's 1971 best seller whose title, *Bury My Heart At Wounded Knee*, drew from Benét. Black Elk, an Oglala Sioux holy man who witnessed that confrontation, recognized that something more than the lives of 250 Sioux ended in that remote South Dakota valley. In *Black Elk Speaks*, he offered an epitaph to the larger struggle, whose roots stretched back to earliest European colonial settlement and concluded at Wounded Knee:

I did not know then how much was ended. When I look back now from this high hill of my old age, I can still see the butchered women and children lying heaped and scattered all along the crooked gulch as plain as when I saw them with eyes still young. And I can see that something else died there in the bloody mud, and was buried in the blizzard. A people's dream died there. It was a beautiful dream. . . . The nation's hoop is broken and scattered. There is no center any longer and the sacred tree is dead.

The Need for a Solution

The expansion of the American population westward during the first century of the national experience was breathtaking in its celerity and scope. Surging outward from the Atlantic seaboard and across the Appalachian chain, Americans moved with intense and unyielding determination to acquire and settle a vast western domain: first east of the Mississippi, then west of the Mississippi. By 1850, the United States had realized its Manifest Destiny. The nation stretched from the Atlantic to the Pacific—"from sea to shining sea," as Americans heralded jubilantly. Many dreamed of adding Canada, more of Mexico, and various Caribbean islands, such as Cuba, to the growing republic.

Each year Americans filled in the frontier until finally, in the late nineteenth century, the superintendent of the census for the United States declared that the frontier had ceased to exist. A Census Bureau bulletin, "Distribution of Population According to Density: 1890," concluded: "Up to and including 1880 the country had a frontier of settlement, but at present the unsettled area has been so broken into by isolated bodies of settlement that there can hardly be said to be a frontier line." In a twist of irony, the announcement came in the same year as the battle at Wounded Knee.

This staggering migration of people, acquisition of territory, and settlement of the frontier was one of the greatest forces shaping the nation's history. In 1893, three years after the superintendent of the census's pronouncement, a young historian named Frederick Jackson Turner presented a paper in Chicago before the convention of the American Historical Association entitled "The Significance of the Frontier in American History." The paper and its thesis established the reputation of Turner, who became one of the most respected scholars of his generation. A good selection of Turner's work and ideas may be found in *Frontier and Section: Selected Essays of Frederick Jackson Turner*. The settlement of the frontier also proved to be the foremost source of a near constant state of friction and hostility between the United States government, its citizens, and the Indians. The vast locales acquired and settled by Americans were home to various native groups, and they did not long forbear the newcomers who moved with such resolve to displace them, regulate them, and occupy their patrimony. In the face of this aggressive thrust westward, the pattern most representative of United States–Indian relations was set early. It was subject to the ebb and flow of events and to differing views of policy, but through it ran a strain of unremitting determination to dislodge the inhabitants of the western lands. Government might from time to time relent. Americans wanting land never did.

The Indians' resistance to westward expansion and the response of Americans combined to produce periods of desperate violence. Throughout these years, the United States followed three fundamental goals: one, promoting westward expansion and settlement; two, protecting its citizens and their business ventures; and three, guaranteeing Indians' property and treaty rights. The goals, however, were inherently in conflict. Faced with intense and unyielding pressure to support and defend Americans, their interests, and their aspirations, officials found it impossible to pursue the goals simultaneously and impartially. The Indians were marked as the eventual losers. In 1879, a Wyoming newspaper reflected upon this eventual outcome. "The same inscrutable Arbiter that decreed the downfall of Rome, has pronounced the doom of extinction upon the red men of America. To attempt to defer this result by mawkish sentimentalism . . . is unworthy of the age."

The rapidly shrinking frontier and the interracial tension and conflict caused by expansion meant that the United States could not temporize with the Indian question. From the birth of the republic, one central, overriding question was forced upon the managers of the nation's westward expansion and the architects of federal Indian policy: What should be done with the Indians? Most whites considered them a serious and dangerous impediment to the republic's territorial, cultural, and economic aspirations. "For a hundred years the United States has been wrestling with the 'Indian question,' " noted Commissioner of Indian Affairs John Quincy Smith in 1876 at the conclusion of the Plains Wars. Many answers to this question were advanced, both in and out of government. Some suggested creating a geographic boundary, much as the British had done in 1763 when they designated a permanent frontier line along the Appalachians, so that Indians might maintain their accustomed way of life free from white encroachment. Others suggested that acculturation and assimilation of the Indians into the dominant society was the wisest course; although, as Brian W. Dippie suggested in *The Vanishing American*, "This gift of civilization—the ultimate gift, to the whites' way of thinking . . . always seemed to please the donor more than the recipient." And sufficient numbers of Americans, such as Montana Territorial Governor James M. Ashley, applauded extermination. "The Indian race on this continent has never been anything but an unmitigated curse to civilization," Ashley suggested in a letter he published in a national newspaper in 1870, "while the intercourse between the Indian and the white man has been only evil [and will remain so] until the last savage is translated to that celestial hunting ground for which they all believe themselves so well fitted, and to which every settler on our frontier wishes them individually and collectively a safe and speedy transit."

Suggestions, prudent and foolish, mean-spirited and generous, were offered in abundance because most Americans acknowledged that a solution to the Indian question was needed desperately. Generations of federal officials struggled to fashion a lasting one, even though the permanent resolution they sought remained elusive. Reflecting the exasperation this produced in generations of Americans, General William T. Sherman remarked to General John M. Schofield, "The whole Indian question is in such a snarl, that I am utterly powerless to help you by order or advice." This question of what means could solve the Indian question, and the ensuing search for an answer, shaped, reshaped, and to this day continues to affect the relationship of the federal government with Indians. The search, advancement, application, and abandonment of a series of "solutions" aimed at solving the Indian question permanently is at the heart of understanding the relationship between the United States and the Indians.

Possibly no time period affords the student of United States–Indian relations a better vantage point for observing the complexities of this relationship, especially the government's search for the final solution to the Indian question, than the nineteenth century. Three principal solutions characterized this century. The first, the *policy of Separation*, was the answer of the 1830s to the Indian question: eastern tribes would be forcibly colonized beyond a line separating them from areas of expected white settlement. Following implementation, the Indian presence on lands east of the Mississippi River was drastically curtailed, which opened this area for exclusive use by the American population. This solution was not, however, the panacea Americans expected and predicted it to be.

The second solution, the *policy of Concentration*, emerged after massive American migration and territorial expansion in the trans-Mississippi West during the 1840s destroyed the rationale upon which the policy of Separation was based. The government's new solution to the Indian question called for the drastic reduction of Indian landholdings in the West and the compulsory relocation of tribes to federal reservations where permanent residency, under strict governmental, judicial, and cultural control, would be enforced. Indian resistance to this policy, and Washington's commitment to it, resulted in the titanic struggle of the 1860s and 1870s, known as the Plains Wars.

The *policy of Americanization* was the third solution advanced in the nineteenth century. With its tandem programs of land reform and education, it was the government's answer to the Indian question, following the Plains Wars and the reality of the military subjugation of the Indians. This policy, implemented by President Rutherford B. Hayes and his Interior Secretary Carl Schurz, although not translated into effective reform within the terms of office of these men, became the policy of the federal government until the 1930s, when John Collier, Franklin D. Roosevelt's Indian Commissioner, judged this policy a failure and sought another solution to the Indian question: the *policy of Self-determination*.

The search for a solution to the Indian question forms an organic whole transcending the history of United States–Indian relations. The republic was little more than a half-century old when the United States government settled upon the first solution, but the question of how to define it stretched back to the first days of the national experience.

Gradualists and Removalists

The nascent government of the United States hoped to avoid warfare with tribes and provide for the orderly westward expansion of the nation by the wise management of Indian affairs. Congress, because of plenary power over treaty making and the regulation of commerce granted it under Article 1, Section 8, of the new Constitution, exercised sweeping control over Indian matters. It did so by two procedures: one, by ratifying formal treaties with Indians to nullify their title to land, a practice established by England and the other European imperial powers and followed by the United States, which recognized tribes as sovereign nations holding title to land by right of occupancy; and two, by legislation, in particular a series of Trade and Intercourse Acts passed between 1790 and 1834. These laws, delineated in Francis Paul Prucha's *American Indian Policy in the Formative Years: The Indian Trade and Intercourse Act, 1790–1834*, regulated white settlement on Indian land, controlled white trade in liquor with tribes, provided a detailed definition of Indian country, managed the sale of Indian land, and established a network of government-operated trading houses known as factories. The goals of this legislation were to gain the confidence and loyalty of tribes on the frontier, control them economically, and decrease sources of conflict so as to promote harmonious relations between them and American settlers as the nation expanded westward. The government also planned to develop a program that would work to the mutual benefit of the Indian and white races. As early as 1776 the Continental Congress had approved a resolution that concluded that "a friendly commerce between the people of the United Colonies and the Indians, and the propagation of the gospel, and the cultivation of the civil arts among the latter, may produce many and inestimable advantages to both." While Americans agreed that a positive program was necessary and advantageous, they disagreed over its content. Almost from the birth of the republic, two groups emerged with different opinions of the proper course of federal policy to achieve peace with Indians. Ultimately the fate of eastern tribes was shaped by the battle between these groups to dominate the national government, as each sought to influence the policy toward Indians. One group is referred to as "the Gradualists"; the other, "the Removalists."

The Gradualists advocated peaceful coexistence between the whites and Indians until a steady assimilation of Indians into the dominant society occurred, especially through missionary work, education, and reordering Indian land usage. Their program called for a total transformation of Indian society in the absolute confidence that the transfiguration would in all ways be superior to the life-style that had preceded it. This group stressed the absolute necessity for nonagriculturalist Indians to change their subsistence pattern from hunting, which required extensive territory and periodic migration, to farming, which would require much smaller tracts of land and encourage a sedentary life-style. "Excess" land could then be acquired peacefully by whites. As Thomas Jefferson explained: "While they are learning to do better on less land, our increasing numbers will be calling for more land, and thus a coincidence of interests will be produced between those who have land to spare, and want other necessaries, and those who have such necessaries to spare, and want land." When conversion into farmers was joined with changes brought about by educational and missionary efforts, Indians would possess the economic, cultural, and religious wherewithal to be acceptable and productive neighbors for the white settlers about them. But first, Indians must abandon their native culture, the tribal order, and their belief in communal ownership of property. "They cannot much longer exist in the exercise of their savage rights and customs," declared William H. Crawford, James Madison's secretary of war. "They must become civilized, or they will finally ... become extinct."

The Gradualists foresaw no unsolvable problems with those Indians unwilling to alter or abandon either nonagricultural subsistence patterns or their accustomed life-style. They suggested to critics that the steady movement of the American agricultural frontier toward the Mississippi would deplete the wild game that these Indians depended upon for survival. When they could not find sufficient food, they would be compelled to move out of the settlers' way. The Gradualists confidently expected their program to achieve two critical objectives: It would civilize and assimilate a sizeable number of Indians, while facilitating peaceful relations between them and white settlers on the frontier as the westward movement proceeded.

Thomas Jefferson, as well as the other presidents of the "Virginia Dynasty," offered unswerving support for the Gradualists' program. Jefferson, in his annual messages to Congress, offered vigorous praise and support for those measures that would advance "the arts of civilization" among Indians. He reiterated this view in messages to the Indians. The president stated to the Miamis, Weas, and Potawatomies on January 7, 1802: "We shall with great pleasure see your people become disposed to cultivate the earth, to raise herds of useful animals and to spin and weave, for their food and clothing. These resources are certain, they will never disappoint you, while those of hunting may fail, and expose your women and children to the miseries of hunger and cold. We will with pleasure furnish you with implements for the most necessary arts, and with persons who may instruct how to make and use them."

Yet if Indians refused the opportunities provided by white society to civilize themselves, Jefferson would demand that they be evicted. "This then is the season for driving them off," he wrote, whose "ferocious barbarities justifies extermination."

The Removalists argued the other side of the issue. They, too, sought peaceful relations between Americans and Indians, but they were never sufficiently persuaded that the plan advanced by the Gradualists held much likelihood of success. "There seems to be a deep rooted superstition ... that the Indians are really *destined*, as if there were some fatality in the case, never to be christionized, but gradually to decay till they become totally extinct," one missionary surmised. The Removalists contended that most Indians were little interested in being "civilized." Perhaps the actual problem, they speculated, really was not one of disinclination, but of incapacity.

Most Americans, concluded George W. Manypenny, who held the post of commissioner of Indian Affairs from 1853–1857, regarded Indians as "irreclaimable, terrible" savages. The scientific community validated this belief. "Do what we will," emphasized Dr. Josiah C. Nott, one of the South's leading surgeons, "the Indian remains the Indian still. He is not a creature susceptible of civilization. ... He can no more be civilized than the leopard can change his spots. ... He is now gradually disappearing, to give place to a higher order of beings." Nott reiterated this conclusion in *Types of Mankind*, which he co-authored with George R. Gliddon, an expert on ancient Egypt: "It is as clear as the sun at noon-day, that in a few generations more the last of these Red men will be numbered with the dead. ... It is in vain to talk of civilizing them. You might as well attempt to change the nature of the buffalo." Dr. Charles Caldwell, a University of Pennsylvania medical professor, an influential lecturer and author, a leading phrenologist, and founder of a medical school in Kentucky, concluded the same. After examining a variety of Indian skulls, he analyzed that "when the wolf, the buffalo and the panther shall have been completely domesticated, like the dog, the cow, and the household cat, then, and not before, may we expect to see the full-blooded Indian civilized, like the white man."

To accept this line of reasoning required one to reject the Gradualists' program. Indians, incapable of being civilized, were doomed to extinction and therefore any effort to civilize them must prove futile. This judgment was not malicious, only common sense. It also led to another matter of contention: Did uncivilized and uncivilizable people enjoy any inherent right to the land they occupied? Most Americans thought not. For example, the noted author Hugh Henry Brackenridge, arguing in his article "The Animals, Vulgarly called Indians" that tribes had no right to the soil, asserted that it was as ridiculous to "admit a right in the buffalo to grant lands" as it would be to bestow the same right on "the Big Cat, the Big Dog, or any of the ragged wretches that are called chiefs and sachems." Brackenridge concluded his argument with a question: "What would you think if going to a big lick or place where the beasts collect to lick saline nitrous earth and water, and addressing yourself to a great buffalo to grant you land?" The answer, he expected confidently, was obvious to all discerning people.

The Removalists, unlike the Gradualists, also concluded that the unrelenting westward thrust of white settlement would occur too rapidly to permit peaceful coexistence on the frontier for any satisfactory length of time, or for that matter, perhaps for any time at all. It was common knowledge—to settlers, to frontier politicians, and to officials in the federal Indian office in Washington—that taking too much tribal land at one time led inexorably to warfare. To avoid further bloodshed and depravations of the frontier and, equally as important, to throw open more Indian land for white settlement and enterprise, the Removalists offered their own solution: Indians must exchange their lands east of the Mississippi for territory in the West. If some tribes proved recalcitrant, as might be anticipated, they suggested forced removal as an appropriate option for government. This solution, too, was not maliciousness, only common sense. They judged removal as a benevolent, not a malevolent, course—one predicated on the assumption that Indians would remain "savages," perpetuating their accustomed way of life. Removal therefore was the best way of assuring peaceful relations between Americans and Indians. But what if Indians resisted removal? Some Americans took a hard line. Congressman David Levy of Florida contended that Indians were "demons, not men. They have the human form, but nothing of the human heart. . . . Horror and detestation should follow the thought of them. If they cannot be emigrated, they should be exterminated."

Toward a Policy of Separation

Forces stimulating American expansion were never long dormant, and during the early nineteenth century the frontier pushed relentlessly beyond the Appalachian chain into Indian country. It pressed deeper into the Old Northwest with the collapse of significant Indian resistance under the leadership of Tecumseh and his brother Tenskwatawa, the "Shawnee Prophet." It spread across the Old Southwest, especially with the rapid expansion of the Cotton Belt. By 1820 settlers had pushed as far west as the valley of the Mississippi River. The census of that year indicated that almost one-fourth of the American people lived in the trans-Appalachian West, and there was no hint that the human flow would diminish.

This activity fanned interracial conflict and, for a growing number of Americans, solidified the conviction that gradualism could not solve the Indian question. For the first two decades of the nineteenth century, the Gradualists had dominated the national government and the formation of Indian policy. But proponents of removal charged that the program of the Gradualists failed to solve the Indian question. It had failed to prevent warfare on the frontier or to bring natives in any appreciable numbers into the American mainstream. Unacculturated Indians remained on the much coveted land of the frontier, impeding white settlement. For most Americans this situation evidenced its greatest failing. It seemed clear that the two races could never live harmoniously in propinquity with each other. "The deep rooted prejudices, and malignity of heart, and conduct, reciprocally entertained and practised on all occasions by the Whites and Savages will ever prevent their being good neighbors," surmised one official. "Either one or the other party must remove to a greater distance." Removalists stepped up calls for Washington to initiate a comprehensive plan to colonize eastern Indians on lands west of the Mississippi River.

In those same years Gradualists also concluded, slowly and painfully, that colonization might be appropriate. This development did not signal an abandonment of their beliefs and goals. It did, however, reflect their doubts about the possibility of success of their program amidst the swirl of settlement on the frontier. They could not refute charges that, so far, most Indians would not, or could not, be civilized. Even when some did alter their life-style, few were accepted in white society. More often than not, their attempts only heightened tensions with white neighbors. The Gradualists also knew that these Indians were the exception. Most Indians experienced increasing distress, privation, and societal disintegration. "Two centuries have gone round," observed Thomas L. McKenney, President Monroe's Indian commissioner, after travelling among the tribes in the Old Northwest, "and the remnants of these people, that remain, are more wretched than when they were a great and numerous people." His report described the depth of their debasement: "They catch fish— and plant patches of corn; dance, paint, hunt, fight, get drunk when they can get liquor and often starve. . . . There is no sketching that can convey a clear perception of the misery and degradation in which [they are] involved."

In light of this dismaying reality, removal took on new significance and purpose for Gradualists. Because their long-term objective remained the incorporation of detribalized, acculturated Indians into white society, removal seemed the only means of achieving that end. It became the panacea to the Gradualists, but its success and the mitigation of the trauma to tribes, which removal would certainly cause, depended on future contingencies, as scholar Bernard Sheehan points out in *Seeds of Extinction: Jeffersonian Philanthropy and the American Indians.* "The Indian must be allowed a period free from the pressure of the frontier, and the civilizing program must move west with the tribes. Should these expectations be fulfilled, the inconvenience of removal . . . would have been only incidental to the long-run accomplishment." Increasingly, Gradualists believed that not only did the ultimate success of their program seem to rest on supporting removal, but the very survival of the eastern Indians depended on it as well. The Gradualists and the Removalists, for different reasons, found themselves occupying common ground. Henry School-craft, for years an Indian agent at Sault Sainte Marie, Michigan Territory, echoed mounting public opinion. "It is now evident to all, that the salvation of these interesting relics of Oriental races lies in colonization west," he wrote. "Public sentiment has settled on the ground; sound policy dictates it; and the most enlarged philanthropy for the Indian race perceives its best hope in the measure [forced removal]."

President James Monroe, like his mentor Thomas Jefferson, supported the Gradualist program as the best course for saving the Indians and promoting peaceful relations between them and whites. Monroe stressed that to civilize the Indians it was "indispensable that their independence as communities should cease," their accustomed life-style and cultural values be abandoned, and the government provide "some benevolent provisions." Congress responded to his calls with the Indian Civilization Act of 1819. It appropriated $10,000 annually to employ "capable persons of good moral character" to educate the Indians in reading, writing, arithmetic, and agricultural techniques. But were these measures too late to save the Indians in the East? The president, increasingly troubled by reports from Commissioner McKenney and others about the deterioration among many tribes, finally acknowledged that settlement "on every side by the white population" would not allow sufficient time for acculturation programs to improve

the situation. Like other Gradualists, he concluded that removal, to be followed by government-assisted civilization programs in the West, offered the best solution.

In 1824, Monroe proposed a plan for the relocation of
tribes westward. "The hunter or savage state requires a greater
extent of territory to sustain it, than is compatible with the
progress and just claims of civilized life, and must yield to it,"
Monroe explained, offering Congress his rationale for advocating relocation. "It was right that the hunter should yield to
the farmer, for the earth was given to mankind to support the
greatest number of which it is capable, and no tribe or people
have a right to withhold from the wants of others more than
is necessary for their own support and comfort." He stressed,
however, that relocation must be voluntary on the part of
eastern tribes and that their new western land must equal the
extent and quality of that forfeited in the East. The government's plan for the Indians did not rule out persuasion, but
at this juncture it did not contemplate force. Forced removal,
Monroe declared emphatically, would be "revolting to humanity, and utterly unjustifiable." The direction charted by
the president mollified the Removalists, but it displeased them
that it left the choice of relocation up to the Indians. The next
chief executive's attitude did not satisfy them at all.

The crusty, honest New Englander John Quincy Adams
succeeded Monroe. Like his predecessor, Adams acknowledged
voluntary relocation as an appropriate solution to the Indian
question, although he showed far less enthusiasm for the plan.
Also like Monroe, he refused to force tribes westward against
their will, but he opposed the idea with greater vehemence
than Monroe. Adams was not sentimental regarding Indians,
and he held no illusions about the present state of Indian–
white affairs. The president, an ardent legalist, categorically
rejected forced removal because it meant rejecting earlier treaties with tribes; which Adams considered to be an unconscion-
able violation of the nation's solemn pledge.

Although not coerced by the Adams administration, tribes
of the Old Northwest during the 1820s began forfeiting their

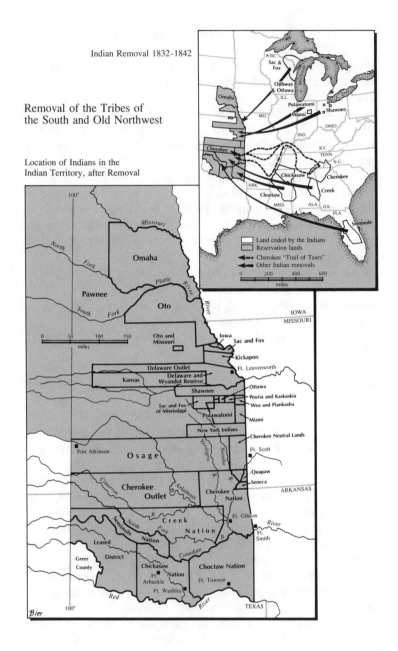

Indian Removal 1832-1842

Removal of the Tribes of
the South and Old Northwest

Location of Indians in the
Indian Territory, after Removal

remaining lands, agreed to removal treaties, and started re-locating beyond the Mississippi to lands that later became Kansas. Many factors compelled them. Harried by settlers, many corrupted by alcohol and other aspects of white culture, and void of strong leadership like Tecumseh's, the Indians acknowledged continued resistance as futile. Most had already abandoned hope of saving themselves and remaining in their lands by accepting the Gradualists' civilization measures. The inevitable could be forestalled only so long. One Wyandot chief chided federal officials, saying he saw little point in supporting acculturation or urging his people to make progress toward that goal when it was clear that whites intended to evict them whether they were civilized or not. Some individuals resisted removal by hiding, marrying whites, and even suicide. Most abandoned the Old Northwest between 1829 and 1843, with-drawing to the trans-Mississippi West.

In sharp contrast, while some southern Indians emigrated to the West by the late 1820s, a significant majority of the region's tribes refused voluntary removal and elected to stay on their lands, most especially the five major tribes of the region: the Cherokees, Chickasaws, Choctaws, Creeks, and Seminoles. That decision made them a target for southern Removalists. Americans residing in the southern states re-garded the Indians as barriers to settlement and economic gain. They demanded the elimination of the Indians to open the fertile lands for agriculture, particularly cotton.

In the face of mounting demands for their eviction, the tribes devised various strategies to buttress the right to remain in their homelands. For example, they changed their tradi-tional forms of government. The Cherokees, Chickasaws, and Choctaws, between 1808 and 1829, fashioned systems of na-tional laws based upon a written constitution. National judicial systems and national police forces also were inaugurated in the same period. Another strategy was supporting the interests of the United States. During the War of 1812, for example, parties of the Cherokees, Creeks, Chickasaws, and Choctaws came to the aid of General Andrew Jackson, assisting his militia to guard the southern frontier against British invasion and to combat anti-American tribal factions, such as the Red Stick Creeks.

Perhaps the most salient strategy was altering their lifestyle to make it more acceptable to white neighbors. In this the Cherokees provide the most distinct illustration. Occupying fifteen million acres in northern Georgia, southwestern North Carolina, northwestern Alabama and eastern Tennessee, many Cherokees used housing and clothing typical of white society. Some sent their children to white schools, a few being sent as far away as the foreign mission school at Cornwall, Connecticut, which the American Board of Foreign Missions opened in 1817. After 1821, the Cherokees had a written language of their own, utilizing the eighty-five symbol syllabary developed by Sequoia, and they published their own newspapers: the *Cherokee Phoenix*, edited by the mixed-blooded Elias Boudinot and first appearing in 1828, the most widely read and well known of their publications. Boudinot printed the paper in both the Cherokee and English languages. Historian Arrell Morgan Gibson reported that the Cherokees achieved near total literacy in their own language in less than half a decade. In 1827 the Cherokees drafted and adopted a written constitution, modeled after the United States Constitution, that reaffirmed their nation's sovereignty. Increasingly, they conducted political affairs in much the same manner as Americans. Like their white neighbors and some members of other major southern tribes, some Cherokees owned Black African slaves. The Cherokee nation also developed a thriving economy, monopolized by the mixed-bloods, based on stock raising, grain and lumber mills, and a plantation agricultural system. A northern visitor during the 1820s observed that they lived "in comfort and abundance, in good houses of brick, stone, and wood," admitting that the Cherokees "seemed to have more money than the whites in our own settlement."

Americans who opposed forced removal applauded these advancements, often exaggerating their extent among tribal members to bolster support for gradualism and for their contention that Indians could acculturate. Those favoring forced removal often discounted reports about the level of civilization achieved by the Cherokees and other southern tribes. One Southerner declared, for example, that it was "a mistake to imagine a nation civilized because it has black cattle, or plants a few potatoes in the weeds, or spins a gross of broaches of very indifferent cotton." Misleading reports about Indian advances, Removalists argued, did not mitigate the need to acquire more Indian land or the right to require their eviction.

Secretary of War John C. Calhoun noted the irony of the situation in the South to President Monroe. "It cannot be doubted," he wrote, "that much of the difficulty of acquiring additional cessions from the Cherokee nation, and other southern tribes, results from their growing civilization and knowledge, by which they have learned to place a higher value upon their lands than more rude and savage tribes." Calhoun was correct in his assessment. As southern Indians became more acculturated, they became more conscious of a unitary tribal identity, eventually combining it with the white man's concept of national sovereignty.

Certainly the Cherokee nation was more determined than ever not to yield to the Removalists. "The Cherokees have long since come to the conclusion never again to cede *another foot* of land," declared Principal Chief John Ross. To protect Cherokee landholdings, in 1819 the Cherokee nation made the unauthorized sale of lands by Cherokees to whites a capital offense. Georgians, on the other hand, declared the actions of the Cherokee nation to be a threat to state sovereignty. An earlier compact between Georgia and the United States further complicated the knotty situation in that state. In 1802 Georgia waived its claims to western lands, thus reducing its territory to that of the present-day state. For this cession, the state coaxed the federal government into promising that title to all Indian lands within its borders would be conveyed to Georgia. No other state managed to extract such a concession. But Georgia's triumph proved more frustrating than satisfying. For twenty years the federal authority made broad grants of Indian land to Ohio, Indiana, Illinois, Kentucky, North Carolina, Tennessee, Alabama, and Mississippi. Georgia watched anxiously, and with increasing anger, while almost one-third of the state remained in the hands of Indians.

Separation and the "Trail of Tears"

Southern state officials could do little in the 1820s except harass the Indians to remove themselves because the presidents simply refused to force them west against their will. James Monroe ignored mounting demands from fellow Southerners and steadfastly refused to budge from his position of strong disapproval of forced removal. And John Quincy Adams, deeply troubled by developments in Georgia, had little sympathy for Southerners' cupidity for Indian land, guaranteed to Indians, as he pointed out, by solemn federal treaties. Then the fate of the southern tribes reversed as a result of the 1828 election. Adams lost his bid for a second term to Andrew Jackson of Tennessee, an advocate of forced colonization of the southern tribes. The Cherokees were well aware of what the ascendency of Jackson forbode. "A crisis seems to be fast approaching when the final destiny of our nation must be sealed," predicted John Ross. He addressed the situation in his annual message of 1829 to the Cherokee nation:

The preservation and happiness of the Cherokee people are at stake, and the United States must soon determine the issue—we can only look with confidence to the good faith and magnanimity of the General Government, whose precepts and profession inculcate principles of liberty and republicanism, and whose obligations are solemnly pledged to give us justice and protection.

President Jackson gave personal attention to passage of federal legislation authorizing forced removal, stressing in his annual messages the need for Congress to endorse a policy of Separation to solve the Indian question. He might have been troubled by betraying tribes that had come to his aid during the War of 1812, when the survival of the republic was at stake. Chief Junaluska, who had saved Jackson's life when a hostile Red Stick Creek sneaked into the general's tent and tried to stab him, now reacted with bitterness: "If I had known that Jackson was going to drive us from our homes, I would have killed him that day at the Horseshoe." Chief John Ross likewise was appalled. "I have known Genl. Jackson from my boyhood—my earliest and warmest friends in Tennessee are generally his advocates—during the late war [the War of 1812] I held a rank [lieutenant] in the Cherokee regiment and fought by his side," he wrote the legendary frontiersman Davy Crockett. "How the President of the U[nited] States can reconcile it to his feelings to withdraw from us the protection pledged by treaty, and to allow the state of Georgia to usurp from us the rights and liberties of freemen . . . I cannot understand."

Andrew Jackson was a hybrid, not a pure Removalist. In his proposed agenda for the Indians he coalesced the Removalist and the Gradualist positions, producing the policy of Separation. Like Monroe, Adams, and earlier nineteenth-century presidents, Jackson believed firmly that Indians were capable of acculturating, and could be assimilated. They were not unreclaimable savages. But, considering the desperation with which whites coveted their lands and the virulence directed against them by many Americans, achieving these results was impossible as long as the Indians remained east of the Mississippi. Unlike his recent predecessors in the White House, Jackson would not leave the choice up to the Indians. Relocation was no longer an option for Indians to accept or reject as they wished, the United States government would mandate the choice. Indians would be forcibly relocated to the western wilderness by the federal authority, separating them from Americans, so that they could not impede white settlement and enterprise, and so that Gradualists would have the necessary time to implement their civilization measures successfully. When, far in the future, white settlement again reached the Indians, thought Jackson, they would be culturally, religiously, politically, and economically ready to take their place in the dominant society. For these reasons, the president stressed, a policy of Separation was the only solution to the Indian question, and Congress must affirm this.

Andrew Jackson saw himself a true friend and protector of the Indians, acting with paternalistic wisdom in their best interest, as Michael Paul Rogin argued in *Fathers and Children: Andrew Jackson and the Subjugation of the American Indian*. Although the policy of Separation appeared to be "an act of *seeming* violence," Alfred Balch, a Jackson supporter, wrote the president, "it will prove in the end an act of enlarged philanthropy." Andrew Jackson concurred emphatically:

May we not hope . . . that all good citizens, and none more zealously than those who think the Indians oppressed by subjection to the laws of the States, will unite in attempting to open the eyes of those children of the forest to their true condition, and by a speedy removal to relieve them from all the evils, real or imaginary, present or prospective, with which they may be supposed to be threatened.

The debates in Congress over proposed legislation to ratify the policy of Separation sparked rancorous debate and strong sectional antagonism, as much of the North lined up in opposition. Northerners identified Southerners as bullies and bigots; Southerners were convinced that Northerners, having already eliminated Indians from their states, were pious hypocrites. Lewis Cass, Jackson's secretary of war, echoed Southern opinion when asserting in the *North American Review* that "it is difficult to conceive that any branch of the human family can be less provident in arrangement, less frugal in enjoyment, less industrious in acquiring, more implacable in their resentments, more ungovernable in their passions, with fewer principles to guide them, with few obligations to restrain them, and with less knowledge to improve and instruct themselves [than the Indians]." He concluded his argument, stating that one could not find "upon the face of the globe, a more wretched race than the Cherokees. . . . Many of them exhibit spectacles as disgusting as they are degrading." Elias Boudinot, writing in the *Cherokee Phoenix*, attacked these ideas in his criticism of Georgia's manifesto, which demanded the immediate eviction of the Cherokees for reasons similar to those advanced by Cass.

What a pernicious effort must such a document . . . have on the interests and improvements of the Indians? Who will expect from the Cherokees a rapid progress in education, religion, agriculture, and the various arts of civilized life when resolutions are passed in a civilized and Christian legislature (whose daily sessions, we are told, commence with a prayer to Almighty God) to wrest their country from them, and strange to tell, with the point of the bayonet, if nothing else will do? Is it in the nature of things, that the Cherokees will build good and comfortable houses and make them great farms, when they know not but their possessions will fall into the hands of strangers & invaders? How is it possible that they will establish for themselves good laws, when an attempt is made to crush their first feeble effort toward it?

More attention was aroused by the speech of Theodore Frelinghuysen on the floor of the Senate. "We have crowded the tribes upon a few miserable acres on our southern frontier; it is all that is left to them of their once boundless forests; and still, like the horseleech, our insatiated cupidity cries give!" The senator from New Jersey continued, "Our fathers successfully and triumphantly contended for the very rights and privileges that our Indian neighbors now implore us to protect and preserve to them." None of this, however, could move Southern legislators and those Northern colleagues who supported their efforts. To them, perhaps above all other justifications for forced removal, the interests, indeed the rights, of the individual states were paramount, regardless of federal treaties. Thus, in the end, they carried the day; the Indian Removal Bill, having passed in the House, was ratified in the Senate by a margin of eight votes. President Jackson signed it into law on May 28, 1830, effecting the policy of Separation. The government of the United States was empowered legally to appropriate tribal lands by negotiating a set of new treaties and to exile the Indians of the South to the trans-Mississippi West.

The South's triumph in the removal fight—over justice for the Indians and over formidable opposition from the North—forbode an alarming future, however. The North, increasingly resentful of two generations of Southern control of Congress and the presidency, was frustrated by its defeat to the South on the removal question. As one of the fruits of its victory, the South carried a heavier burden of anxiety about the possibility of more Northern political "assaults" upon the region's economic and territorial aspirations and its institutions, for someday would not the question of Negro rights be raised as Indian rights had? Its fears soon materialized, as determined Northern anti-slavery agitation mounted in the aftermath of heightened sectionalism caused by Indian removal. A year after passage of the Removal Act, William Lloyd Garrison of Boston established his controversial abolitionist newspaper, *The Liberator*. Then, in 1833, abolitionists formed the American Antislavery Society with its goal the immediate, uncompensated ending of slavery in the United States.

Within two years of the passage of the Indian Removal Act, three of the five major southern tribes had forfeited their lands. The Choctaws in 1830 and then the Chickasaws and the Creeks in 1832 concluded treaties with the federal government mandating their resettlement; an eventuality that would prove horrific for all three tribes. Only the Cherokees and the Seminoles remained. While each selected different tactics, both tenaciously resisted removal. The Seminoles rejected their removal treaty and withdrew into the depths of the Florida swamps where, from 1835 to 1842, they fought courageously but unsuccessfully against the United States Army. When military operations finally halted, the government had removed most of the tribe to the Indian Territory (present-day Oklahoma), although several hundred were never apprehended and remained in Florida.

The Cherokees were equally determined to resist removal. "The Cherokees are not foreigners but original inhabitants of America," a delegation of tribal members declared to the secretary of war. "They now inhabit and stand on the soil of their own territory ... and the states by which they are now surrounded have been created out of land which was once theirs." The Cherokees no longer relied solely on appeals to conscience, which had failed them in the states, in Congress, and at the highest executive office. They decided to seek redress in the federal courts. "Nothing can and nothing will sattisfy [sic] this nation upon the subject of the controversy which has been forced upon them by Georgia, than a fair and honest decision upon the principles of the Constitution, laws & Treaties of the U.S. by the Supreme Court," John Ross replied to William H. Underwood, who had inquired of the chief what response the Cherokees would offer to the threat of forced removal.

The Cherokee appeal was no routine matter. American courts can at any time be "seized" of questions for which there are neither clear laws nor established precedents. State courts had jurisdiction in state matters, federal courts in federal matters. But what was the status of an Indian nation? Certainly it had treaty rights. These were sometimes disregarded, but they were not rejected. Moreover, the Constitution was clear that an international treaty supersedes an act of Congress. But a number of Southerners, Jefferson, Madison, and Calhoun among them, believed that the states must be judges of the constitutionality of federal acts. The vexed question of the Cherokees' status would be settled by the United States Supreme Court. In *Cherokee Nation* v. *the State of Georgia* (1831), the court under Chief Justice John Marshall ruled in the Cherokees' favor, stating that Indians were not subject to state law and so affirmed the right of the Cherokees to hold their land in the state of Georgia. Although he made no secret of his sympathy for the Cherokees, the chief justice delivered a blow to their claims to sovereignty, ruling that they were not independent but a "domestic dependent nation in a state of pupilage"—in other words, wards of the United States government. Still, the Cherokees received the decision with rejoicing, for had not the highest tribunal in the land ruled to quell those who aspired to crush them? John Ross announced to his nation: "Our adversaries are generally down in the mouth—there are great rejoicings through the nation on the decision of the supreme court upon the Cherokee case." A year later, the Supreme Court in *Samuel A. Worcester* v. *the State of Georgia* (1832) again ruled against Georgia. The Cherokees dared to hope that protections guaranteed them by treaty were safeguarded. What could block access to their rights?

Unfortunately Andrew Jackson could. The president may have said, as so often quoted, "John Marshall has made his decision; *now let him enforce it!*" The rejoinder is probably apocryphal, but it accurately depicts his attitude and his behavior—he simply refused to enforce the court's decision. When it became clear to Georgia that President Jackson would not fulfill his constitutional duty, but instead would ignore a federal court, the state quickly turned the Cherokees' domain over to white land speculators. A malleable tribal faction, led by Major Ridge and encouraged by state and federal officials, signed a removal treaty at New Echota, Georgia, the Cherokee capital, on December 29, 1835. On behalf of the Cherokee nation they ceded to the United States all the lands owned, claimed or possessed by them east of the Mississippi River, and agreed to remove west of that river. Their action exacerbated Cherokee factionalism, as the overwhelming majority of the tribe, led by Principal Chief John Ross, refused to vacate their homeland.

Three years later it fell to President Martin Van Buren, Jackson's hand-picked successor, to implement his mentor's design for these people. On April 10, 1838, Van Buren ordered the reluctant Major General Winfield Scott to the Cherokee homeland to remove the inhabitants beyond the Mississippi River. For Scott it was a sad task, but one from which he could not shrink. Although he made clear to his troops that compassion must be shown to the Cherokees as they were rounded up and held in detainment camps until the journey westward commenced, too often this was not the troops' behavior. Ethnologist James Mooney gathered firsthand accounts from survivors of the ensuing ordeal. In his words:

Families at dinner were startled by the sudden gleam of bayonets in the doorway and rose up to be driven with blows and oaths along the weary miles of trail that led to the stockade. Men were seized in their fields or going along the road, women were taken from their wheels and children from their play. In many cases, on turning for one last look as they crossed the ridge, they saw their homes in flames, fired by the lawless rabble that followed on the heels of the soldiers to loot and pillage.

Soldiers surrounded houses to make sure that no one escaped. In one typical example, a woman, seeing herself trapped, called her chickens for their last feeding. Then taking one child on her back and leading two others by the hand she joined her husband and followed the soldiers. Cattle, hogs, horses, household effects were all lost. The Cherokees were to start with nothing but the clothes on their backs. A Georgia volunteer, Private John G. Burnett, later a colonel in the army of the Confederate States of America, remembered: "I fought through the civil war and have seen men shot to pieces and slaughtered by thousands, but the Cherokee removal was the cruelest work I ever knew." Some Cherokees did evade the dragnet and fled into the mountains of North Carolina. Scott did not pursue them vigorously. Their descendants now reside on a reservation located in the northwestern portion of that state just south of the Great Smokies National Park.

General Scott, hoping that the removal would be carried out with the least possible pain to the emigrants, agreed to allow John Ross and leaders of his faction to supervise the operation. A number of Cherokee parties, numbering at most a few hundred individuals in each case, had already made the trip to the West; hence Scott, Ross, and others found little reason not to believe that this removal could be made without too much difficulty. But those who had already emigrated were relatively few in number and had chosen the time for departure and, to some extent, the route. The movement of a body of people numbering well into the thousands would be much more difficult.

Following a delay of almost half a year, the Cherokee migration began in October 1838. Despite Scott's hope for an endurable journey, the rigors of the operation could hardly be mitigated. The trek westward, a trying one even under the best of conditions, was handicapped by a lack of sufficient provisions. In addition, a terrible drought blasted the Southeast through the early fall of 1838, a drought that would have hindered even a much smaller migration. To herd a party of eighteen thousand people through hundreds of miles of blasted vegetation and dried-up streams with only the minimum of provisions and comforts was to invite disaster. Because of the excruciating horror of death and suffering through which they trudged, the Cherokee trek is recalled as "The Trail of Tears." The missionary Elizur Butler, witness to a portion of the odyssey, confessed, "I have felt I have been in the midst of death itself." A reporter for the *New York Observer*, under the heading "A Native of Maine, traveling in the Western Country," recorded his impressions: "When I past [sic] the last detachment of those suffering exiles and thought that my native countrymen had thus expelled them from their native soil and their much loved homes, . . . I turned from the sight with feelings which language cannot express." Four thousand of those who left their Georgia homes died on the dreadful trail—about one-quarter of those who set out. Thomas H. Crawford, Van Buren's commissioner of Indian Affairs, reflected a different reality in his official report: "Good feeling has been preserved, and we have quietly and gently transported 18,000 friends to the west bank of the Mississippi."

In 1840 the lands east of the Mississippi had been lost by those people who had lived in them for centuries. By then, federal officials and the American public overwhelmingly were convinced that the policy of Separation solved the Indian question. A few individuals did not share their optimism. Jared Sparks, editor of the *North American Review*, mused that "after all, this project only defers the fate of the Indians. In half a century their condition beyond the Mississippi will be just what it [was] on this side. Their extinction is inevitable." Jeremiah Evarts, corresponding secretary of the American Board of Commissioners for Foreign Missions, predicted that another solution would "soon be necessary." Evarts offered his rationale:

If the emigrants become poor, and are transformed into vagabonds, it will be evidence enough, that no benevolent treatment can save them, and it will be said they may as well be driven beyond the Rocky Mountains at once. If they live comfortably, it will prove, that five times as many white people might live comfortably in their places.

Most Americans preferred to trust Andrew Jackson's judgment, not that of these doomsayers. He exuded confidence that the policy of Separation had successfully dealt with the Indian question: It provided safety for Americans and the United States, and prevented the annihilation of the Indians. "The States which had so long been retarded in their improvement by the Indian tribes residing in the midst of them are at length relieved from the evil," Jackson assured a grateful nation, "and this unhappy race—the original dwellers in our land—are now placed in a situation where we may well hope that they will share in the blessings of civilization and be saved from degradation and destruction."

We do not think of the great open plains, the beautiful rolling hills, and winding streams with tangled growth, as "wild." Only to the white man was nature a "wilderness" and only to him was the land "infested" with "wild" animals and "savage" people. To us it was tame. Earth was bountiful and we were surrounded with the blessings of the Great Mystery. Not until the hairy man from the east came and with brutal frenzy heaped injustices upon us and the families we loved was it "wild" for us. When the very animals of the forest began fleeing from his approach, then it was for us the "Wild West" began.

LUTHER STANDING BEAR, OGLALA SIOUX

CHAPTER TWO

Western Expansion Forces a New Solution

And so tribes from the East arrived in the western wilderness, a foreign land that they now called home. "Your father has provided a country large enough for all of you," President Andrew Jackson promised. "There your white brother will not trouble you; they will have no claim to the land, and you can live upon it, you and all of your children, as long as the grass grows or the water runs, in peace and plenty. It will be yours forever." To provide a solution to the nation's Indian question, the United States in the 1830s settled on a policy of Separation, uprooting and removing, often by force, more than fifty thousand Indians beyond the Mississippi River. They yielded approximately 100 million acres in the eastern United States in return for some thirty-two million western acres.

The question of whether or not to implement a policy of Separation had stirred heated debate. But once the policy became an accomplished fact, the American public overwhelmingly judged it a workable and humane solution to longstanding and vexing problems between Indians and whites.

They backed the policy in the faith that separation of the races was the best solution that could be had, and certainly that it was the best possibility for the Indians. The Euro-American experience of several centuries had demonstrated conclusively, so they believed, that neither race could live peacefully in proximity with the other. With the bulk of eastern woodland tribes located beyond the Mississippi, warfare with them and conflict over land use in the East became a problem of the past. Other, less palatable reasons also helped sanction the policy of Separation: racial and cultural biases, political expediency, and perhaps above all, the enormous profits to be reaped from the confiscated Indian lands. By 1840, with the removal of these tribes accomplished, Americans, although compelled by different reasons in their support of the policy, believed that the government had solved the nation's Indian question.

Fashioning the Indian Territory

The decision to implement Separation and forcibly remove the Indians of the South and the Old Northwest required that federal officials allocate land for their colonization. This issue raised a fundamental and far-reaching question: Once organized, what was the best method of guaranteeing this colonization zone for exclusive use by Indians and of preventing white intrusion?

During the concluding years of James Monroe's presidency, the federal government developed a plan to create a permanent Indian domain from lands not included within the boundaries of any state or organized federal territory. The idea for an Indian country or state was not new. For decades it had been bantered about in a variety of forms, most notably by Thomas Jefferson, who considered the newly purchased Louisiana Territory as the best locale. In the early 1820s John C. Calhoun of South Carolina resurrected Jefferson's idea, focusing government's attention on the Louisiana Purchase for an Indian country.

West of the Mississippi River, and comprising nearly seven-eighths of the Louisiana Purchase, lay millions of acres of unorganized federal territory stretching over endless prairies and plains to the Rocky Mountains. Beyond the Louisiana Territory lay Mexican and British possessions. The American public in those years, secure in the belief of "national completeness," agreed they would never desire this area west of the Mississippi for settlement. Americans considered the land east of the Mississippi River fully adequate for the needs of the republic, especially its agricultural needs, and so were satisfied that the United States encompassed its suitable territorial limits. There seemed little, if any, reason in the foreseeable future for settlement to press much beyond the Mississippi. Because Americans perceived the western prairies and plains worthless and forever uninhabitable for an agricultural society, this area became an obvious solution to the problem of where to establish an Indian country for the Indians of the South and the Old Northwest. By settling the removed tribes on a portion of this great expanse, American society could expand without interference from Indians on the habitable lands east of the Mississippi. Indian society, concentrated on the "wild" land of the prairies and plains west of American settlement, could flourish in its own way by adaptation to an economy and way of life alien to white societies. The rationalization appeared flawless to Americans of that era.

To state that Americans could never exist west of the 95th meridian and east of the Rockies seems incredible today, but such was the belief of the time. During the first half of the nineteenth century, virtually all Americans believed that the Great Plains were dry, barren, and forbidding. In 1820, Major Stephen H. Long led an expedition that explored the central and southern portions of this area, journeying up the Platte River and returning through present-day Oklahoma on the Canadian River. He described the region as "almost wholly unfit for cultivation and of course uninhabitable by a people depending upon agriculture for their subsistence.... The scarcity of wood and water ... will prove an insuperable obstacle in the way of settling the country." In spite of his discouraging assessment, Major Long did see some attributes to this locale. "Viewed as frontier," he suggested, this region "may prove of infinite importance to the United States, inasmuch as it is calculated to serve as a barrier to prevent too great an extension of our population westward." Major Long judged the area so worthless that he dubbed it "The Great American Desert." Although erroneous, the name stuck—along with the misconception.

Secretary of War Calhoun, partly because of Long's report, urged Congress to set aside the area west of Missouri and Arkansas as a huge compound for Indians. Subsequent administrations acted on Calhoun's idea, and during the 1830s Congress withdrew millions of acres from potential American settlement, fashioning out of them the "Indian Territory." Here the colonized eastern tribes, as well as western tribes living within the jurisdiction of the United States, would reside. By 1840 the boundary of this sanctuary, after some adjustments, had been determined. The government reserved for Indians an enormous parcel of land west of the states of Louisiana, Arkansas, and Missouri. On the north, the Platte River bounded the Indian Territory and on the south the Red River defined it. The western border of the United States as of 1840 also served as the western boundary of the Indian Territory: the one hundredth meridian running northward from the Red River to the Arkansas River, then westward along the Arkansas to the Rockies.

The federal government, in those same years, took steps to protect all Indians residing within the Indian Territory against white encroachment and aggression from other tribes. Congress passed legislation that limited white settlement in much of this area, thus buttressing the right of Indians to its exclusive possession. Responsibility rested with the United States Army for safeguarding the Indian Territory, and especially for protecting the colonized Indian communities against attack by more numerous western tribes which resented the intrusion of these refugees on their hunting ranges. Soldiers were garrisoned in a chain of installations established along the eastern frontier of the Indian Territory. The forts extended southward from Fort Snelling on the Mississippi in what became in 1849 the territory of Minnesota, to Forts Atkinson and Leavenworth along the Missouri on the central plains, to three posts in present-day Oklahoma—Forts Gibson and Smith on the Arkansas River and Fort Towson on the Red River, ending at Fort Jesup near the western border of the state of Louisiana. This line of forts with their available military personnel would, in the judgment of the government in Washington, "both insure the safety of the western frontier, and enable the government to fulfill all its treaty stipulations, and preserve its faith with the Indians."

In that portion of the Indian Territory north of thirty-seven degrees latitude (the present border separating the states of Kansas and Oklahoma), the Indians from the Old Northwest were colonized, including the Wyandots, Delawares, Potawatomies, Kickapoos, Sac and Fox, and Shawnees. Weakened and traumatized by their removal, and now located precariously close to the hunting ranges of the Plains Indians, the refugee tribes experienced frequent assaults from the powerful Cheyennes, Arapahoes, and Sioux. Missionaries toiled among them, trying to improve their condition. They believed the best means was education, especially manual labor schools where, in addition to instruction in reading, writing, basic arithmetic, and Christian precepts, the Indians would be taught how to "build and live in houses, to sleep on beds; to eat at regular intervals, to plough, and sow, and reap; to rear and use domestic animals; to understand and practice the mechanic arts; and to enjoy, to their gratification and improvement, all the means of profit and rational pleasure that are so profusely spread around civilized life." In 1839, the Methodists established a school at their Shawnee mission in present-day eastern Kansas. It became the model that the Indian Affairs Office copied elsewhere in the Indian Territory.

Residing near the Indians of the Old Northwest were a number of local tribes, such as the Osage and Kansa, whom the government had resettled on reduced territory to make room for the immigrant tribes. West of the Missouri and straddling the Platte River in the northernmost portion of the Indian Territory lived other local tribes, among them the Pawnees, Otos, Missouris, Omahas, and Iowas—who for centuries were agriculturalists, but who in more recent times had adopted many of the characteristics of the Plains Indians' buffalo and horse culture. Life for these tribes had become increasingly precarious by the early 1840s. Plains tribes constantly harried them, seeking to evict them from choice hunting grounds. "They were," wrote agent Thomas Fitzpatrick, "completely invested by enemies so much so that they are in danger of losing their scalps as soon as they put their heads outside their mud hovels; and it seems to me that their feasting on buffalo, are nearly at an end. The Platte River, the headwaters of the Kansas, and even south west to the Arkansas were formerly the great hunting grounds of the Pawnies [sic]; but now those of the Sioux, Cheyennes, and Arapahoes, who are all gradually nearing the Pawnies, with a full determination of wiping them out."

The government set aside the southern part of the Indian Territory, below thirty-seven degrees latitude, for the Cherokees, Chickasaws, Choctaws, Creeks, and Seminoles. After arrival in their new western lands, the surviving members of these tribes, with quiet heroism, began to reconstruct their lives from the ashes of their past. Diligently and energetically they set themselves to the awesome task of rebuilding their society, economic base, and governments; and they accomplished an astonishing, phoenix-like recovery. Within a few short years of their arrival, they transformed the wilderness of the southern Indian Territory into a flourishing and prosperous homeland. Towns, farms, plantations, and ranches provided the base for a thriving economy. They established an educational system for their children. Soon after arrival these tribes reestablished their constitutional governments, fashioning five independent Indian republics, each with a national capital: Tahlequah for the Cherokees, Tishomingo for the Chickasaws,

Doaksville for the Choctaws, North Fork Town for the Creeks, and Seminole Agency for the Seminoles.

William Armstrong, federal superintendent of the Western Territory, greatly impressed by the remarkable progress of the five tribes, noted with approval in 1840: "Where but a few years past the forest was untouched, in many places good farms are to be seen; the whole face of the country evidently indicating a thrifty and prosperous people, possessing within themselves the means of raising fine stocks of horses, cattle, and hogs, and country producing all the substantials of life." Their extraordinary efforts and achievements, and the manner of society, government, and economies fashioned in the southern portion of the Indian Territory by these five republics led to their designation by Americans as "The Five Civilized Tribes." If Americans needed an example to verify the wisdom of the policy of Separation, they pointed readily to these republics as evidence of the potential for Indians to adapt to the ways of the dominant society, especially when the unyielding pressure from white settlement was eliminated. "There was nothing to distinguish appearances from those of many of our border people," Ethan Allen Hitchcock noted in 1841 during an investigative trip for the government, "except the complexion and superior neatness."

The Tribes of the Great Plains

To the west of the tribes residing in the eastern end of the Indian Territory—from roughly the one hundredth meridian to the Rocky Mountains, in 1840 the far western edge of United States territory—lay the domain of the Great Plains tribes. Some of these tribes had just recently made room, often with belligerent protests, for the relocated Indians from the East, whom they viewed as intruders and competitors for the already limited food resources of the region. Although these Indians were nominally under the jurisdiction of the United States since the Louisiana Purchase of 1803, federal officials so far had few dealings with these tribes—a state of affairs that would change soon, as much of the government's attention in Indian affairs for the next half-century would focus on these people. Most Americans were only vaguely aware of the Great Plains tribes, if they knew of them at all: "picturesque but unimportant savages" might be the most accurate characterization of public perception. Those who had direct contact offered impressive descriptions. For example, the artist George Catlin in 1834 recorded his observations of the Cheyennes. His portrayal would have applied as accurately to the other bison-hunting tribes of the region.

There is no finer race of men than these in North America, and more superior in stature, excepting the Osages; scarcely a man of the tribe, full grown, who is less than six feet in height. The Shiennes [Cheyennes] are undoubtedly the richest in horses of any tribe on the Continent, living in a country as they do, where the greatest numbers of wild horses are grazing on the prairies. . . . These people are the most desperate set of horsemen, and warriors also, having carried on almost unceasing war with the Pawnees and Blackfeet, time out of mind.

Sedentary farming peoples, like the Mandan, Hidatsa and Arikara, occupied the timbered Missouri River valley and some of its major tributaries on the eastern plains. Nomadic bison-hunting societies, collectively referred to as the Plains Indians, dominated the remainder of the region. The Dakota, or Sioux, controlled the northeastern portion of the plains. Numbering twenty-five thousand people, which by far made it the largest group on the Great Plains, the Sioux had three principal tribal divisions. The Sisseton, or Santee, lived in present-day Minnesota, a Dakota word meaning "waters many." To their west, spanning the Missouri River on the prairies of what is now South Dakota, were the Yankton and Yanktonai. The most populous division resided to the north and west. These were the Teton, comprising seven divisions or subtribes: Blackfeet, Brule, Hunkpapa, Miniconjou, Oglala, Sans Arc, and Two Kettles. The Teton Sioux's strength of numbers made them a formidable obstacle to any white expansion on the northern plains. On the lands along the western Missouri River and ranging on both sides of the United States–

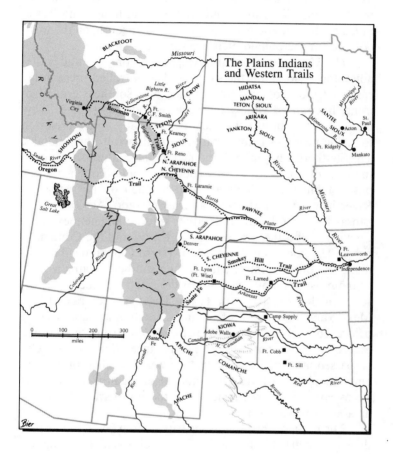

The Plains Indians
and Western Trails

Canadian border were the Blackfeet, Assiniboines, and Atsinas. The Crow inhabited the Bighorn Mountain country of what became Wyoming and Montana, although the Teton Sioux challenged them for control. To their south, on the western edge of the buffalo plains, resided the Shoshonis.

The Cheyennes and the Arapahoes, long comrades and allies and residing on the same lands, controlled present-day eastern Colorado, western Kansas, and southeastern Wyoming, but ranged widely over the central plains. The Cheyennes had two branches. The Northern Cheyennes preferred to reside near the Teton Sioux and trade with other Indians. The Southern Cheyennes remained on the central plains, trading directly for white man's goods at Bent's Fort, a trading post established by William Bent in 1834 on the Arkansas River in what is now southeastern Colorado. Across the Arkansas River to the south lived the traditional enemies of the Cheyennes and the Arapahoes: the Kiowa and the Comanche tribes. The Kiowas lived in northwestern Oklahoma. The Comanches, the dominant tribe on the southern plains as well as the most populous with seven thousand members, resided south of the Red River in Texas. Together they raided into Mexico and Texas for horses, mules, and human captives long before coming into contact with settlers from the United States. Over the southwestern plains ranged the Apaches. Unsurpassed at guerrilla warfare, they were a match for any enemy, Indian or white. They hunted and gathered from the Pecos River in New Mexico over the northern Rio Grande area and eastward into Texas.

The nomadic bison-hunting tribes of the Great Plains produced a remarkable synthesis of political, social, and religious characteristics, especially when one considers the size of the region and the diverse geographical origins of these tribes. The Plains Indians had recently mastered the "buffalo and horse culture," ironic perhaps since that culture became so completely identified with these tribes (and often generalized to all North American Indians) in the minds of Americans and Europeans.

The highly specialized way of life they developed, reaching its climactic form in the nineteenth century, centered on two animals: buffalos (bison), which were native to the plains, and domesticated horses, which were not. Just when they obtained horses is not certain, but by 1700 most tribes had acquired them. All the Indians that the French and the English encountered west of the Missouri River in the eighteenth century rode horses. The Plains Indians first obtained the horse from the Spanish. Both Coronado and DeSoto had them on their treks to the Great Plains, as did the Spanish settlers and soldiers in Mexico. Through thefts, sales, or escape, horses ultimately made their way northward into the possession of the plains tribes, and from that time on they rapidly and thoroughly made the horse an integral part of their lives. Before the buffalo and horse cultural period, few tribes actually lived on the Great Plains. Those who did kept close to the fertile valleys of the major rivers—the Missouri, Platte, Red, and Canadian Rivers—rarely leaving those locales unless to venture out onto the plains in search of buffalo and other sources of wild game. Then around 1700, coinciding with the spread of the horse, more than two dozen tribes moved out onto the plains, abandoning most, and in many cases all, of their previous cultural traits, to forge the buffalo and horse culture.

The horse transformed two main elements of the life of Indians on the Great Plains: transportation and food gathering. Before the introduction of the horse, they lived a meager life always near the brink of want, whether farmers or hunters. They travelled and hunted on foot. On the march they carried their gear on their backs, on the backs of their dogs, or on a *travois*, an A-shaped device that could be strapped to the dog. Travel was slow, tedious, and difficult. The horse changed these conditions forever. It freed them from bondage to the periphery of the plains and allowed them to move at will over its immense reaches. It also transformed the Plains Indians into formidable fighters: American military personnel characterized them, often with awe, as the "finest light cavalry in the world." Use of the horse increased competition among tribes for territory and game, and intensified intertribal warfare as raiding parties could move with much greater speed and tactical dexterity against enemies. Horses were so valuable that the plains tribes ultimately measured wealth by the number owned.

The coming of the horse altered the food gathering process as well. Archaeological and historical evidence indicates that buffalo was always an ingredient in the diet of the plains people, as well as antelope, elk, and smaller game. But these animals were hard to catch in sufficient quantity by hunters on foot. Wild seeds, grains, dried berries, and edible roots were also part of the diet. All provided an unreliable minimum. But with the horse, a hunter could kill in a day of buffalo hunting what had previously required a week or even more. The horse not only discouraged tendencies toward a more sedentary life, it strengthened roving and migratory habits in the pursuit of the great buffalo herds. The Plains Indians "have no fixed habitations. Hunting and fighting they wander incessantly, through the summer and winter," noted Francis Parkman. "Some follow the herds of buffalo over the waste of the prairie; others traverse the Black Hills, through the dark gulfs and sombre gorges, and emerging at last upon the 'Parks,' those beautiful but most perilous hunting grounds." The buffalo, found in enormous herds throughout the region, became the dietary staple of the mounted Plains Indians. The buffalo also satisfied most of their material needs. From hides came clothing, robes, moccasins, saddles, walls of tepees, bedding, vessels to hold water, boats to cross streams. The hooves were made into glue, horns were carved into cups and spoons, and muscle tendon was made into bowstrings, cordage, and trailropes for their horses. Dried manure—"buffalo chips"—provided fuel. Stomachs were fashioned into water bottles. "The buffalo supplies them with the necessities of life," Parkman also observed. "When the buffalo are extinct, they too must dwindle away." So vital were the buffalo and the horse to the Plains Indians' way of life, that during the Plains Wars of the 1860s and 1870s the United States Army made it a military objective to eradicate the buffalo herds and kill the Indians' horses.

Migratory Fever and Manifest Destiny Jeopardize the Policy of Separation

Both the American public and the United States government believed that the policy of Separation assured a state of longterm peaceful relations with Indians. They believed it because most tribes under United States jurisdiction resided either in the Indian Territory or on land west of it, and because Americans saw no value in these lands for future settlement. Their anticipation proved frustratingly brief. Within a decade of the implementation of the policy of Separation, events in the trans-Mississippi West undermined the premises upon which it rested. Two factors contributed most to its rapid collapse. The first is called Migratory Fever. The second came to be called Manifest Destiny. Their effects ignited a new Indian question for the nation, which in turn compelled another search for a solution.

The 1840s witnessed a dramatic increase in westward movement by the American people. Phrases such as "Oregon Fever" and "California Fever" aptly portrayed the ardent spirit of exploration that compelled thousands of citizens to migrate from their homes in the East and cross the Indian Territory and the domain of the plains tribes to settle the Far West. This uncontrolled stream of population destroyed forever the undergirding of the policy of Separation: a sanctuary where Indians could be left to themselves in lands of their own. By the early 1840s, reports had spread eastward of the abundance of fertile, almost empty lands beyond the Rocky and Sierra Nevada Mountains. Americans did not take long in resolving to fashion new and better lives for themselves and their families in these lands, or businessmen to recognize the commercial opportunities inherent in this situation, or the national government to see advantages in securing the region for the United States.

The first noteworthy trail to carve its way across the Great Plains in this era led to the Oregon Territory, and from its destination took its name—the Oregon Trail. Although trappers and fur traders had been exploiting the rich natural bounty of the region for some time, the first real American interest in Oregon came as a result of the activities of Protestant missionaries. They labored diligently, although with considerable lack of success, to convert local Indians to Christianity. Perhaps more important, reports of their evangelizing efforts were carried east, including the missionaries' enticing descriptions of the beauty and economic potential of Oregon. Religious journals and secular newspapers printed and reprinted the observations, stimulating increasing interest in migration. The Oregon Territory, well watered and forested, appealed in particular to New Englanders and midwestern farmers, especially those who had been hurt so badly by the recent depression—the Panic of 1837. To these people who longed for a new start in life, Oregon seemed an answer heaven-sent. As reports spread of this bountiful locale, Americans caught Oregon Fever. It started as a trickle, but by 1843 the first substantial migration had begun. With each passing year thousands of covered wagons wound their way down the trail, crossing the Indian Territory and the Great Plains in order to reach the Oregon country.

Other trails soon developed. In the same decade, a persecuted religious group resolved to migrate to the West, beyond the jurisdiction of the United States. The Church of Jesus Christ of Latter-Day Saints, more commonly known as the Mormons, by the mid-1840s had endured nearly twenty years of persecution by other Americans because of their beliefs. To escape hostility they had moved their community several times: from New York State to Ohio, to Missouri, to Illinois. Finally, in 1846, their new leader Brigham Young organized and led a fifteen-hundred-mile trek from Illinois to Mexican territory in Utah. By successfully completing the journey they created a second major trail across Indian country, called the Mormon Trail. Earlier in the decade the explorer John C. Frémont said the region possessed "good soil and good grass, adapted to civilized settlements." Instead the Mormons found a barren, sun-baked plain, "the paradise of the lizard, the cricket and the rattlesnake." It seemed to them that Stephen Long, not John Frémont, had been the more accurate observer. Dismayed, many urged their leaders to forsake this "dry, worthless locality" and press on for greener lands along the Pacific coast. Other Americans crossed the plains with the Mexican province of California as their destination. Some overland immigrants followed the Oregon Trail to the Pacific Northwest, then headed southward into California. Others followed the Mormon Trail to the Great Salt Lake. From there they pushed across the Nevada desert and over the Sierra Nevadas to the Pacific, thus forging the California Trail.

The stream of Americans journeying through Indian country became a human deluge after James Marshall discovered gold at Sutter's mill in northern California in January of 1848. Few words had the capacity to evoke greater tumult and rapacity than "GOLD!" "Never, I think," commented a local resident, "has there been such excitement in any country of the world." One San Francisco editor, noting with displeasure how thousands had abandoned their daily work to become gold hunters, wrote, "The whole country, from San Francisco to Los Angeles, and from sea shore to the base of the Sierra Nevada, resounds with the sordid cry of '*gold!* Gold! *GOLD!*' while the field is left half planted, the house half built, and everything neglected but the manufacture of shovels and pickaxes." Within six months Californians had rushed to the area of the American River to "strike it rich," and by the end of 1848 news of a gold strike in California had reached the East. The next year the "forty-niners" swept across the overland trails in numbers never seen before. Fourteen-thousand non-Indians lived in California before the gold strike; nearly half a million occupied it two years later, when California became the thirty-first state. Subsequent discoveries of gold and silver in western territories prompted even greater numbers to migrate across Indian country and try to make their fortunes in the mountains of the Far West.

No sooner had Americans reached the Oregon country, California, and other western locales, than the seeds of international crisis began to sprout. Settlers, supported by an increasingly large following back in the United States, did not wish to abide British or Mexican rule. By the mid-1840s, calls for the United States to annex these regions, with military force if necessary, reached a crescendo throughout a vast arc from Oregon down through California and over to the Republic of Texas. Their demands found ideological impetus in the set of ideas called Manifest Destiny. John L. O'Sullivan, the influential editor of the *New York Morning News* and *The Democratic Review*, initially coined the phrase in an 1845 political editorial. According to O'Sullivan, American expansionism

... is by the right of our manifest destiny to overspread and to possess the whole of the continent which Providence has given us for the development of the great experiment of liberty and federative self-government entrusted to us. It is a right such as that of the tree to the space of air and earth suitable for the full expansion of this principle and destiny of growth.

This celebrated belief also proclaimed the superiority of American culture and institutions of which Manifest Destiny was the slogan and emblem of divine sanction and providential direction. Congressman Robert C. Winthrop of Massachusetts, addressing Congress, echoed the public's widespread support of the tangent ideas of American exceptionalism and American geographic determinism: "The right of our Manifest Destiny, ... a right for a new chapter in the laws of nations." International events and the rationalizations that clustered under the rubric of Manifest Destiny soon radically undercut the policy of Separation and the reasons for establishing and maintaining the Indian Territory.

James K. Polk of Tennessee, a young Democratic protégé of Andrew Jackson, ran for president as an outspoken expansionist and a vigorous proponent of American Manifest Destiny. His victory in the election of 1844 made expansion inevitable. While Polk was clearly willing to provoke a war with Mexico to obtain the Southwest (as he would soon demonstrate), he just as clearly wished to avoid an armed conflict with Great Britain if possible. In 1846, Great Britain and the United States agreed to divide the Oregon Territory at the forty-ninth parallel of latitude. The English retained that portion north of the compromise line; Americans acquired sole right to the territory south of it down to the border of California.

In the spring of 1846 escalating American-Mexican tension over the southwestern border of Texas erupted in war. American troops put the capstone on more than a year of successful and brilliant campaigning when Mexico City fell to them in the fall of 1847. The Treaty of Guadalupe Hidalgo in 1848 ended the conflict and required the Mexican government to sell the entire Southwest (from New Mexico to California) to the United States for $15 million. The Treaty added 1.2 million square miles of land to the area of the United States. As Polk apprised Congress in his annual message of 1848, the Mexican War secured "a country more than half as large as all that which was held by the United States before their acquisition." America's east-west boundaries now extended from the Atlantic to the Pacific Ocean, in the Far West encompassing a great crescent of territory from Oregon to Texas. The acquisition of these lands dramatically altered the American perception of the Indian sanctuary on the prairies and plains, established as part of the policy of Separation. In the 1830s it was viewed by Americans as advantageous to the United States because it provided part of the solution to the nation's Indian question. But a decade later, it had become an impediment to unifying a transcontinental nation, an open space that someday had to be filled.

The fruits of Migratory Fever and Manifest Destiny proved exceedingly bittersweet. Certainly their foremost consequence was to overheat sectional animosity by raising enormously divisive questions: Will the recently acquired land be free or slave? Should Congress open these lands to slavery or ban the institution from them? Southern and Northern efforts to resolve this concern to their section's satisfaction created a chain of events that in little more than a decade led to secession, then civil war. Probably a lesser concern to most Americans than the extension of slavery was the effects of overland migration and territorial expansion on relations with Indians. The events of the 1840s severely jeopardized the policy of Separation and the nation's solution to the Indian question by placing considerable stress on the tribes in the Indian Territory and those on the plains, disrupting their lives and environment, heightening intertribal hostilities, and reawakening interracial tensions.

Amid the array of forces transforming the Far West, one thing remained constant, at least for the moment: Americans did not desire Indian lands on the prairies and plains. Later mythology of American western settlement idyllically pictured fruitful prairies as far as the eye could see with "endless waves of grain" sustaining hearty pioneer families. But in fact, Americans looking for homes in the West during the 1840s pushed quickly beyond the plains to more familiar terrains, such as Oregon. They hastened westward along the overland trails partly from excited anticipation of a better life awaiting them at their destination, but also out of a primal terror of Indians. It affected all people on the overland trails. "We had been told," Heinrich Lienhard confessed in his diary, "that somewhere along the Little Blue there was a large camp of [Indians] whose hostility toward the whites was generally feared. . . . Everybody kept his rifle loaded and ready." To the vast majority of Americans of this era, living in what they still called the Great American Desert held absolutely no appeal. "What this God-forsaken country was made for," concluded one exasperated voyager, "I am at a loss to discover." Why challenge Indians for it? This locale was to be crossed, and as fast as possible. The throngs of westward immigrants had no desire to disturb the equilibrium established over the previous decade between Indians and whites. And yet the mere act of crossing disrupted the Indians and the policy of Separation on which this equilibrium rested.

One area of disruption occurred with the buffalo. The immense size of the herds astonished Americans on the overland trails. The large, lumbering beasts seemed to be everywhere. "Every acre was covered, until in the dim distance the prairie became one black mass from which there was no opening, and extending to the horizon," noted one traveller on the Santa Fe Trail in 1846. The never-ending tide of immigrants moving over the well-trod, developed trails panicked the herds roaming the central plains. The animals soon avoided these trails, restricting their grazing to areas either to the north or south of them. White hunters also began their assault on the herds. In 1846 Thomas A. Harvey, western superintendent of Indian affairs, noticed the disappearance of buffalo from some areas of the plains. "All experience proves that game rapidly disappears before the firearms of the white," Harvey concluded. "He kills for the sake of killing." So intimately were the cultures and physical existence of the Plains Indians tied to the buffalo that the disruption of the herds, and in many instances the complete elimination of buffalo from tribal hunting ranges, produced a corresponding massive disruption in the Indians' lives. It forced tribes to secure new hunting areas by driving away those Indians who presently relied on them. Three years later Subagent John E. Barrow reported to superiors: "Our old friends, the Pawnees, have had a hard time of it during the past winter. When they returned from their hunting grounds, their trail could be followed by the dead bodies of those who starved to death. Children, young men, and women have shared this fate." It is little wonder that tribes increasingly identified the overland travellers as the source of their mounting misfortune. Harvey, in 1848, addressed the nature of the rapidly worsening situation for tribes:

The immense traveling of emigrant companies over the prairies, and the consequent increased destruction of buffalo, has excited the anxiety of several of the western tribes for some years past. . . . The country occupied by the buffalo is gradually and rapidly being circumscribed, which shows their great diminution. The time cannot be distant when they will be insufficient to subsist the numerous tribes that now depend upon them for food.

Harvey also urged the government to begin considering new solutions for the Indians, because a crisis was fast approaching as Migratory Fever eroded the premises that grounded the old solution of Separation.

New diseases introduced by the white migration and American expansion created more misery and disruption. Separated from the Old World for thousands of years, Indians had no natural immunities to diseases such as measles, whooping cough, and scarlet fever. These diseases were seldom fatal to whites, but they drove the Indian population into sharp decline. Epidemics of smallpox and cholera, which also plagued white settlements, added to the Indians' tribulation. The epidemics swept through the various tribes, devastating them with deadly speed and deadly results. A series of epidemics ravaged tribes along the Pacific coast from Oregon to California, eventually spreading across the Southwest. Historian William T. Hagan points out the frightful Indian casualties from an epidemic that struck the Upper Missouri. "Of 1,600 Mandans, only about 100 survived a smallpox epidemic which also struck down perhaps half of the Blackfeet," he records. "More than half of the Kiowas and Comanches were the victims of Asiatic cholera, and other plains tribes suffered proportionally." Agent Henry Schoolcraft set the number of Mandan survivors at 13, noting also that Minnetarees, Assiniboines, Crows, and Arikaras likewise were struck hard. White-introduced disease devastated the Pawnees and other tribes along the Platte. Schoolcraft, calling smallpox "the scourge to the aborigines," described uninhabited villages where wolves roamed "fattening [themselves] on the human carcasses that [lay] strewed about." Other afflictions, such as venereal disease, became common too among people previously uninitiated to its horrors, rapidly proving itself a plague of a different variety.

Disease, not warfare with whites, was the great devastator of the Indian population. Don Russell, in "How Many Indians

Were Killed" (*American West*, July 1973), estimated that Indians suffered roughly four thousand deaths in warfare with American soldiers between 1789 and 1898, less than one percent of their population during that time span. Death from disease produced catastrophically higher figures, perhaps as high as 30 to 40 percent of their population, and even more among some tribes. "The vast preparations for the protection of the western frontier are superfluous," one American wrote from New Orleans in 1838 following the Indian smallpox epidemic of that year. "Another arm has undertaken the defense of the white inhabitants of the frontier; and the funeral torch, that lights the red man to his dreary grave, has become the auspicious star of the advancing settler." Disease proved the most accurate and deadly harbinger of advancing white settlement to tribes.

Perhaps worse even than epidemics was the introduction of alcohol on a scale that proved corrupting, demoralizing, and destructive to bodies and cultures not accustomed to it and its effects. "In epidemic form," stated historian Bernard Sheehan, "it ravaged tribe after tribe until the drunken, reprobate Indian became a fixture of American folklore." Studies in the 1970s postulated possible explanations for Indian drinking patterns, ranging from physiological causes (Jerry McLeod and Stanley Clark, "It's in the Blood," *Canadian Welfare*, September-October 1974) to a method of protesting white domination (Nancy Oestrich Lurie, "The World's Oldest On-Going Protest Demonstration: North American Indian Drinking Patterns," *Pacific Historical Review*, August 1971). The Oklahoma Center for Alcohol-Related Research suggested that genetic factors lay at the root of the drinking habits of many Indians ("A Metabolic Clue to Indian Endurance and Intolerance for Alcohol," *Psychology Today*, July 1972). Whatever the actual cause, many Indians were ardently attracted to the white man's alcohol. Commentators as diverse as Jesuit missionaries in Canada during the seventeenth century and the influential nineteenth-century American politician Lewis Cass made similar reports that "Indians in immediate contact with our settlements, old and young, male and female, the chief and the warrior, all give themselves up to the most brutal intoxication, whenever this mad water can be procured." Cass recounts an especially telling episode of a Potawatomie chief's pitiful pleas during treaty negotiations at Chicago in 1821: "Father, we care not for the money, nor the land, nor the goods. We want the whiskey."

Reformers, missionaries, government officials all agreed that whiskey was socially and physically injurious to the Indians. Perhaps more important to them, alcohol severely undermined their attempts to improve the condition of the Indians. "I cannot too strongly impress upon you," Indian Commissioner William Medill wrote one of his agents in 1846, "the importance of the duty imposed upon you. The prevention of the use of strong drink has almost been the one thing needful to ensure the prosperity of the Indian race and its advancement in civilization. The use of it has tended more to the demoralization of the Indians than all other causes combined." The Indian Affairs Office forbade the introduction of liquor into the Indian country and the sale of it to Indians. White traders generally disregarded the injunction for two simple reasons: they reaped enormous profits from liquor sales to Indians and, if they were caught, the government imposed a minimal penalty. "The profits of the trade are so great," said Commissioner Medill, summing up the problem, "that the risk of detection and loss of the article is, and will be incurred without hesitation."

Migratory Fever, by introducing liquor and catastrophic diseases, coupled with the mounting disruption that it caused to the tribes' ecological base, irrevocably altered Indian-white relations in the trans-Mississippi West. Although early overland travellers had wanted to avoid contact with Indians as they crossed the Great American Desert, they nevertheless left a devastating imprint. It distressed few Americans, however. Medill saw the Indians' mounting problems and misfortunes as nothing more than the natural consequence of approaching civilization. "The injury complained of," he concluded, "is but one of those inconveniences to which every people are subjected by the changing & constantly progressive spirit of the age." And although Indians may not have immediately grasped the significance of Manifest Destiny, by the end of the decade they were confronted with the emerging popular conviction of the need of Americans to control and inhabit all land between the Atlantic and the Pacific.

Dashed Hopes, a New Indian Question, and a New Solution

The developments of the 1840s—Migratory Fever and the overland trails, Manifest Destiny and territorial expansion—opened a door to a succession of consequences in Indian-white relations that could never be closed. The rationale for the policy of Separation and the reasons for establishing and maintaining an Indian sanctuary on the western prairies, which sounded so convincing and so immutable in 1840, were crumbling fast as the decade wore on.

Those Indians who observed the first stream of covered wagons passing through their lands could little have imagined the cumulative effect this migration would have on their people and on the continuance of their way of life. At first, the tribes showed little concern, reacting placidly to the overland travellers. But by the mid-1840s, as trails through the central plains became fixed and more attractive to migrants, and as these migrants increasingly disrupted the Indians' economy, ecology, and lives, leaving in their wake untold masses of sick, dying, or dead people, Indian reaction changed. Steadily unease and bitterness mounted among increasing numbers of Plains Indians. John C. Frémont, while en route to California, noted unrest among the powerful Teton Sioux, and especially their mounting anger toward the overland travellers whom they blamed for driving away the buffalo. In 1846, Sioux along the Oregon Trail approached agents of the federal government, asking that restrictions be placed on the haphazard killing of game on the plains by whites, and requesting either payment from the travellers or compensation from the government for use of trails through their lands. Some Brules and Oglalas complained directly to President Polk:

For several years past the Emigrants going over the Mountains from the United States, have been the cause that Buffalo have in great measure left our hunting grounds, thereby causing us to go into the Country of Our Enemies to hunt, exposing our lives daily for the necessary subsistence of our wives and Children and getting killed on several occasions. We have all along treated the Emigrants in the most friendly manner, giving them free passage through our hunting grounds. . . . We are poor and beg you to take our Situation into Consideration, it has been Customary when our white friends make a road through the Red man's country to remunerate them for the injury caused thereby.

The government did nothing to appease the Sioux, who therefore took it upon themselves to demand and collect "tolls" from travellers. Prudently, the emigrants usually paid the fee required of them, but rarely with grace or with any feeling that the payment was just.

Americans who stayed home were no more sympathetic to the Indians' claims. The idea that these unimportant "savages" had grounds for their claims was ludicrous and presumptuous. Complaints and petitions flooded the offices of congressmen and filled the pages of frontier newspapers, demanding that the government guarantee the right of free and unmolested passage on all trails through Indian country. "The advance company of emigrants, which were for Oregon, . . . comprising forty wagons, *were stopped in the road*, on arrival at Laramie by the Sioux, and not *permitted to pass until tribute had been paid*," went one complaint. Another American grumbled: "The Sioux say they must have tobacco, &c., for the privilege of travelling through their country. . . . This may cause trouble, and Government should attend to it at once." Western editors snapped to the task of offering advice to Washington. "We think it is high time the attention of the Government was called to the matter," the *St. Louis Reveille* editorialized, "and that they should take some other measures with the Indians than making them presents and smoking with them the peace pipe."

The Indian question again faced the nation, and once more Americans expected a solution. Haltingly, the government in Washington responded. Compelled by growing demands for action, officials dispatched negotiators such as Major Philip Kearny to reason with tribes on the central plains, but the government's principal response was to establish forts along the overland trails and then charge the army with guarding travellers and punishing those Indians who annoyed or threatened them. "Such a course I am convinced would have a very salutary effect," applauded Thomas Fitzpatrick, agent for the Upper Platte and Arkansas, "and be the cause of accomplishing more good to the Indians . . . than all the treaties and councils that could be invented." Officials anticipated that Indians would be intimidated and thus kept away from the overland trails.

This new procedure went into effect in 1847 with the establishment of forts along the trail to Oregon, manned by mounted rifle units called "dragoons." Campaigns against those Indians living near the trail commenced according to plan, but the soldiers' efforts met with little success. The Indians proved too elusive on the wide expanse of the plains, and as mounted warriors they were superior to the soldiers sent to suppress them. The military's increased presence on the central plains simply failed to intimidate the tribes. The dragoons' work had one chief effect: it sharply increased native hostility toward the United States government and the migrants on the overland trails. Retaliatory attacks on soldiers and travellers escalated alarmingly.

By the late 1840s the plains bustled with change and movement, no longer just from emigrants and various travellers, but also by speculators planning to build railroads across the Great Plains. With increasing attacks on overland travellers, the intrusion of large-scale commerce, and the specter of full-scale war with Indians, the region took on a new status and a new burden for the government. Federal officials took a hard look at the situation, realizing they must do something quickly. They had conspicuously few alternatives: the premises of the policy of Separation must be rejected or affirmed. Either Americans must be permitted unhindered access to the region, or the right of Indians to hold this land indisputably and to live upon it undisturbed by whites must be protected by the federal authority.

The proposal offered by Indian Commissioner Medill in 1848 began the reversal of the government's earlier decree and initiated a sequence of federal decisions that three years later culminated in the government's new solution to the Indian question: the policy of Concentration. Medill speculated that the answer to the dilemma lay in establishing two large Indian colonies, one on the northern and the other on the southern plains. Seven years earlier, in 1841, Thomas H. Crawford, Indian Commissioner for Presidents Van Buren, Harrison, and Tyler, suggested the same idea. But in the face of mounting turmoil beyond the Mississippi, Medill settled on a more expeditious plan: treaties with potentially hostile tribes to secure a right-of-way through their lands. But he never had the time to implement the idea. Zachary Taylor's victory in the 1848 election placed federal patronage under the control of the Whig party. Redistribution of political spoils soon swept Medill and other Democrats from government service.

Secretary of Interior Thomas Ewing, one of the new president's most trusted advisors, personally directed Indian affairs for the Taylor administration. Indian Commissioner Orlando Brown simply executed Ewing's agenda. In dealing with the turbulent trans-Mississippi state of affairs, the secretary decided to go beyond Medill's plan of right-of-way treaties. Instead, Ewing recommended accords with the plains tribes to establish areas with well-defined boundaries as their residence and hunting grounds. This plan, he felt, would limit Indian-white contact, reduce intertribal warfare, and provide government the means to limit negative white influence on tribes. A bill encompassing Ewing's recommendation was submitted to the Senate on March 18, 1850. The proposed legislation passed quickly in the Senate, which gave its approval in late April 1850. The House, however, embroiled in fierce debates over the question of the extension of slavery into the lands of the Mexican War cession, tarried on a final decision. By the time that body took up the Ewing proposal later that year, new leadership directed federal Indian affairs.

Zachary Taylor died unexpectedly on July 9, 1850, less than a year and a half into his term of office. He was succeeded by his vice president, Millard Fillmore, who brought Alexander H. H. Stuart into his cabinet as secretary of interior, replacing Ewing. Luke Lea, whom Taylor, just before his death, appointed head of the Indian Bureau as a patronage reward, remained as commissioner of Indian Affairs. Secretary Stuart considered the policy of Separation no longer tenable. He demanded a new solution to the Indian question. The Indians were "encompassed by an unbroken chain of civilization; and the question forces itself upon the mind of the statesman and the Philanthropist, what is to become of the aboriginal race?" asked Stuart. "This question must now be fairly met. . . . The policy of removal [Separation] except under peculiar circumstances, must necessarily be abandoned."

Commissioner Lea set to the task. Proceeding from Medill's and Ewing's ideas, he formulated a comprehensive plan to address the new Indian question. Lea, in his annual report of 1850, explained the policy of Concentration and the new course to be followed in Indian affairs by the federal government:

There should be assigned to each tribe, for a permanent home, a country adapted to agriculture, of limited extent and well-defined boundaries; within which all [Indians], with occasional exceptions, should be compelled constantly to remain until such time as their general improvement and good conduct may supersede the necessity of such restrictions. In the mean time the government should cause them to be supplied with stock, agricultural implements, and useful material for clothing; encourage and assist them in the erection of comfortable dwellings, and secure to them the means of facilities of education, intellectual, moral, and religious.

Lea worked closely with Robert W. Johnson, chairman of the House Committee on Indian Affairs, to assure congressional approval. In February 1851 Congress passed the Indian Appropriation Act, sanctioning the new policy and appropriating $100,000 to negotiate Concentration treaties.

Responsibility for administering and enforcing the policy of Concentration rested with agents of the Indian Bureau and the United States Army. To provide both the necessary civilian personnel and an efficient organization for the task, Lea also reorganized and enlarged the Indian Bureau. He established three superintendencies to administer the region east of the Rockies to the Indian Territory. Responsibility for the upper plains rested with the northern superintendent, the central plains with the central superintendent, and the Indian Territory with the southern superintendent. To complete his reorganization and to improve administration in the region acquired under the banner of Manifest Destiny during the Polk presidency, Lea, in addition to agents already posted to California and Oregon, now assigned agents to administer the tribes in Utah and New Mexico Territories.

Seeking to safeguard overland traffic, as well as to open up new areas in the trans-Mississippi West to American settlement and enterprise, the Indian Bureau moved with deliberation to implement the policy of Concentration by concluding comprehensive treaties with the western tribes. Although not fully realized until after the American Civil War, Washington during the 1850s took important steps toward effecting the policy. By 1856, under the direction of Lea and his successor George W. Manypenny, over fifty treaties had been negotiated that extinguished Indian title to 174 million acres of land. The first major council to implement Concentration provides a good example of what happened to tribes when negotiators appeared in their land with a treaty to sign.

In September 1851, the largest gathering of natives seen on the Great Plains until that time participated in a council held near Fort Laramie in southeastern Wyoming. Its purpose was to organize the northern plains and secure the important

Oregon Trail for American travellers. Almost ten thousand Indians—Cheyennes, Arapahoes, Teton Sioux, Assiniboines, Shoshonis, Crows, and Arikaras—came in for this council. The Kiowas and the Comanches did not attend, refusing to meet with their tribal enemies. The government's negotiator, David D. Mitchell, asked the Indians to allow free, unmolested travel over the Oregon Trail; to stop all intertribal warfare; and to agree to the establishment of exact territorial boundaries for each tribe. "In times past you had plenty of buffalo and game to subsist upon, and your Great Father well knows that has always been your favorite amusement and pursuit," Mitchell explained to the gathered tribes. "Your condition has changed, and your Great Father desires you will consider and prepare for the changes that await you." The government, perhaps aware of what it asked, did attempt to use such natural boundaries as existed on the northern plains, such boundaries as the Arkansas, Powder, North Platte, and Yellowstone rivers, in making its determination. In return for signing this crucial treaty, the tribes were guaranteed an annuity payment of $50,000 a year in food and goods for the next fifty years, permanent right to their defined lands, and peace with the United States. When the Fort Laramie Treaty came before the United States Senate for ratification, the senators considered the terms too generous, hence the length of time for the annuity was reduced from fifty to fifteen years.

Franklin Pierce's Democratic victory in 1852 assured the departure of Commissioner Lea and other Whigs from the federal bureaucracy. Just before leaving office, Lea evaluated the government's new solution to the Indian question and addressed the ethical considerations raised by the policy of Concentration. "When civilization and barbarism are brought in such relation that they cannot coexist together, it is right that the superiority of the former should be asserted and the latter compelled to give way," he wrote in his final annual report. "It is, therefore, no matter of regret or reproach that so large a portion of our territory has been wrested from its

aboriginal inhabitants and made the happy abode of an enlightened and Christian people."

Concentration in the Indian Territory and Texas

George W. Manypenny, recommended to Franklin Pierce by
members of the Ohio Democratic delegation to Congress, assumed his duties as the new commissioner of Indian Affairs
within a month of the presidential inauguration in March
1853. Although commissioners tended to have little contact
with Indian matters after leaving the post, Manypenny developed a life-long concern with Indian affairs, Indian welfare,
and the government's relationship with and treatment of
tribes. He summarized his ideas in *Our Indian Wards*, published in 1880.

During Manypenny's four-year tenure in the Indian Bureau, government emissaries succeeded in negotiating fifty-two
treaties with western tribes, significantly advancing the implementation of the policy of Concentration. In 1853, however,
as Manypenny assumed his duties, the Indian Territory on the
eastern edge of the Great Plains remained untouched, a situation that would soon change. By the early 1850s the public's
perception of the region had changed. What had been considered the Great American Desert was perceived as the nation's
heartland. Settlers discovered that this area, long thought of
as unproductive, could support certain types of farming. Lust-
ing after real estate in the Indian Territory, Americans complained bitterly that there was more land there than the Indians
could ever use productively. Increasingly they demanded that
Washington move to concentrate the Indians and organize the
region into a federal territory in preparation for statehood.

The American business community also had plans for the
locale, and its aspirations probably carried the greater influence
in the nation's capital. Railroad companies, backed by western
senators David R. Atchison of Missouri and Stephen A. Douglas of Illinois, chairman of the influential Senate Committee
on Territories, were making long-range plans to build a trans-

continental railroad across the Great Plains. They anticipated that the line would originate at a western city, perhaps Chicago, St. Louis, Memphis, or New Orleans, and from there it would run westward across the Great Plains to California. Railroad executives exerted enormous pressure upon the federal government to open the Indian Territory for their use. Outgoing President Millard Fillmore, bowing to their lobbying efforts, asked permission of Congress to negotiate treaties with all tribes residing in the northern portion of the Indian Territory for the cession of their lands and relocation to diminutive reservations. Congress gave authorization on March 3, 1853.

In August 1853, Secretary of Interior Robert McClelland charged Commissioner Manypenny with the responsibility of implementing the plan. He dutifully carried out his orders, but the assignment gave him pause for reflection and, so it seems, for remorse as well. "By alternate persuasion and force," reflected Manypenny, "some of these tribes have been removed, step by step, from mountain to valley, and from river to plain, until they have been pushed halfway across the continent. They can go no further; on the ground they now occupy the crisis must be met, and their future determined." The commissioner did as duty demanded, however, spending the final months of 1853 implementing "the new order of things," as he called it, with the Delawares, Iowas, Kaskaskias, Kickapoos, Miamis, Missouris, Omahas, Otos, Sacs and Foxes, Shawnees, Peorias, Piankashaws, and Weas. At last he reported that tribal leaders, "without enthusiasm," had completed cession accords, thus opening that portion of the Indian Territory north of thirty-seven degrees latitude to whites.

As a result of the treaties, these tribes forfeited over fifteen million acres to the United States. Their new reservations provided them with less than 1.5 million acres. One year later, the Congress of the United States passed the Kansas-Nebraska Act, which established two large federal territories from what previously was the northern portion of the Indian Territory. Americans eagerly rushed in to claim this bonanza, which until 1854 had been withheld from them by Congress. By the end of the decade, 136,000 had settled in those territories, mostly in Kansas. It soon became known as "Bleeding Kansas," as violent confrontation erupted among white settlers in that territory over the extension of slavery question. George Manypenny noted sardonically that Indian deportment contrasted "favorably with the disorderly and lawless conduct of many of their white brethren, who, while they have quarrelled about the African, have united upon the soil of Kansas in wrong doing toward the Indians!"

The once immense Indian Territory had now been reduced by the policy of Concentration to the domains of the republics established south of Kansas by the Five Civilized Tribes. In light of past events, they had cause to wonder just how much longer Washington would maintain the sanctity of their nations. Troubling signals already abounded. "Necessity will soon *compel* the incorporation of their [the five Indian republics'] country into the Union," one federal official concluded. The Cherokee newspaper scathingly predicted that soon, no doubt, "a Commissioner will be sent down to negotiate, with a pocket full of money and his mouth full of lies. Some chiefs he will bribe, some he will flatter and some he will make drunk; and the result will be . . . something that will be called a treaty." Many in positions of leadership within the governments of the five republics realized the need to secure an ally capable of helping defend their nations against encroachment by the United States. The eventual answer to their desperate situation proved ironic, but not surprising. It appeared in 1861 with the onset of the Civil War in the form of the Southern Confederacy.

If the policy of Concentration was to solve the Indian question, as officials in Washington confidently expected, its success would rest on one of two exigencies: either unilateral enforcement by the United States government, probably through its military arm, or bilateral resolve and forbearance by Indians and Americans. Indians would have to cooperate by living and hunting in their specified territory, and Americans would have to utilize the land accorded to them and refrain from trespassing on tribal lands. Unfortunately, too seldom did either side cooperate with the government's expectations. To the distress of Americans, many western tribes still moved about freely, as they had always done, without heed to boundaries or borders, over lands now reserved for white settlement and enterprise by recent treaties. In turn, Indian resentment increased as the number of whites who attempted to displace them from areas within their specified territories grew. The behavior of both parties exasperated Manypenny, but especially that of his fellow citizens, theoretically the more civilized of the two groups. "Trespasses and depredations have been committed on the Indians," the commissioner stated with displeasure in 1856. "They have been personally maltreated, their property stolen, their timber destroyed, their possession encroached upon, and divers other wrongs and injuries done them." Years later, in 1881, Interior Secretary Carl Schurz explained why so little cooperation came from Americans. "The average frontiersman looks upon the Indian simply as a nuisance that is in his way," he surmised. "It would be difficult to convince [many] that it is a crime to kill an Indian, or that to rob an Indian of his lands is not a meritorious act."

Nowhere were the difficulties of making the policy of Concentration a workable and permanent solution to the Indian question more apparent than in Texas. Here, during the previous decade, the United States had inherited a vicious and ongoing struggle between Texans and Indians—fruits of Migratory Fever and Manifest Destiny. The Texas situation cried for resolution. Washington, understandably, applied its new solution of Concentration, but the policy failed to solve the Indian question in Texas. But this failure did little to shake federal officials' confidence in the efficacy of the policy. Perhaps it should have, because Texas foreshadowed United States–Indian affairs in the 1860s and 1870s, two of the most turbulent and violent decades in the history of Indian-white relations.

Americans under Stephen Austin settled along the Colorado River in Coahuila-Texas, a northern province of Mexico, in the early 1820s. Over the next decade the Mexican government prohibited further American colonization, outlawed Negro slavery, and attempted to strengthen Mexican central authority over the American settlers in Texas, prompting revolution to break out in 1835. Almost as soon as Texans achieved independence the following year, they requested annexation by the United States. Northern politicians blocked the attempt, fearing that Texas would be divided into numerous slave states. The Lone Star Republic therefore remained an independent nation.

Sam Houston, the hero of the recent revolution, became the first president of the Republic of Texas. He moved quickly to establish peaceful and harmonious relations with the Indians of Texas, who included Kiowas, Comanches, Lipan Apaches, Wacos, Caddos, and Wichitas. Of these, the Comanches, inhabiting the northern and western portion of the republic, were both the most populous and the dominant tribe. Their lives consisted almost exclusively of hunting and raiding. In earlier times they had raided Spanish, then Mexican, settlements. Recently they had turned to the newer Texas settlements with enthusiasm. In 1837 Houston successfully concluded a treaty with the Indians guaranteeing them their lands in western Texas. Texans, disregarding the treaty, unceremoniously shoved their president's wishes and promises aside and pressed into the forbidden land. Warfare soon swept across the west Texas frontier as tribes brutally retaliated against the land-hungry settlers.

In 1838 Sam Houston lost his bid for reelection, and the new president of Texas, Mirabeau Lamar, carried out his campaign promise to conduct a war of extermination against the Indians. Terrible fighting engulfed western Texas for the next four years, until weariness prompted the people to turn again to the peace-minded Sam Houston. He sought an enduring peace by creating a boundary line within the republic to separate the two warring races. He charged the Texas Rangers with the responsibility of guarding the border and keeping whites out. Had President Houston been able to effect this measure, peace might have been secured since Indians would live west of the boundary line while Texans would remain east of it. Most Texans, however, refusing to recognize the Indians' right to any land in Texas, claimed homesteads in Indian territory and threatened to "shoot the first Indian that came on the land." The Texas Rangers compounded the difficulty by haphazardly enforcing Houston's plan. As a result whites continued to overrun the lands reserved for the Texas tribes. The Indians, convinced that Houston and the Texas government had betrayed them, increased their efforts to repulse the settlers.

The United States assumed the troubles in Texas when it annexed the Republic of Texas in 1845 and made it the twenty-eighth state. The federal government faced another, more immediate problem: Texans, intense supporters of states' rights, were not eager to submit to federal authority on the Indian question. Washington was handicapped because it lacked ownership and jurisdiction over public lands in the state. As one of the conditions of annexation, Texas retained "all the vacant and unappropriated lands lying within its limits, to be applied to the payment of the debts and liabilities of said Republic of Texas, and the residue of said lands, after discharging said debts and liabilities, to be disposed of as said State may direct." Immediately Texas's attitude toward the Indians conflicted with the policy of the United States government, which recognized the Indians' claims to land in Texas by right of occupancy. Texans were highly critical of such an assertion by the federal authority. The state legislature angrily countered by declaring that it did not and would not recognize any Indian right to land within Texas.

The situation in Texas between 1846 and 1854 split into a series of interrelated conflicts between the United States government, the Texans and their state government, and the Indians of Texas. The United States attempted to bring lasting peace to Texas by negotiating a series of peace initiatives with the Indians, while trying to placate Texans. The first talks took place in 1846. Two United States commissioners, Pierce M. Butler and M. G. Lewis, convened a council of the Texas tribes on the Brazos River at a spot known as Council Springs. The treaty they negotiated offered "perpetual amity and friendship" with the Indians by promising to remove them from the jurisdiction of the state of Texas. It also pledged that the United States would protect both Texans and Indians. Texas took a vigorous states' rights position, bitterly denouncing federal interference in an internal matter and federal usurpation of a state's prerogative to administer Indian affairs within its borders. The state government declared it did not recognize the validity of the federal treaty. Hostilities resumed. The Indians quickly recognized that Texans intended not only to take all of their land, but to conduct a war to exterminate them. They responded by vicious attacks against white settlements in Texas. The Comanches, angered by the ineffectualness of the United States government in fulfilling its treaty promises, bitterly addressed their concerns to special federal agent Robert Simpson Neighbors:

For a long time a great many people have been passing though [our] country; they kill all the game, and burn the country, and trouble me very much. The commissioners of our great father promised to keep these people [Texans] out of our country. I believe our white brothers do not wish to run a line between us, because they wish to settle this country. I object to any more settlements.

The federal government was obliged to acknowledge its failure to protect the Indians of Texas. Just as clearly it also realized that Texas would not protect the Indians, especially when, in the summer of 1847, the state granted white speculators vast tracts of public land, even though Indians resided there. This recognition, coupled with ongoing hostilities, prompted American authorities to apply the new policy of Concentration within Texas. Only in this way, they concluded, could Indians be protected from further white aggression. After long delay and arduous negotiations, the United States in early 1854 finally assumed a tenuous jurisdiction over the Texas tribes, only after the state legislature agreed to the establishment of two large federal Indian reserves within the state. The Indian Bureau under Manypenny created one reserve on the Clear Fork of the Brazos River for the Comanches and a second on the main fork of the Brazos for the smaller tribes. But no sooner was this accomplished than Texans decided they wanted to settle this portion of the state themselves. Whites soon entered the federal reserves in an attempt to eliminate the Indian presence completely.

In a desperate attempt to protect the Indians from the Texans, frustrated federal officials sanctioned the complete removal of all Indians from that state in 1859. The United States had made a bitter enemy of the Comanches. Even so, the tribe had been treated with such ruthlessness by Texas that even after the long confrontation ended, Comanches never failed to distinguish between Americans and their most despised enemy, Texans.

As the decade closed, the western tribes were adjusting to the changes forced on them. Minor altercations occurred between troops and Indians, but there was no serious outbreak of violence. Federal officials confidently maintained that the policy of Concentration was the solution to the Indian question. While conceding that the policy had failed in Texas, they judged that episode an anomaly, not an augur. If anything, officials believed Texas taught an important lesson about the policy of Concentration: Washington could not count on the resolve and forbearance of either Indians or Americans. To solve the Indian question, the United States would have to enforce the policy unilaterally. But that question seemed unimportant now to the federal bureaucracy as other, more serious problems confronted the nation. At the end of the decade, with the United States moving rapidly toward a civil war, governmental attention to Indian affairs all but disappeared. The Indian question did not, however. The Civil War years exacerbated it, reinforced the lesson of Texas and, unexpectedly for the federal authority, further advanced the Concentration policy.

Yes; they fight among themselves—away off. Do you hear the thunder of their big guns? No; it would take you two moons to run down to where they are fighting, and all the way your path would be among white soldiers as thick as tamaracks in the swamps of the Ojibways. Yes; they fight among themselves, but if you strike at them they will all turn on you and devour you and your women and little children just as the locusts in their time fall on the trees and devour all the leaves in one day.

LITTLE CROW, SANTEE SIOUX

CHAPTER THREE

The Civil War Years

Ominously, one event had built upon another during the 1850s, straining sectional antagonism to the breaking point. Then came the election of 1860 and the crisis that lengthened into the American Civil War. Abraham Lincoln's victory and the ascendency to power of the Republicans, a purely Northern party dedicated to preventing the extension of slavery into the West, posed a threat too great to many Southerners. Before Lincoln took office as sixteenth president of the United States in March 1861, seven Cotton Belt states dissolved their ties with the federal union and, at Montgomery, Alabama, quickly proceeded to establish the Confederate States of America.

Lincoln was no sooner inaugurated than the emergency focused on Fort Sumter, a three-story pentagon-shaped masonry stronghold towering fifty feet above low water, constructed upon a shoal in the harbor of Charleston, South Carolina. Confederates demanded the immediate evacuation of the garrison. Lincoln not only rejected the ultimatum but dispatched a convoy of merchant ships to reprovision his troops.

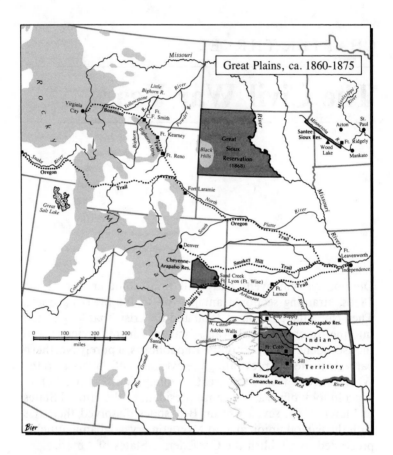

Great Plains, ca. 1860-1875

"The gage is thrown down," responded the *Charleston Mercury*, "and we accept the challenge." In the early morning hours of April 12, 1861, shore batteries around the harbor commenced a massive bombardment of Sumter. After thirty-four hours of shelling, federals lowered the flag of the United States and surrendered the fortress. Lincoln declared the Deep South to be in a state of rebellion and immediately issued a call for seventy-five thousand army volunteers. Four states of the Upper South, seeing Lincoln's call as an act of war, also seceded from the United States and joined the Confederacy.

A wave of war fever swept across the North and the South when people heard the news of Fort Sumter. People cheered. Bands played. Flags waved. "The military excitement here is intense," Senator John Sherman of Ohio wrote from Washington. "Civil War is actually upon us, and strange to say, it brings a feeling of relief: the suspense is over." Northerners and Southerners alike expected the war would be but a few glorious battles; people repeatedly fixed estimates of its duration at sixty days. In a short time, however, as Americans grimly battled Americans, the terrible reality of this destructive struggle settled over the land.

The combination of military, political, racial, social, cultural, economic, demographic, and constitutional consequences wrought by the Civil War made it pivotal in the national experience. It also proved crucial in Indian affairs. Here too the events of the Civil War years produced several important outcomes. After the five Indian republics allied with the Confederacy, the United States gained license to "solve" the Indian question in the Indian Territory, as it judged appropriate. The land taken from the five republics after the Civil War provided the government with the means in the postwar years to designate a zone for further implementation of the Concentration policy. In the absence of federal authority, white westerners tried to adjust Indian matters themselves, increasing hostility between the two groups. The heightened Indian hostility toward whites convinced the United States government that it must vigorously pursue and enforce the Concentration policy, which helped to precipitate the Plains Wars of the 1860s and 1870s.

Civil War in the Indian Territory

While the West paled in military significance to the eastern theater of the Civil War, both the United States and the Confederate States judged that region as strategically important. The government in Washington, determined to hold its western domain, was especially concerned with protecting the supply of gold and silver from western mines, which it vitally needed to help finance war against the Southern states. The government in Richmond, driven by its own vision of Manifest Destiny, intended by force of arms to acquire territory in the West for the expansion of its institutions, especially slavery; areas that, to the South's bitter aggravation, were denied to it before the war by the federal government. Additionally, the Confederacy aimed to secure a land corridor to the Pacific, stretching westward from the Confederate state of Texas across New Mexico and Arizona to California. Finally, it was determined to seize the Union's western silver and gold mines to shore up its pitiful lack of capital to prosecute the South's war for independence.

Since early in 1861 Southern officials had been forwarding overtures to leaders of the five Indian republics in the Indian Territory. "Your people, in their institutions, productions, latitude, and natural sympathies, are allied to the common brotherhood of the slaveholding States," argued Arkansas Governor Henry M. Rector in a letter he sent to Principal Chief John Ross of the Cherokees, hoping to coax this crucial leader over to a pro-Confederate position. "Our people and yours are natural allies in war." Similar messages went out to the other tribes. The Lincoln administration tried to counter the Confederates' arguments, especially on the slavery question. William P. Dole, Lincoln's Indian commissioner, hoping to hold their allegiance, wrote the tribes that "the government would under no circumstances permit the smallest interference with their tribal or domestic institutions." He cautioned them that Confederate agents were spreading an "erroneous impression" about the Republicans' position on slavery. Dole's reassurances never reached the tribes, however; Southern agents intercepted them en route.

To help realize his nation's objectives in the trans-Mississippi theater, Confederate Indian Commissioner Albert Pike travelled to the Indian Territory in 1861. There he hoped to draw the Five Civilized Tribes into the conflict against the Union. Pike had fertile ground on which to work. Many tribal members still harbored deep animosity toward the United States for the removal trauma of the 1830s, as well as for the federal authority's general nonobservance of treaty obligations in the years following removal. Economically the five republics had much stronger ties to the South than to the North. A number of the Indian republics' citizens were slaveholders, providing yet another factor. They felt a natural affinity for the Confederate cause and a like dread of the alleged threat posed by Lincoln and the Republicans to the maintenance of slavery in the United States.

The case against the Union did not end here. Confederates exploited several other provocative issues in an attempt to compel the Indian republics to sign treaties of alliance. One was the threat posed by the United States to the tribes' sovereignty and sanctity. Pike and his agents apprised the tribes of the recent campaign promises of William H. Seward, a leading New York Republican who now served as Lincoln's secretary of state. During the 1860 election Seward, in a speech at Chicago, had advocated the appropriation of the land of the Five Civilized Tribes so as to open it to white homesteaders. "The Indian Territory . . . south of Kansas, must be vacated by the Indians," rang his declaration. Confederates also reminded tribes of how the United States government had forsaken them. In the spring of 1861 the federal Indian Bureau withdrew all Indian service agents from the Indian Territory and Secretary of War Simon Cameron ordered the abandonment of Forts Washita, Arbuckle and Cobb in the Indian Territory, transferring their garrisons to Fort Leavenworth in Union-held Kansas. Confederate forces now occupied the installations. This action not only freed the five republics of their treaty obligations to the United States, Confederate agents argued, it also left the tribes vulnerable and fully exposed to assault from the Confederacy, which surrounded them on three sides and maintained troops within their homeland. "Indeed," reflected Union Commissioner Dole, acknowledging the convincing nature of the Confederate arguments, "the only matter of surprise to me is, that they [the five republics] have not more readily and heartily espoused the cause of the rebels."

There seemed few alternatives for the Five Civilized Tribes. In fact there appeared to be a number of advantages in allying with the Confederates, in part because they promised more liberal treaties than the United States ever had extended to the five tribes, but also because the Confederacy pledged to preserve and defend the independence of the Indian republics. The Chickasaw government, reflecting a strong desire among the great majority of its citizens to ally with the Confederacy, made its decision on May 25, 1861. "The Lincoln Government, pretending to represent said Union, has shown by its course toward us, in withdrawing from our country the protection of the Federal troops, ... a total disregard of treaty obligations," the Chickasaw legislature concluded. "Therefore, Be it resolved," it continued, declaring independence from the United States, "that the dissolution of the Federal Union ... has absolved the Chickasaws from allegiance [while] the current of the events of the last few months has left the Chickasaw Nation independent [and] the people thereof free ... to take such steps to secure their own safety, happiness, and future welfare as may to them seem best."

Like the Chickasaws, citizens of the Choctaw nation also overwhelmingly supported the proposed alliance. It took formal action against the United States on June 14, 1861. On July 12 delegates of both nations signed a joint treaty with Albert Pike committing their governments to the Confederate cause. The turn of events in the Indian Territory did not surprise Pike's Union counterpart, William Dole. In his annual report for 1861 the commissioner of Indian Affairs concluded:

Cut off from all intercourse with loyal citizens; surrounded by emissaries from the rebels, who represented that the government of the United States was destroyed, and who promised that the rebel government would assume the obligation of the United States and pay their annuities; assailed by threats of violence, and seeing around them no evidence of the power of the United States to protect them, it is not surprising that their loyalty was unable to resist such influence.

Not all tribes in the Indian Territory possessed the same certitude of action as the Chickasaws and Choctaws. Whatever fragile unity had existed since removal within the Creek, Seminole, and Cherokee tribes was shattered by the Southern overtures. Deeply divided over the question of allying with the Confederacy, each tribe split along factional lines with one side supporting an alliance and the another demanding neutrality. Albert Pike, in July 1861, at last won over influential mixed blooded chiefs, among them Daniel McIntosh, who allied the Creek nation with the South. But many Creeks, led by the respected full-blooded chief Opothleyahola, resisted interfering in this "white man's war," and so declared themselves neutral. During the factional struggle within their tribes that spring and summer, this group sought support from Washington. None came. Now, with their people split over the question of allying with the South, the neutrals bitterly condemned the Union's actions as a betrayal. Opothleyahola, in a long letter to Abraham Lincoln, demanded to know why they did not hear from him. The chief reminded the president that previous chief executives promised that "in our new homes, we should be defended from all interference from any people, and that no white people in the whole world should ever molest us unless they came from the sky." Perhaps Southern agents were correct after all, he stated briskly. Perhaps the "Government represented by our Great Father at Washington has turned against us."

The stand of Opothleyahola and his followers put them in a precarious, even perilous, position. Hoping to avoid a confrontation, the neutrals decided it wise to distance themselves from those Indians who backed the Confederacy. They journeyed into the northern portion of the Creek nation and established a camp along the North Fork of the Canadian River near the present town of Eufalaula, Oklahoma. The number in camp soon swelled to between eight and twelve hundred people with the arrival of neutral Seminoles under chiefs John Chupco and Billy Bowlegs, who had separated from their pro-Confederate kinsman.

No less severe was the bitter split within the Cherokee nation. Here the long-standing feud was between the Ross party and the Ridge, or Treaty, party. Back in Georgia during the 1830s, John Ridge had painfully come to see the hopelessness of the Cherokees' position in retaining their homeland, especially following the refusal of President Jackson to enforce the Supreme Court's *Worchester* v. *Georgia* decision. Believing that the Cherokee nation's only salvation lay in surrendering its land and relocating quietly in the West, he moved cautiously but purposefully to line up influential support within the tribe for a removal treaty. In this he ultimately succeeded. Ridge persuaded his father, Major Ridge, one of the wealthiest Cherokees and speaker of the nation's ruling body, the Cherokee National Council, as well as Stand Watie and his brother Elias Boudinot, editor of the tribal paper, the *Cherokee Phoenix*. The Ross party, led by Principal Chief John Ross, opposed them. This group categorically rejected removal and strenuously denounced both the Ridge party and all federal advances to sign a removal treaty. Understandably, officials in Washington turned to the Ridge party to consummate its design. Disregarding the wishes of the majority of Cherokees, the Ridge party signed the Treaty of New Echota, which sold the tribe's homeland for $5 million and authorized removal of the Cherokee people to the Indian Territory.

The Cherokees carried the feud from Georgia to the Indian Territory, and now in 1861 the Ross and Ridge parties again engaged in an intense struggle to chart the national course for the Cherokees. Stand Watie, following the assassinations of the Ridges and Boudinot in retaliation for their signatures at New Echota, inherited leadership of the Ridge party. He supported the Confederacy and pressed for an alliance. John Ross, as in the old days in Georgia, opposed him absolutely. The Civil War terrified Ross. He worried that the sea of violence that now drowned Americans might also engulf his own people in fratricidal conflict. The principal chief saw no alternative but to declare the Cherokee nation's neutrality. "I am—the Cherokees are—your friends," he reassured Confederates, "but we do not wish to be brought into the feuds between yourselves and your Northern Brethren. Our wish is for peace. Peace at home and Peace among you." At the same time he enjoined his people to the "faithful observance" of treaties with the United States and requested that they abstain from "partisan demonstrations."

The Creek and Seminole neutrals applauded John Ross's decision. Not unexpectedly, reaction from within the Cherokee nation was severely divided. Watie, sensing a growing public shift to his pro-Southern position, especially after the Union military catastrophe at Bull Run in April 1861, moved quickly to shape events. Watie offered military assistance to the Confederacy on behalf of the Cherokees and, in return, on July 12, received a commission in the Confederate Army at the rank of colonel. General Ben McCulloch, Confederate military commander in the Indian Territory, then authorized him to raise a regiment of Cherokees.

The Chickasaws and Choctaws, less than a month after allying themselves with the Confederacy, also organized a regiment of "mounted rifles." On August 1, 1861, Commissioner Pike notified Confederate President Jefferson Davis that the Indian regiments stood ready for battle. Later that month they went into action for the first time at the Battle of Wilson's Creek, fought near Springfield, Missouri. There a Confederate army, with the aid of the Indian regiments, although Watie himself was not present, mauled Union forces under General Nathaniel Lyon. The news of victory and the performance of its sons thrilled the Cherokee nation. Just as war fever swept across the North and the South that spring following Fort Sumter, martial ardor now mounted throughout the Indian Territory in the late summer.

Watie's actions and Cherokee participation in the victory at Wilson's Creek effectively reversed John Ross's declaration of neutrality. Desperately hoping to block the ascendency of Watie, Ross dramatically altered his stance. On August 21, 1861, two weeks after Wilson's Creek, he addressed his nation, telling the Cherokee people that he would seek an alliance with the Confederacy. General McCulloch reported jubilantly on August 31: "The Cherokees have joined the South." The Cherokee nation formally dissolved its ties with the United States on October 7 by signing a reciprocal treaty of alliance with the Confederate States. Both parties pledged "perpetual peace and friendship, and an alliance, offensive and defensive." After the signing ceremony Ross and Watie shook hands as a demonstration of tribal solidarity.

Those Cherokees who still maintained that the only satisfactory course for their nation was neutrality went into exile. Bearing the news of John Ross's defection, the neutrals sought haven with Opothleyahola. All too soon the worst fears of Ross came to pass. The specter of civil war among his people loomed unmistakably as Confederate Indians organized an expedition to assault the neutral's encampment, hoping to put the "traitors" to flight. Ross, in a letter that fall to Opothleyahola, pleaded with the neutrals' leader: "Brother—My advice and desire, under the present extraordinary crisis, is for all the red Brethren to be united among themselves in the support of our common rights and interests by forming an alliance of peace and friendship." But time had run out.

The internal strife in the Indian Territory burst forth on November 19, 1861, when Confederate Indians supported by Texans under Colonel Douglas H. Cooper engaged the neutrals at the Battle of Round Mountain. Less than a month later the two sides clashed again at Chusto Talasah. The decisive engagement came on December 26. Now reinforced by sixteen hundred Southern cavalrymen, the Confederate Indians routed Opothleyahola's neutrals; destroyed their camp, belongings, supplies, and livestock; and drove them from the Indian Territory. They fled up the Verdigris River, ultimately settling in refugee camps in Kansas where they faced destitution throughout the next three years. William Coffin, Southern superintendent for the United States, visited the camps. What he saw profoundly moved him: "The destitution, misery, and suffering amongst them is beyond the power of any pen to portray; it must be seen to be realized." Army surgeon A. B. Campbell witnessed the plight of the refugees, too. After visiting the Verdigris River camp during the refugees' first winter in Kansas, he tried to convey the agony of the experience: "It is impossible for me to depict the wretchedness of their condition. Their only protection from the snow upon which they lie is prairie grass, and from the wind scraps and rags stretched upon switches; some of them had some personal clothing, most had but shreds and rags, which did not conceal their nakedness; and I saw seven, ranging in age from three to fifteen years, without one thread upon their bodies." After arrival in Kansas their leaders cast off neutrality and offered to assist the United States.

The year 1862 proved fateful for the Confederate Indians and Southern fortunes. The hopes that the alliances with the South offered and the excitement of the early victories began to fade. In early spring, while Ulysses S. Grant battered Confederate defenses along the Tennessee and Cumberland rivers, Union forces to his south prepared to battle for control of Missouri and northern Arkansas. The showdown came on March 6, 1862, as blue and grey armies collided at Elkhorn Tavern, Arkansas. Samuel R. Curtis's ten thousand Union troops withstood an assault on the first day of the Battle of Pea Ridge by Earl Van Dorn's sixteen thousand Confederates, whose troops included thirty-five hundred Indians. Although outnumbered, General Curtis counterattacked on the second day, inflicting heavy casualties on the Southerners and forcing them into full retreat. The performance of Colonel Watie's

Cherokee Mounted Rifles proved to be one of the few bright spots during the Confederate debacle at Pea Ridge. Watie's men captured a strategic Union artillery position that raked Southern lines and later skillfully covered the Confederate withdrawal. General Curtis noted in his report on Pea Ridge how impressed Union officers were with "the hordes of Indians, cavalry, and infantry that were arrayed against us."

Confederate fortunes in the western theater continued to plummet that spring as Union land forces captured the Upper Mississippi and Admiral David Farragut's fleet blasted its way up the Lower Mississippi and seized New Orleans. These victories doomed the Southern cause in the West. Thereafter Confederates abandoned conventional tactics in the border states of Kansas, Missouri, and Arkansas and waged their fight through guerrilla warfare. General McCulloch relied heavily upon Colonel Watie and his Cherokees, whom he ordered to "destroy everything that might be of service to the enemy." Many of the forays came from guerrilla bases within the Indian Territory, as raiders under commanders like Stand Watie and Charles Quantrill attacked Union border settlements and disrupted federal supply lines and bases. Unlike the atrocities committed by Quantrill's band, Watie rejected such tactics. As a result of his notable war record, in 1864 his superiors promoted him to brigadier general.

Meanwhile, the Confederate defeat at the Battle of Pea Ridge opened the Indian Territory to invasion from Kansas. The United States saw two principal advantages in this tactic. One, as Lincoln told Congress, was to lead the Confederate Indians back into the Union. "It is believed that upon the repossession of the country by the federal forces," the president explained, "the Indians will readily cease all hostile demonstrations, and resume their former relations to the government." The second advantage, one pressed for fervently by the two United States senators from Kansas, James Lane and Samuel Pomeroy, was to hasten the removal of the refugee Indians from that state.

Opothleyahola and other pro-Union chiefs met with General David Hunter in February 1862 and agreed to assist with the invasion. A month later the commander of the Department of the Mississippi received his orders: "It is the desire of the President . . . that you should detail two regiments to act in the Indian country, with a view to open the way for friendly Indians who are now refugees in Southern Kansas to return to their homes and to protect them there. Five thousand friendly Indians will also be armed to aid in their own protection and you will please furnish them with necessary subsistence." By spring, cavalry and infantry regiments from Ohio and Wisconsin arrived, swelling the ranks of the invasion force. Superiors attached them to troops from Kansas and the pro-Union Indians to form the "Indian Expedition."

Pushing southward during the summer of 1862, the federals and their Indian allies advanced into northeastern Indian Territory as far as Tahlequah, capital of the Cherokee nation, where they arrested John Ross without incident. Thousands of Cherokees, realizing the futility of supporting the Southern cause, defected to the Union. The government sent Ross to Fort Leavenworth, Kansas, then to Philadelphia. There, with great personal relief, he repudiated his nation's alliance with the South. For the remainder of the war he directed a pro-Union Cherokee government in exile, ultimately serving as emissary to the United States. Not to be undermined by his rival, Stand Watie disavowed Ross's actions and declared himself rightful chief of the Cherokees. A meeting of Cherokees at Tahlequah on August 21, 1862, elected Watie principal chief and reaffirmed the treaty of alliance with the South.

John Ross, upon his arrival in the East, immediately sought to develop a cordial relationship with Abraham Lincoln and to secure aid for his people. Interior Secretary Caleb Smith wrote to Lincoln, asking permission for Ross to visit the White House. The president responded coolly. "I will see Mr. Ross at 9 A.M. to-morrow, if he calls." The chilly demeanor continued in the meeting. The two met on September 12, 1862, and Ross reaffirmed the Cherokees' loyalty to the United States. He explained to Lincoln that the Cherokees signed the treaty with the South under duress, only after the United States failed to protect his people under obligations set forth in earlier treaties. The arguments failed to sway Lincoln. The president disclaimed any failure of the national government, nor was he satisfied with Ross's reasons for the alliance. Lincoln closed the meeting assuring Ross that he would investigate the matter thoroughly.

Later that year Ross again approached Lincoln to seek a pardon for the Cherokee people. After a special meeting with his cabinet, Lincoln assured Ross that he would do everything in his power to protect pro-Union Cherokees; however, any determination of the fate of those who had aided the rebel cause must wait until the war's conclusion. It would be placed on the government's Reconstruction agenda. The United States eventually granted a parole to John Ross, but, to Ross's distress, the victorious Union punished his nation and the other Indian republics more harshly than it did the states of the defeated Confederacy.

Federal troops and pro-Union Indians followed their successful invasion of 1862 by launching another operation against the Indian Territory in the summer of 1863. At the Battle of Honey Springs, fought on July 17, the Indian Expedition defeated the rebel army and its Indian allies. Then it advanced steadily southward, at last reaching the Canadian River, which separated the Cherokee and Creek nations from those of the Choctaws and Chickasaws. The Confederate Indians, fleeing in disarray in the wake of the invading force, eventually reassembled in refugee camps further south and west, not unlike those in which their kinsmen languished in Kansas. The Indian Expedition might have pressed deeper into the Confederate Indians' territory and claimed absolute victory if military developments in the East had not intervened. Earlier that month in Pennsylvania, Union and Confederate soldiers assaulted each other at the Battle of Gettysburg. Robert E. Lee withdrew his battered forces back into Virginia and prepared for the inevitable Union counteroffensive. Lincoln soon ordered General U. S. Grant in from the western theater, assigning him responsibility for directing what the president hoped would be the conclusive operation against the Confederacy. Consequently, Northern and Southern commanders chose to abandon operations in the Indian Territory and the border states and reassign men to the more critical eastern theater.

The Canadian River now stood as the rough boundary line separating Indian combatants. The Indian Territory descended into its own bloody and destructive fratricidal struggle, as pro-Union and pro-Confederate Indians assailed one another. Each side swept back and forth across the river for the next two years, turning the once bountiful Indian Territory into a no-man's-land of terror, disruption, and desolation. At last the Civil War concluded as Union forces triumphed. General Lee surrendered his army on April 9, 1865. Over the next six weeks other Confederate commanders capitulated to the Union. Stand Watie was the last Confederate general to succumb. He signed articles of surrender on June 23, 1865, near Doaksville, the capital of the Choctaw nation.

Like the South, the Indian Territory was prostrate after the terrible fighting of the Civil War years. Great portions of it lay devastated: homes destroyed, fields overrun or untended, stock dead or running loose. The war left countless families bereft, while thousands from the five republics suffered as refugees. One can sense from John Ross the feelings of anguish and dislocation so widespread among members of the Five Civilized Tribes as he travelled back to the Indian Territory. "I know that I am fast approaching my country & my people," he wrote from Arkansas in late August 1865, "but, where is that delightful Home . . . the family Homestead ruthlessly reduced to ashes by the hand of rebel incendiaries. And whilst the surviving members of our family circle are scattered abroad as refugees—I am here journeying as it were, alone to find myself, a stranger & Homeless, in my own country."

Reconstruction under Abraham Lincoln might have been less calamitous for the Five Civilized Tribes and for the South, but by war's end he was dead from an assassin's bullet. Instead of a spirit of conciliation, one of vindictiveness toward the vanquished too often prevailed in Washington and characterized post-war dealings with the Five Civilized Tribes. The federal government, virtually charging the tribes with treason, asserted that they "had compromised their rights under existing treaties." James Harlan, Andrew Johnson's Secretary of War, made clear to Indian Commissioner Dennis N. Cooley the government's agenda in reconstructing the Five Civilized Tribes: "The President is willing to grant them peace, but wants land for other Indians, and a civil government for the whole Territory." Thus the Civil War provided a resolution, unplanned but not unwelcomed, to certain Indian problems that lingered from the 1850s. Through the process of Reconstruction the United States would advance the policy of Concentration.

To reestablish their relationship with the United States, Washington required each of the five tribes to sign a Reconstruction treaty. Following preliminary discussions with a federal peace commission headed by Indian Commissioner Cooley at Fort Smith, Arkansas in the fall of 1865, representatives of each tribe came to Washington in 1866 to sign the documents. In most respects all treaties were similar. Their terms allowed the United States to solve, in its judgment, the long-standing Indian question in the Indian Territory with the Five Civilized Tribes and provide for new contingencies. The treaties contained five major provisions. They established peace with the United States and among the five Indian republics; they abolished slavery, granted tribal citizenship to Negroes formerly held in bondage, and ordered their integration into the five tribes on an equal footing; they acknowledged preliminary steps for a unified government in preparation for territorial status and possibly an Indian state; and they mandated tribal acquiescence to rights-of-way for future railroad construction across the Indian Territory.

The fifth provision dealt with land occupancy. The Indian Reconstruction treaties contained substantial land cessions by all five tribes. Their collective forfeiture amounted virtually to the western half of present-day Oklahoma. The United States planned to advance the policy of Concentration in this area. After reducing by half the five Indian republics' domains, Washington set aside roughly the western third of the Indian Territory for future use as federal reservations. A central corridor in the Indian Territory was also organized as a zone to settle tribes such as the Kickapoo, Pawnee, Potawatomie, Sac and Fox, and Shawnee, among others. A quarter-century earlier the United States had removed them under the policy of Separation from the East to the northern part of the Indian Territory. In the 1850s Commissioner George Manypenny dissolved that portion of the Indian Territory and concentrated them on lands that became Kansas. Congress, at the end of the Civil War, now evicted them from Kansas in answer to the successful lobbying of senators Lane and Pomeroy of that state and provided them with another "permanent" home, this time in lands once granted in perpetuity to the Five Civilized Tribes.

The burden of peace, like that of the war years, proved heavy for the people of the Indian Territory. John Ross concluded that the "victory perched upon the banners of the United States . . . has been achieved at the sacrafice [sic] of hundreds of precious lives, the loss of wealth and resources of the [Cherokee] Nation and amid pain, suffering and destitution hitherto unknown to our people." Elias C. Boudinot succinctly summarized the net effect of the Civil War—the "white man's war" that Ross, Opothleyahola, and others so desperately tried to avoid—on the Five Civilized Tribes in a letter to Stand Watie in 1866: "We have been beaten."

The Santee Sioux Uprising

The Five Civilized Tribes were the only Indians actually drawn into the Civil War itself. The Civil War was not, however, the only arena of Indian-white conflict between 1861 and 1865. Other severe altercations erupted as well, although none related directly to the war. The United States government, locked in a struggle with a determined Southern Confederacy, of necessity was forced to give Indian affairs a low priority. Having little effort to spare for policing its own regulations in an area far removed from the arena of conflicts between the states, Indian affairs suffered. Settlement of the trans-Mississippi West, although slackening slightly, continued throughout the war years. Under the buffeting of those Americans who looked for land to farm or gold to dig, Washington found it increasingly difficult to maintain the integrity of treaty obligations and the areas defined in the 1850s under the policy of Concentration. Indians, who complained of many uncorrected injustices, now exacerbated by the absence of federal authority, took advantage of the recall of army regulars from frontier posts to adjust matters themselves. This situation resulted in two eruptions of interracial violence. One involved the Sioux, the other the Southern Cheyennes. Both incidents posed a significant threat to the Concentration policy and convinced the federal government that it would have to enforce the policy unilaterally in the post-war years.

While the Union and Confederate armies battled through the opening years of the war, the first serious outbreak of the trouble occurred in Minnesota involving the Santee Sioux. The tribe had agreed to two sets of treaties with the United States during the 1850s when the federal government began the policy of Concentration. Both sets of treaties contributed to the events in the late summer of 1862. In the first of the treaties, concluded at Traverse des Sioux in 1851, the tribe ceded twenty-four million acres to the United States and, in turn, were allotted two reservations along both sides of the Upper Minnesota River, measuring twenty miles wide by 150 miles long. In 1858, the Santee Sioux saw this reservation reduced by half as they forfeited the territory north of the river in the second treaties. Both sets of treaties contained assimilation measures that directed the government to build blacksmith shops and saw mills, establish manual labor schools on the reservations, and introduce the concept of private property among the Santees by allotting eighty-acre farm plots to individual families. "The theory, in substance," explained Thomas J. Galbraith, the Santee Sioux's agent, "was to break up the community system among the Sioux; weaken and destroy their tribal relations; individualize them by giving each a separate home and having them subsist by industry—the sweat of their brows; till the soil; make labor honorable and idleness dishonorable; or, as it was expressed in short, '*make white men of them*,' and have them adopt the habits and customs of white men."

It did not take long for problems to arise on the reservation. The assimilation measures of the recent treaties provided one source of intratribal tension, producing antagonism between the "farmer" and "blanket" Santees, who disagreed over whether to shed or keep the old tribal ways. Food shortages among the Santee Sioux produced the second problem. A constantly increasing white population in the rich Minnesota Valley during the 1850s and early 1860s steadily diminished the amount of game on or around the reservation. This development, coupled with the Santees' mounting inability to grow sufficient food to feed themselves on their compressed reservation, made it inevitable that government annuity payments came to mean the difference between survival and starvation. Tribal members typically used annuity monies to purchase food supplies.

The Civil War destroyed many things, among them the federal government's plan for feeding the Santee Sioux. Ever since that conflict broke out, the United States, preoccupied with prosecuting the war and needing every dollar available, had become increasingly tardy in providing annuity payments. Combined with bad harvests, it produced severe food shortages in the early 1860s. Hunger on the reservation increased, as did the Santee Sioux's hostility toward white settlers who, it seemed, had forged lives of plenty on former Sioux lands while they slipped from deprivation to destitution. By the summer of 1862, the severe hunger precipitated a catastrophe in Minnesota.

By early August of 1862, the Sioux were desperate. Santees from the Upper Agency, the northern portion of their reserve, broke into the government's warehouse and, with the reluctant approval of their agent Thomas Galbraith, took enough pork and flour to save their people from starvation. Less than two weeks later Santees from the Lower Agency requested emergency food allotments. Galbraith rejected their appeal. A local contingent of armed traders backed him up. Andrew Myrick, one of the more vocal, closed the discussion by suggesting contemptuously, "So far as I am concerned, if they are hungry, let them eat grass or their own dung."

Soon many young warriors talked openly of trying to drive white settlers out of the Minnesota River valley and back across the Mississippi. The Lincoln administration's recall of units from the region to fight the Confederates made the success more plausible to them. A local missionary reported that stories about the white man's war "operate very powerfully upon the . . . Indians." But this talk was checked by Little Crow, or Taoyateduta, chief of the Mdwekanton, a tribal division of the Santee Sioux. Little Crow solemnly warned the angry young men that any engagement would be nothing short of suicide. "We are only little herds of buffalo left scattered, the white men are like the locusts when they fly so thick that the whole sky is a snowstorm," he explained. "You may kill one—two—ten; yes, as many as the leaves in the forest yonder, and their brothers will not miss them. . . . Count your fingers all day long and white men with guns in their hands will come faster than you can count." For the moment the young warriors heeded Little Crow's warning.

An uncertain peace lasted for two weeks. Then the inevitable explosion occurred on August 17—"like a spark of fire, upon a mass of discontent, long accumulated and ready for it," characterized Minnesota Lieutenant-Governor Ignatius Donnelly—near the town of Acton, Minnesota, forty-five miles north of the Santee's reserve. A small hunting party of Sioux stole eggs from settlers, quarreled with them, and in a mindless act of revenge murdered five. That evening they returned home and went immediately to Little Crow recounting the deed. He called a meeting of chiefs of the Lower Agency for later that night to decide what action should be taken. After heated debate between a war and a peace faction, the majority decided upon a preemptive strike before whites could retaliate for the murders. Little Crow agreed to lead the fight against the settlers of Minnesota, even though he acknowledged it to be a lost cause.

The attacks began during the early morning hours of August 18. The Santees initially struck at settlers residing at nearby farms. One of the first to die was the trader Andrew Myrick who, when found later, had prairie grass crammed into his mouth. The warriors sent overtures to followers of the peace faction chiefs to join in the rampage, but they firmly rejected the offer. As the day advanced, the range of the massacre, with its accompanying raping and plundering, widened. The Santees' attack caught settlers by surprise. "We were beginning to regard the poetry of the palisades as a thing of the past," one settler recalled to John Nicolay, Lincoln's personal secretary, "when, suddenly, our ears were startled by the echo of the warwhoop, and the crack of the rifle, and our hearts appalled by the gleam of the tomahawk and the scalping knife, as they descended in indiscriminate and remorseless slaughter, on defenseless women and children on our border."

Fighting frantically, the Santee Sioux swept down the Minnesota Valley trying to eliminate all settlers. Minnesota Governor Alexander Ramsey wired Secretary of War Edwin Stanton, apprising him with alarm: "The Sioux Indians on our western border have risen, and are murdering men, women, and children." Many in Washington feared, incorrectly, that the uprising was a Confederate conspiracy to disrupt the Union war effort. Interior Secretary Caleb Smith was one such official: "I am satisfied the chief cause is to be found in the insurrection of the southern states." While the United States and Minnesota prepared to respond, Little Crow, in a wise tactical move, suggested directing a concentrated attack against the strategic Fort Ridgely. Here, guarding the populous valley, terrified settlers had sought shelter. The younger warriors overruled him, preferring to loot and plunder, a serious and ultimately fatal error because it allowed reinforcements to swell the number of defenders at the fort. Not until August 20, the third day of the uprising, did the Santees assault Fort Ridgely. The garrison repelled the attack after three days of intense fighting. With their path to advance through the valley blocked, the Sioux changed direction and raided to the northwest. Between four hundred and eight hundred citizens of Minnesota perished in what Commissioner Dole called "the most atrocious and horrible outbreak to be found in the annals of Indian history."

Responsibility for carrying the war to the Santee Sioux fell to Governor Ramsey and to General John Pope, commander for the newly created military Department of the Northwest. "Attend to the Indians," Lincoln advised upon hearing of the uprising, "necessity knows no law." The general concurred. "It is my purpose utterly to exterminate the Sioux if I have the power to do so," Pope declared. His orders to Colonel Henry Hopkins Sibley, commander of the Third Minnesota Volunteer Regiment, were blunt and explicit: "Destroy everything belonging to them and force them out to the plains, unless, as I suggest, you can capture them." Although there was little need to elaborate on such orders, Pope apparently felt a need to add to the savagery. "They are to be treated as maniacs or wild beasts," he exhorted. The Minnesota militia defeated the outmatched Santee Sioux in a pitched battle at Wood Lake, Minnesota, on September 23, 1862. Large numbers of Sioux surrendered. Little Crow and many of the hostiles escaped into the Dakotas to join their plains cousins, the Teton Sioux.

The rest of the tribe did not flee. For many, staying was natural, since they had not been belligerents and supposed they would be treated as neutrals. They understood clearly that those who had rampaged could hardly expect much mercy from the whites. In October John Pope informed Henry W.

Halleck, general-in-chief in Washington, that he had taken about fifteen hundred Santee prisoners. Pope adamantly recommended "executing the Indians who have been concerned in these outrages." Minnesotans agreed, demanding vengeance against the perpetrators. "Exterminate the wild beasts," urged Jane Swisshelm, editor of the *St. Cloud Democrat*, "and make peace with the devil and all his hosts sooner than with these red-jawed tigers whose fangs are dripping with the blood of the innocents." Pope faced a tricky problem in meting out justice. "I don't know how you can discriminate now between Indians who say they are and have been friendly, and those who have not. I distrust them all." Undeterred, he convened a military court of justice that, in ten days, tried 392 Indian prisoners accused of committing crimes during the uprising. When it finished its work the commission had sentenced sixteen to imprisonment and condemned 303 to death by hanging.

Abraham Lincoln was not convinced that justice had been served in Minnesota and ordered that no executions be made without his sanction. On November 10, he sent a request by telegram to General Pope: "Please forward, as soon as possible, the full and complete record of these convictions." Pope obeyed and dispatched the transcripts to Washington so the president and his attorneys could review them. The general also warned Lincoln: "The people of this State . . . are exasperated to the last degree, and if the guilty are not all executed I think it nearly impossible to prevent the indiscriminate massacre of all the Indians—old men, women, and children." Episcopal Bishop Henry B. Whipple, taking an extremely unpopular stand in the eyes of fellow Minnesotans, vigorously interceded with Lincoln on behalf of the condemned Sioux, launching an illustrious career as an Indian reformer. Indian Commissioner William Dole and Interior Secretary Caleb Smith likewise threw their support behind efforts to prevent the mass executions. After a review of the verdicts, Lincoln authorized the hanging of less than forty of the condemned Santee Sioux. All had either participated in the massacre or raped women. Lincoln's goal, as he told the Senate, was neither to act "with so much clemency as to encourage another outbreak, on the one hand, nor with so much severity as to be real cruelty, on the other." A large gathering watched as thirty-eight Santees died on a single scaffold at Fort Mankato, Minnesota, on the day after Christmas, 1862.

Those Santees remaining in the state had little to hope for at the hands of Minnesotans. As the Civil War had provided a solution to the Indian question in the Indian Territory, the tragic events of 1862 served the same end in Minnesota. The state's representatives in Washington urged Congress to authorize the immediate expulsion of all Indians from Minnesota; not just the Santees, but the Winnebagos as well, whose fertile land in Blue Earth County white settlers coveted. Congress acquiesced. On February 21, 1863, it authorized the eviction of the Winnebagos. The Santee removal bill of March 3, 1863, revoked the earlier treaties with the tribe and by "right of conquest" extinguished title to their land in Minnesota. The government ordered the two tribes removed to a desolate tract of land at Crow Creek near Fort Randall on the Missouri River, in the Dakota Territory. There the army could keep them under close scrutiny.

On May 4 and 5, 1863, thirteen hundred Santee Sioux, mainly women and children, boarded two steamboats that carried them into exile. While one of the vessels was docked at St. Paul taking on supplies, whites on shore, in a final act of reprisal, hurled rocks at the hated passengers. In addition to banishment, Washington suspended the tribe's annuity payments for four years and converted them to reimburse the damage claims of citizens of Minnesota. Well before this four-year period ended, crop failures at Crow Creek, coupled with a severe lack of essential supplies, reduced hundreds of Santees to starvation and death. Luckily for the Winnebagos, the Indian Bureau had relocated them from Crow Creek to the Omaha reserve in Nebraska in 1864.

As for Little Crow, his stature in the eyes of his followers diminished rapidly after his flight into the Dakotas, and his attempts to organize another attack on Minnesota from the land of the Teton Sioux failed. By July 1863, the discredited chief was back in Minnesota attempting to steal horses. On the afternoon of July 3, a farmer named Chauncey Lamson shot and killed Little Crow while the Santee was picking raspberries. The shooting took place to the south of Acton, where all the violence had begun the previous year. Little Crow's head was cut off and displayed at St. Paul. His body was disposed of in the refuse pit of a local slaughterhouse in Hutchinson. For his marksmanship, the state legislature awarded Lamson $500.

Fears of a widespread Indian war permeated the northern frontier in the aftermath of the Santee Sioux uprising. "From all indications and information, we are likely to have a general Indian war all along the frontier," predicted General Pope. Governor Samuel Kirkwood of Iowa notified Secretary of War Edwin Stanton, "I have reliable information that the . . . Indians on our western border, north of the Missouri River, have joined with the hostile Indians of Minnesota, and threaten our whole northwestern border." Already the Teton Sioux, after hearing tales of the events in Minnesota from the renegade Santees, made it known that no longer would whites be allowed to pass through their lands. "If you have no ears, we will give you ears," they warned those who refused to heed their admonition.

In the spring of 1863 General Pope, hoping to exert authority over the northern frontier, ordered two columns of troops into the Dakota Territory to deal with the Teton Sioux. The thrust was unsuccessful. The troops managed only to engage the Tetons in a few inconsequential battles. The Sioux, in turn, infuriated by what they judged as invasion of their country, lashed out at whites. They made good their threat to halt traffic on the Upper Missouri and on the overland roads across the Dakota Territory, and in the spring of 1864 Sioux raiding parties struck hard at settlers along the Minnesota-Iowa border. The fires of war on the upper plains, ignited in the aftermath of the Santee Sioux uprising, blazed throughout most of the next two decades, not to be extinguished until the battle at Wounded Knee. Meanwhile, further to the west, another severe struggle had erupted in Colorado.

Colorado and Sand Creek

In 1858, gold was discovered in the Pike's Peak region of present-day Colorado, on the western edge of the Southern Cheyennes' country. As with all gold discoveries, it caused dramatic changes to the land and the Indian people near the strike. The Pike's Peak gold strike set in motion events that destroyed the Concentration measures implemented by the Lea and Manypenny's Indian Bureau in the 1850s and led to all-out war on the central plains by the mid-1860s. That the discovery produced no results did not deter the swarms of gold hunters who cascaded across Cheyenne lands flaunting the slogan, "Pike's Peak or Bust." For all but the luckiest miner, Pike's Peak was a bust.

In 1859 a second find, near Clear Creek, sent even greater numbers rushing to make their fortunes. In that year alone over one hundred thousand people travelled to these fields along the new Smokey Hill Trail, which ran directly westward through the center of Cheyenne-Arapahoe territory as defined by their Concentration policy treaty. A decade earlier, when it implemented this policy with the Fort Laramie Treaty of 1851, Washington had pledged the grasslands between the North Platte and Arkansas rivers to the Southern Cheyennes and Arapahoes. This trespassing was a source of irritation compounded by the multitude of Americans who actually spilled off the trail and squatted in the midst of Indian land, numbering over thirty-four thousand by 1860. With the government's energies directed toward crushing the Confederacy, the United States again proved unresponsive to the needs of Indians and undependable regarding its treaty obligations.

In 1860 and 1861, white population and business enterprises increased dramatically in this region. "We have substantially taken possession of the country and deprived [the

Indians] of their accustomed means of support," assessed Indian Commissioner Alfred B. Greenwood. In response to such
rapid growth, the United States organized the Southern
Cheyenne-Arapahoe lands into the territory of Colorado in
preparation for statehood. Again the government had to secure
land cessions from them. By the terms of a new treaty in 1861,
the Treaty of Fort Wise, ten chiefs and delegates representing
the Southern Cheyennes and Arapahoes relinquished all of
their tribes' extensive landholdings except for a small, trian-
gular tract along the Arkansas River in southeastern Colorado,
designated the Sand Creek reservation. The treaty's civilization provision called for the land at Sand Creek to be allotted
in severalty to individual tribal members. With government
assistance, the Southern Cheyennes and Arapahoes were expected to forsake the buffalo and horse culture and become
self-supporting farmers. Most tribal members had no interest
in becoming farmers or abiding the new direction for them as
outlined in the treaty. Instead they preferred to continue raiding, hunting the buffalo, and moving about freely on their
former lands.

The same elements that had produced calamity and death
in Minnesota quickly emerged in the Colorado Territory: The
clash of convictions within the tribes between forsaking or
keeping the old ways, white demands for the Indians to stay
off the land ceded at Fort Wise, and mounting food shortages
among the Southern Cheyennes and Arapahoes caused by the
physical conditions of the reservation: a sandy, barren, agri-
culturally sterile piece of land. The scarcity of food at Sand
Creek during 1862 made it inevitable that more men would
secure food by hunting outside its bounds, on their former
ranges. There was even greater hunger in the following year.
No buffalo, the staple of these people's diet, could be found
within two hundred miles of the reservation, reported their
agent, Samuel G. Colley. Disease, brought in part by the lack
of food, plagued the Southern Cheyennes and Arapahoes during that summer. Finally, out of desperation, the Indians re-
verted to raiding local farms and passing wagon trains; not

necessarily to kill—there were remarkably few casualties as a result of the attacks—but to secure food. "Most of the depredations committed by them are from starvation," wrote agent Colley. "It is hard for them to understand that they have no right to take from them that have, when in a starving condition." William Gilpin, Colorado's first territorial governor and ex officio superintendent of Indian Affairs in the region, and his successor, John Evans, recognized that the Indians must be forced to remain at Sand Creek and convinced to adopt the government's civilization measures before a more dangerous situation arose.

Then in April 1864, a small, rather typical, frontier incident turned into a crisis. It began with the arrival of a disturbing report at Camp Sanborn, Colorado. The report came from a rancher who charged that a party of Cheyennes had stolen horses and livestock from his land near Bijou Creek. Colonel John Chivington, Methodist minister, local politician, and militia commander of the District of Colorado, dispatched forty soldiers to disarm these Cheyennes and recover the allegedly stolen animals. North of Denver the militiamen encountered a group of Cheyennes herding horses and mules. The militia afforded them no opportunity to explain where they had obtained the animals, and a clash quickly erupted. The Cheyennes drove the soldiers off, then unleashed their anger with raids against ranches on the South Platte.

Governor Evans, outraged, decided that a swift and concentrated display of force was necessary to protect Colorado settlers and to drive the Cheyennes to Sand Creek. He ordered a large force into the field under the command of Lieutenant George Eayre. Eayre's experience illustrates the difficulty plains commanders had in distinguishing peaceful from hostile Indians. In the spring of 1864 he assaulted a number of Cheyenne encampments in eastern Colorado and western Kansas, destroying clothing, food, weapons, and ammunition. Among Eayre's targets was the large camp of Black Kettle, situated along the banks of the Arkansas River. One of the leading chiefs of the Southern Cheyennes and a staunch advocate of peace and conciliation with the Americans (as were nearly all of the Cheyenne leaders at this time), Black Kettle had participated at the Fort Wise council in 1861 and, in March of 1863, had journeyed to Washington with a delegation of plains chiefs to meet President Lincoln. It was natural, therefore, that Black Kettle did not expect violence at the hands of the militiamen. The sight of soldiers approaching the camp caused little alarm; Lean Bear, a lesser chief, rode out of the camp with his son to greet the arrivals. On his chest Lean Bear proudly displayed a large medal, a token of the friendship of Lincoln. As he neared the soldiers, his hand raised in a sign of peace, he noticed too late that they had formed a skirmish line with artillery in position, facing the camp. When he was within twenty yards of the soldiers, Lieutenant Eayre gave the command to fire on him, his son, and the Cheyenne camp. The volley, immediately killing Lean Bear and his son, rocked the camp. Swiftly, swarms of Cheyenne warriors sprang to their horses and routed the aggressors. The militiamen retreated westward to Fort Larned, Kansas.

The immediate effect of Eayre's raids was to escalate the violence. Cheyenne and Arapahoe war parties launched devastating assaults against the major Colorado trails, the stagecoach lines from Fort Kearney in Nebraska Territory on the Oregon Trail to Denver, and the farms of settlers. They burned ranches, stole livestock, and took settlers as prisoners. In response, the alarmed Governor Evans issued a proclamation on August 11, 1864, authorizing each citizen in the Colorado Territory:

either individually or in such parties as they may organize, to go in pursuit of all hostile Indians on the plains; [and] to kill and destroy as enemies of the country wherever they may be found, all such hostile Indians, and further, as the only reward I am authorized to offer for such services, I hereby empower such citizens, or parties of citizens, to take captive, and hold to their own private use and benefit, all the property of said hostile Indians that they may capture, and to receive for all stolen property recovered from said Indians such reward as may be deemed proper and just.

Chivington fully agreed with the stern measures authorized by the governor. As Lieutenant Joseph Cramer evaluated his superior: "He [Chivington] believed it to be right and honorable to use any means under God's heaven to kill Indians . . . and 'damn any man that was in sympathy with Indians.' "

Once the Coloradans attacked them, the Cheyennes and Arapahoes reciprocated, escalating their attacks on settlers and cutting telegraph lines between Colorado and the East. By late August other plains tribes had joined in attacking whites. "It will be the largest Indian war this country ever had," Governor Evans predicted, "extending from Texas to the British line involving nearly all the wild tribes of the plains." The Sioux, for example, besieged the area along the Oregon Trail in retaliation for raids directed against them by, among others, the Minnesota militia after the Santee Sioux affair in 1862. The Kiowas, Comanches, and Kiowa-Apaches vented their anger, frustration, and vengeance by raids against traffic on the Santa Fe Trail and against their hated enemies, the Texans. An observer described the volatile events in the West to the *New York Times*, which published the account on September 8. The report alluded to the widespread but incorrect belief that agents of the Confederacy provoked these Indian attacks:

Upon the overland route, devastation, terror, murder, has held a perfect carnival. From Denver to Fort Laramie to the Little Blue in Kansas, and to the Big Sandy in Nebraska, both within 150 miles of the Missouri, the Rebel Indians have swept like a hurricane. In a distance of four hundred miles along this great route they have captured at least 50 trains of merchandise or Government freight, driving stock, plundering and destroying to the value of a quarter of a million dollars. They have murdered two hundred white persons, among them many women and children. The stark bodies lie stripped and mutilated in the glaring sunlight, festering and rotting for want of burial, or half charred, are seen mouldering amid the ruins of ranches, cabins, and stage-stations.

As hostilities increased and the death toll mounted, some level-headed Americans, such as the influential trader George Bent, attempted to reason with both sides, urging them to stop the warfare. Success seemed possible that fall at a council held at Camp Weld near Denver. There Black Kettle, tired of raiding, ready to camp for the winter, and still an advocate of conciliation with whites, acted as spokesman for the other six Cheyenne and Arapahoe chiefs present. He declared that he, the other chiefs, and their people desired peace above all else. Governor Evans, Colonel Chivington, and the other assembled officials doubted the Indians' sincerity and so offered no formal peace arrangements. The council failed, but with an odd twist. Black Kettle and the other chiefs, having misunderstood their interpreter, left Camp Weld believing in the success of their initiatives and confident that conflict with the Coloradans had ended.

Unaware of the misunderstanding, Black Kettle led some five hundred Cheyennes toward the Sand Creek reservation to camp for the winter, where they thought they would be free from attack by the military. They knew nothing of the recent orders of Brigadier General Samuel R. Curtis, commander of the military Department of Kansas from Fort Leavenworth, to Colonel Chivington: "I want no peace until the Indians suffer more!" He was not alone. In Denver Evans prepared for further hostilities.

In the early morning hours of November 29, 1864, Chivington, leading the First Colorado Volunteer Cavalry and one-hundred-day enlistees of the Third Colorado Cavalry, who carried with them four twelve-pound howitzers, attacked Black Kettle's sleeping encampment on the Sand Creek reservation without warning. It was virtually defenseless, filled with old men, women, and children. Most of the young men were miles away in Kansas that night hunting food to bring back for the winter. On a pole over Black Kettle's lodge floated both a white flag and a flag of the United States. Near dawn, the assault began. First the militia ran off all Indian horses so that escape from the coming assault would be near impossible. Next a terrible volley of cannon and rifle shot ripped through the Cheyenne camp. Then the columns charged and encircled the camp, directing point-blank fire at its occupants. Any surviving

Cheyennes who had not fled were subjected to the soldiers, who ravaged them with swords and knives. Men were castrated, and their organs, some soldiers promised each other, were saved as souvenirs to be used as tobacco pouches. Pregnant women's abdomens were sliced open; then both mother and baby were left to die. Children were dragged from their hiding places and murdered. Robert Bent, a local rancher who unwillingly accompanied Chivington, agonized, "There seemed to be indiscriminate slaughter of men, women and children." Some Cheyennes somehow managed to escape, Black Kettle being among the fortunate.

Sand Creek aroused few favorable responses. The most favorable was perhaps the ecstatic welcome of Chivington and his men upon their return to Denver. Cheyenne scalps were exhibited in the opera house, prompting wild enthusiasm. "All acquitted themselves well," proclaimed the *Rocky Mountain News.* "Colorado soldiers have again covered themselves with glory." Chivington's dictum, "nits make lice," allowed locals to feel justified about the slaughter of children. Outside of Colorado, people received the news with less ecstasy. Much of the nation recoiled in horror. The commissioner of Indian Affairs castigated the Colorado militia, referring to its attack at Sand Creek as a massacre in which Cheyennes were "butchered in cold blood by troops in the service of the United States." As public condemnation swelled, calls rang out for a governmental inquiry into what was already being called the "Sand Creek massacre." Two federal committees eventually issued reports. The Joint Committee on the Conduct of the [Civil] War, following its investigation, vilified the Colorado militia and the conduct of Chivington:

Wearing the uniform of the United States, which should be the emblem of justice and humanity; holding the important position of commander of a military district, and therefore having the honor of the government to that extent in his keeping, he [Chivington] deliberately planned and executed a foul and dastardly massacre which would have disgraced the veriest savage among those who were the victims of his cruelty.

The joint congressional special committee agreed fully, concluding about Sand Creek: "The fact which gives such terrible force to the condemnation of the wholesale massacre of the Arapahoes and Cheyennes [was] that those Indians . . . believed themselves to be under the protection of our flag."

The Southern Cheyennes and Arapahoes kept on the move following the Sand Creek massacre. Some merely wandered the plains, avoiding all contact with whites. A number moved north into Sioux territory to reside with that tribe and their brethren, the Northern Cheyennes and Arapahoes. Still others, thirsting for revenge as word of Chivington's deed spread, organized huge war parties that scourged farms, trading posts, stagecoach stations, and wagon trains along the Platte River. Coloradans, anticipating they had "adjusted" one problem at Sand Creek, ignited a far more deadly one for themselves and other whites on the plains. By the spring of 1865 hostilities burned themselves out for the moment, but they had cost "many valuable lives and $40,000,000" the commissioner of Indian Affairs concluded.

In October 1865, Southern Cheyennes and Arapahoes, joined by Comanches, Kiowas, and Kiowa-Apaches, met in council with federal emissaries at the mouth of the Little Arkansas where the United States offered all of them new treaties. The Little Arkansas Treaty required the Southern Cheyennes and Arapahoes to relinquish all claims to their Colorado lands, merely reiterating the Fort Wise Treaty of 1861. It also required that they forfeit the Sand Creek reserve and cede their cherished hunting grounds in western Kansas. In return the government promised the two tribes a new reserve south of the Arkansas along the Cimarron River. A minority of chiefs, including Black Kettle, signed the document. When other tribal members, especially those residing in the north with the Sioux, learned of their action, they expressed consternation and great condemnation. Within a week of finalizing the Cheyenne-Arapahoe accord the government came to agreement with the Comanches, Kiowas, and Kiowa-Apaches, promising them reservations in the panhandle of northern

Texas and the western part of the Indian Territory. None of the tribes received the land pledged at the Little Arkansas. The United States Senate amended the treaties in such a way as to make the clauses granting the new reservations virtually meaningless.

The Civil War proved as much a turning point for the trans-Mississippi West and its Indian population as it did for the nation as a whole. Federal officials solved the Indian question, as they defined it, with the Five Civilized Tribes, while opening half of the Indian Territory for further implementation of the policy of Concentration. And westerners, with the federal authority's attention focused on the Civil War, used the opportunity to open up more land in the trans-Mississippi West for white exploitation and settlement, expelling those tribes that stood in the way. But these actions heightened Indian hostility toward whites and galvanized among many the conviction not to yield further. Tribal leaders who still exhorted their people to follow the path of conciliation with whites found their arguments undermined by events of the Civil War years and their authority waning over younger warriors who would not retreat from confrontation. "Although wrongs have been done me I live in hopes [sic]," Black Kettle reflected. "But since they have come and cleaned out our lodges, horses, and everything else, it is hard for me to believe white men any more."

While the Civil War was in progress it had been the center of Washington's concern. Indian affairs, of necessity, had to wait in the wings. By the summer of 1865 the war had ended and Washington resumed its efforts to solve the Indian question. It had no choice. In the face of the turbulent atmosphere in the West in 1865 and the hardened sentiments of embittered Indians and aggressive whites, federal officials could not delay. The Indians were described as "a set of miserable, dirty, lousy, blanketed, thieving, lying, sneaking, murdering, graceless, faithless, gut-eating skunks as the Lord ever permitted to inflict the earth," in the *Topeka Weekly Leader*, and "whose immediate and final extermination all men ... should pray for." The area was a tinder box, already ignited and about to explode. Although the federal bureaucracy disagreed about the best method of pursuing and fulfilling the goals of the policy of Concentration, none disputed that the Indian question must be solved immediately by that policy.

The country was made without lines of demarcation, and it is no man's business to divide it. . . . Perhaps you think the Creator sent you here to dispose of us as you see fit. If I thought you were sent by the Creator I might be induced to think you had a right to dispose of me. Do not misunderstand me, but understand me fully with reference to my affection for the land. I never said the land was mine to do with it as I chose. The one who has the right to dispose of it is the one who has created it. I claim a right to live on my land, and accord you the privilege to live on yours.

CHIEF JOSEPH, NEZ PERCÉ

CHAPTER FOUR

The Plains Wars, Phase I: The Struggle to Realize the Policy of Concentration

The relentless westward push of humanity and enterprise that followed the Civil War rolled across the remaining Indian land like a tidal wave, with Americans clamoring for more and more of the republic's heartland. The middle of America seethed with activity. Ranchers moved in with growing herds of long-horns, launching great cattle empires. Pioneer families, lured by the Homestead Act of 1862, arrived to establish farms and attempt to bring forth bounty from the sod of the prairies. Miners continued to scour western rivers and mountains, driven by the irresistible dream that a fleck of gold or silver might open the door to untold personal fortune. The wagon trains of settlers, freight companies, and stagecoach lines traversed the region in steadily growing numbers. Construction crews pushed to extend rail lines further onto the western plains. The Union Pacific and Central Pacific, with substantial financial assistance from the federal government, set to the massive task of laying a transcontinental railroad that would cut through the heart of the region connecting Chicago with San Francisco.

Work crews, comprised largely of Irish and Chinese immigrants, labored for six years to join the two lines. In a lively ceremony at Promontory Point, Utah Territory, on May 10, 1869, dignitaries hammered a golden spike in place to complete the railroad. The news thrilled a nation. The settlement of the trans-Mississippi West in the years 1865 to 1900 was the largest migration of people in the history of the United States. Americans settled more land in those years than in any other period of their history. For the western Indians, the claiming of the "last frontier" by Americans became an episode of apocalyptic proportion.

The ever-increasing flood of humanity who moved into the West bred an intense resentment among tribes. As tribal holdings became more restricted, these feelings turned to violence as Indians fought to hold on to their homeland. The government in Washington, acutely aware of the potent, even dangerous, circumstances that expansion caused, could not have held back such overwhelming and burgeoning activity, even if it had wanted to (which it did not), in order to assure peace with western Indians. "If the whole Army of the United States stood in the way," Senator John Sherman of Ohio concluded, "the wave of emigration would pass over it to seek the valley where gold was to be found." As a result, the years spanned by the Sand Creek massacre of 1864 and the Battle of the Little Bighorn twelve years later witnessed some of the bitterest conflicts in the history of Indian-white relations, with the prairies and plains of the West providing the setting for the climactic struggle.

Post–Civil War Indian Policy

The years after the Civil War confronted the United States government with an antagonistic situation on the Great Plains and elsewhere in the West. "What to do with the tribes of that region?" was an urgent question for Washington. Federal officials, by the latter half of the 1860s, envisioned a day not far in the future when the armed threat posed by western Indians to Americans would be eliminated. Only then could national objectives in the West be fully realized. Both the civil and military arms of government recognized early that permanent peace could not be attained so long as tribes maintained their accustomed way of life, free of American hegemony. This realization guided Washington's Indian policy after the Civil War.

While much of the government's enterprise focused on reconstructing the states of the defeated South, federal officials also defined their program for terminating the Indian question. Three principal objectives ultimately characterized their efforts. The first called for Washington to pursue and enforce the policy of Concentration vigorously. This policy would solve the Indian question and further reduce tribal landholdings in the West, thus increasing opportunities for white settlement and enterprises in the region. The policy called for compulsory relocation of western tribes to federal land reserves, where permanent residency under strict government control would be obligatory. The government especially hoped to concentrate the plains tribes, the most formidable group of western Indians, on one of two large reservations: one south of Kansas in the Indian Territory and another north of Nebraska. When the United States cleared the central plains of free-roaming Indians, a wide east-west causeway would be available for white expansion and exploitation. Officials hoped to avoid conflict and the expense of Indian wars by methodically negotiating treaties with western tribes to consummate Concentration. Yet if they failed to yield peacefully, the government was fully prepared to employ the army to enforce the will of white society upon those Indians who resisted.

Loss of land would not be the full extent of the forfeiture. Under the second objective, Indians would be required to give up their accustomed way of life and, with the help of agents, reformers, missionaries, and educators, adopt the life-style of white society. Most Americans contended that Indians would live more satisfying lives by transforming themselves, to all intents and purposes, into whites. On their reserves they would learn the white man's ways, seek the white man's education, herd cattle and plow fields, wear his clothes, speak his language, and practice his Christian religion. Federal officials and reformers acknowledged the near impossibility of achieving these cultural and economic objectives unless the United States circumscribed the Indians' fighting power and ended their capacity for armed resistance.

The third objective specified that absolute control of Indian affairs in the West must be assumed by the national government. Federal Indian officials would replace western governors, and regiments of the regular army would replace state and territorial militias. Although such a transfer of authority would make the region safer for white inhabitants, it angered some westerners. The increase in the role of federal troops meant that militiamen would no longer receive a bounty for fighting Indians. Others, while not adverse to a brief stint in the militia, did not want to serve in the regular army. Its personnel, poor quality of food, low wages, and tough discipline was anathema to many westerners.

In September of 1865, the War Department appointed Lieutenant General William Tecumseh Sherman as commander of the Division of the Missouri. From headquarters at St. Louis he directed military affairs in that portion of the West roughly east of the continental divide. His responsibilities included restoring order and ending the troublesome meddling of western militias and governors, especially with regard to the Indian question, thus establishing the preeminence of federal direction and authority in the region. It was Sherman's conviction that if the West was to be made safe for Americans, no agency but the United States Army would suffice. Western militias and governors, in the general's opinion based on the handling of Indian affairs during the Civil War years, were undisciplined, untrustworthy, and incompetent. "I think I comprehend the motives of some of the Governors," he told Ulysses S. Grant, commanding general of the army, but "I would not entrust [them] with a picket post of fifty men, much less with the discretionary power to call out troops at national cost."

General Sherman emerged from the Civil War a national hero, surpassed in stature only by Abraham Lincoln and Ulysses S. Grant. But recognition often is not the equivalent of acclaim, and the public vilified Sherman as well as idolized him. To Southerners in particular, he was much more than just another former Yankee. They called him a butcher, a despoiler, a man who gloried in war. Not only gloried in it, but raised it to a higher plane of what some called martial creativity and others called ghastliness. Sherman's tactics in the Civil War presaged modern "Total War," a kind of war that spares no one and no thing. "You cannot glorify war in harsher terms than I will," Sherman warned. "War is cruelty, and you cannot refine it." He believed firmly that war must be waged relentlessly and unsparingly against the enemy's army *and* the civilian population and homeland. Many admired him and took him at his word when he protested that war was hell and the only thing to do with it was to get it over as soon as possible. It is unlikely, however, that any observer of his pitiless application of scorched earth tactics as his army slashed across the Deep South during his March to the Sea in 1864 and 1865 would have endorsed Sherman's contention. This is the man who would oversee military operations on the Great Plains, and the cold fury he had directed against the Confederacy would be turned on the tribes of the heartland, so General Sherman promised, if they spurned the policy of Concentration.

Clearly the government's objectives contained two divergent concepts of the federal authority's responsibility in resolving the Indian question. One viewed the government's civil arm, especially the Bureau of Indian Affairs of the Department of Interior, as the mediator with and the agent of acculturation for the Indians. The other saw its military arm, particularly the War Department, as the instrument for subduing western tribes and clearing the way for American settlement. Consequently, federal Indian policy from roughly 1865 to 1877 wavered between the two concepts: Acculturation or Subjugation—the "Peace Policy" or the "Force Policy"—

as the most pragmatic and effective method of realizing the objectives of the policy of Concentration. A contemporary criticized this dichotomy in *The Nation* magazine: "Comprehensively speaking it may be said that hereto the Indian Bureau has *bribed* [tribes] into . . . peace, while the War Department has desired to *frighten* them into permanent quiet; and between the two they have been nearly exterminated."

This divergence between peace and force sparked heated debates in the executive and legislative branches over the attributes or ill-nature of one role or the other. The War Department and its supporters accused Interior of softness, mismanagement, corruption, and ineffectualness in dealing with the Indian question. The Interior Department and its backers countered by charging the War Department with callous, even brutal treatment of Indians that exacerbated, rather than solved, the question. Nonetheless, both groups agreed that they pursued the same objectives: to place the Indians completely under federal authority and transform their way of life to make it acceptable to the American public. Each department, however, believed it alone held the solution, which stirred an intense jurisdictional dispute over control of Indian affairs. Known as the Transfer Issue, the problem centered on the War Department's attempt to assume jurisdiction over the Bureau of Indian Affairs of the Interior Department. Disagreement over control had been unrelenting since 1849, when the bureau was taken from the War Department and given to the newly created Department of the Interior—"for political reasons and to promote party interests," asserted General Nelson A. Miles, reflecting the overwhelming opinion of the military for the transfer.

In a circular sent to military and civilian Indian affairs authorities in May 1865, Senator James R. Doolittle of Wisconsin, chairman of the Senate Committee on Indian Affairs, trying to resolve the heated question, inquired: "Under what department of the government, the War Department or the Interior, should the Bureau of Indian Affairs be placed, to secure the best and most economical administration of it?"

Every army officer who replied favored transferring the Indian Office to the War Department. Not surprisingly, most of the civilians opposed transfer. William P. Dole, first Lincoln's, then briefly Andrew Johnson's, commissioner of Indian Affairs, adamantly fought transfer and strenuously advocated the treaty process as the only method of serving the interests of "humanity, economy, and efficiency." To him, no better system existed "for the management of the Indians" than the Interior's Peace Policy, because the War Department's Force Policy would lead tribes to regard Americans as "merciless despots and tyrants, who have deprived them of their homes and liberties." This conclusion is "so apparent," Dole stressed, "that I can hardly realize that the former is seriously advocated." Such statements drew harsh criticism from transfer advocates such as General John Pope, who in a letter to General Ulysses S. Grant called the treaty process worthless. "It is a common saying with the Sioux," he protested, "that, whenever they are poor and need powder and lead, they have only to go down to the Overland route and murder a few white men, and they will have a treaty to supply their wants." Others in government suggested that to have the Concentration policy solve the Indian question, tribes "needed to feel the strong arm of the government." Senator Samuel Pomeroy of Kansas, who in a resolution introduced in 1865, suggested to colleagues:

The mild, conciliatory, and even magnanimous conduct of our government towards these savages not being understood or appreciated by them, but only construed to be weakness and cowardice, should now be followed by the most vigorous and decisive measures until those hostile tribes are effectually punished for their crimes, and whipped into a wholesome restraint and submission to the authority of the United States.

The transfer issue between the Interior and War Departments did not abate over the next decade. The troubled relations between the United States and some western Indians in those years only heightened the dispute.

Those Who Resisted Concentration

The goal of the Concentration policy was to place all western Indians on federal reservations without recourse to military coercion. Most tribes, all too aware that they could no longer successfully resist the demands of the United States government, accepted their fate. The Ponka, Osage, Snake, Ute, Navaho, Kansa, Shoshoni, Bannock, Arikara, Gros Ventre, Quapaw, and Mandan, among others, signed Concentration treaties and settled on their assigned lands. Except for efforts to avoid being converted into farmers and resistance to government programs to transform their culture, they generally caused Washington few problems. The nomadic buffalo-hunting societies of the plains and certain other western tribes, however, proved to be a markedly different case for one principal reason: Still controlling vast domains in 1865, they possessed the strength of their convictions in combination with superb martial skills to defend their lands against the United States. Their resistance to the Concentration policy and Washington's absolute determination to impose it on them in order to end the Indian question resulted in over a decade of deadly confrontation called "the Plains Wars."

The Plains Indians strove to continue their accustomed way of life of the buffalo and horse culture, which was absolutely dependent on vast space, abundant game, and freedom of movement. They rejected the policy of Concentration because it required abandoning that way of life. Aside from motives such as revenge or retaliation, they fought to prevent American occupation and to defend their cultural life-style. Undoubtedly many material goods of white society appealed to them as an enhancement of this life-style: cotton clothing, woolen blankets, buttons, thread and needle, metal pots and kettles, metal knives, rifles, revolvers, gunpowder, and a host of other items. But the culture of American society as a whole did not appeal to them. Federal officials recognized the plains tribes' attraction to and increasing dependence on white man's goods, and they used this in the treaty process as an inducement to accept Concentration. For example, at the Medicine Lodge Creek proceedings in the fall of 1867, a council to end recent belligerencies and concentrate the tribes of the southern plains in the Indian Territory, negotiators promised clothing, blankets, weapons, ammunition, and an assortment of trinkets. In return, the Americans required these tribes to restructure their lives by accepting concentration on a federal reserve, allotment of the land in severalty, abandonment of the buffalo and horse culture, and mandatory schooling for children.

The American public regarded those tribes that resisted as a dangerous impediment to expansion, enterprise, and settlement. End the Indian question, they demanded of Washington. The overwhelming majority of Americans refused to abide Indian intransigence, as they saw it, to the consummation of national purposes. Therein was the foremost source of the collision: the direct conflict of purposes, culturally and economically. Nor did either side—Indian or white—ever show itself willing or capable of understanding what the other wanted or how the other viewed the predicament. Many people suffered and died because of this virtually unbridgeable gulf of misunderstanding.

Inevitably, with the Peace Policy holding so little promise of success with the Plains Indians, the United States pursued the Concentration policy by force of arms. When these efforts were successful—and that too was inevitable—the government placed these tribes on reservations. No matter how hard they resisted, their struggle was doomed to failure. Far too many factors worked against them. The flood of homesteaders to stake out farms, the growing interest of American and European investment capital in developing the West, the construction of a railroad system throughout the region moving not only people but supplies into the vast interior sustaining white population growth and providing the basis for a durable economy, the precipitous decline of the Indians' subsistence base—all combined to hasten the final outcome. Every advancement of settlement and business enterprise in the West came at the expense of resources, especially the buffalo, crucial to the continuance of the Plains Indians' way of life. Recognizing the role of the tribes' nomadic life in their resistance and the role of the buffalo in their nomadism, General William T. Sherman jested with earnestness to General Philip H. Sheridan that "it would be wise to invite all the sportsmen of England and America ... for a Grand Buffalo hunt, and make one grand sweep of them all." In fact during the early 1870s, the federal government acquiesced in a measure not dissimilar to Sherman's idea. Officials permitted hunters to kill the remaining buffalo herds on the southern plains.

Yet, especially considering the disproportionate advantages apparently held by the United States, why did it take the United States Army over a decade to complete Concentration and accomplish the military subjugation of resisting Indians? The population of the United States in 1870 was almost forty million. Americans in the tens of thousands plied the western mining frontier. Four hundred thousand homesteaders created a permanent farming population on the prairies, while a much larger number tried, then abandoned, this enterprise. By contrast, all Indians residing from the Great Plains westward to the Pacific numbered under 239,000 in 1872. Only a portion of the western Indian population offered armed resistance of any significant measure during the Plains Wars. Moreover, in the area of technology there was little contest. The United States Army had available rapid transportation and communication—railroads and the telegraph—as well as a modern industrial plant capable of mass producing vast quantities of items, particularly those needed to prosecute war. The Plains Indians, on the other hand, lacked the technology to make a wheel, much less the weapons of modern warfare. Additionally, during the Civil War the United States had developed perhaps the finest conventional military in the world. While the military did go into steep decline after that conflict, the War Department could still draw upon the experience and expertise of battle-tested commanders to direct operations against the Indians.

In light of these factors, and others, the anticipation of a quick victory by the army during the Plains Wars would seem reasonable. Nothing could be further from what transpired. Securing conclusive victory proved frustratingly difficult for many years. As Thomas W. Dunlay discussed in his perceptive essay "Fire and Sword: Ambiguity and the Plains Wars" (in *The American Indian Experience*), part of the paradox lies in the fact that those factors that seemed to favor quick victory for the United States were negated by others that aided the Indians and frustrated the U.S. Army.

The physical conditions of the western prairies and plains were one example. Summers on the Great Plains are extremely hot and exceedingly dry, with water often in short supply. Unless Indian scouts accompanied the troopers, directing them to water and other necessary resources, these conditions often took their toll on men and animals. The region's immensity made troop movements time-consuming and arduous, and for years the size of the war's theater decreased the impact and usefulness of railroads for the army. While the railroad could bring soldiers, horses, and supplies into the general vicinity of planned engagements, movement from that point was by foot or on horseback across hundreds of miles where terrain and climate were taxing, and often perilous, to the unaccustomed. The sheer size of the region made it difficult for the army to locate enemy positions, especially when the Plains Indians' nomadic life-style dictated nearly continuous movement, leaving no evidence of permanent villages. When soldiers finally located and engaged the Indians, warriors usually fought only a holding action against the army while the main tribal body escaped and dispersed. In their escapes, it often seemed to soldiers that the vastness of the plains simply swallowed them.

To the tribes of the region, however, this uncompromising land presented no such obstacle. The Plains Indians knew it intimately and used it fully to their advantage. They knew how to subsist on its meager resources; knew where to locate water in the dry season; knew the choice places to hide; knew the best locations for a successful attack or defense. Their nomadic life accustomed them to traverse the region's vast reaches expertly, changing camp sites readily and transporting their material possessions with ease, all of which were designed for rapid, continuous maneuver.

The differences in military training and skills between Indians and soldiers of the U.S. Army played an important role, too. Indian males trained from youth to be warriors. Due to extensive instruction over many years, they were usually superior in horsemanship, endurance, tracking, scouting, and most martial skills when compared to their army counterparts. Soldiers, on the other hand, first encountered military life and training in early adulthood and simply did not have the time needed to master equally the skills needed to fight in the plains environment.

The Plains Indians esteemed courage and placed a high value on martial achievements and honors, and, especially for the latter reason, warfare was endemic to their culture. But they typically refused to involve themselves in massed engagements because of the inevitability of high casualties. When they did fight in this manner—such as Little Crow's assault on Fort Ridgely during the Santee Sioux uprising of 1862, or the Hayfield and Wagon-Box Fights in 1867 during the Powder River War when Sioux and Cheyennes battled army regulars—their deficiency in tactical knowledge and ability often proved ruinous. Plains warriors preferred to engage enemies, Indian or white, in a "hit and run" style, or by using ambush or guerrilla tactics. Because of the relatively small size of the adult male population, they also selected those tactics that preserved the lives of combatants on their side. The United States Army trained its personnel to obey a superior's orders and advance against an enemy, even if this carried the soldier directly into the line of fire and almost certain death. Such conduct puzzled the Indian fighter. An Indian war leader, employing a similar strategy, probably would have lost the confidence of his followers. Death in battle could bring glory, but living to care for your family and to fight another valorous battle was usually judged wiser. Unless the chance of success was overwhelmingly in their favor, or when a village with women and children was threatened, plains warriors usually avoided massed, frontal engagements.

As Dunlay pointed out, "The real handicaps of the army were those inherent in its organization and doctrine. . . . An army organized on conventional, European lines, [intending] to fight similar enemies, was charged with police duties and with combatting foes with a talent for guerrilla warfare in country giving them ample room to take full advantage of their mobility." Only when the army combined conventional tactics with more innovative ones that took advantage of vulnerable aspects of the Plains Indians' way of life—such as General Philip Sheridan's winter campaign with which he defeated the southern plains tribes in 1868–1869 and again in 1874–1875 during the Red River War, and then crushed the Sioux in 1876–1877 following Custer's Little Bighorn debacle—did the military arm of the government finalize Concentration, effectively enforce the policy, and successfully conclude the Plains Wars.

Olive Branch and Sword

The United States government, within a half year of the end of the Civil War, implemented the Concentration policy to end the Indian question. In October 1865, almost a year after the Sand Creek massacre, federal commissioners finalized an agreement with the Southern Cheyennes and Arapahoes, Kiowas, Comanches, and Kiowa-Comanches at the Little Arkansas. Following this council, the officials moved on to the northern plains planning to negotiate with the tribes in the upper reaches of the Missouri, Yellowstone, and Platte rivers. Concentrating these tribes would provide safe overland travel for those Americans involved in the region's burgeoning gold rush and secure a land corridor on the upper plains for future railroad construction. By the spring of 1866 they arranged accords with the Assiniboines and Crows, as well as with the

Missouri River Sioux and a number of Northern Cheyenne and Arapahoe bands. General John Pope, an outspoken critic of the treaty system, expressed his opinion openly that these agreements would not bring lasting peace to the region. "I do not consider the treaties lately made with the Sioux, Cheyennes, and Arapahoes ... worth the paper they are written on," he wrote General Sherman. "I have myself no doubt that hostilities will again break out on the Platte, the Smokey Hill, and the Arkansas rivers before the beginning of winter." Pope's assessment proved to be correct. The objective of post–Civil War Indian policy was to concentrate all western Indians. The circumstances surrounding the next council on the northern plains and the succession of events that followed assured the accuracy of the general's prediction and highlights the dichotomy within the government about the most pragmatic and effective means of achieving that objective and ending the Indian question: "Peace" or "Force."

In June 1866, a second commission travelled to Fort Laramie, situated along the Oregon Trail in southeastern Wyoming Territory. There they planned to meet and finalize crucial treaties with Siouan leaders of the Powder River country. The new accord would alter the terms of the Sioux's initial Concentration treaty, the Fort Laramie Treaty of 1851 (see Chapter Two). The Powder River country, bounded on the east by the Black Hills and the Bighorn Mountains to the west, was a hilly, bountiful land teeming with fish, game, and rich grazing area. The Sioux had wrested this region from the Crows after nearly two decades of warfare. Mainly Oglalas, Miniconjous, and Sans Arcs—tribal divisions of the Teton Sioux—lived and hunted there now. The commissioners knew that negotiations would be difficult, especially with the prickly Oglala Red Cloud, whose exploits and leadership in numerous campaigns against the Crows, Pawnees, and Shoshonis had earned him great respect and political influence among his people. Still, the commissioners confidently expected an agreement could be secured if they handled the meeting with the Sioux carefully. Their efforts would be severely impeded, however, by simultaneous developments in the region involving the military commander of the Great Plains, William Tecumseh Sherman. The War Department charged General Sherman with safeguarding the Great Plains for Americans, as well as enforcing the reduction of tribal landholdings and moving the Plains Indians even further north and south away from white travellers, homesteaders, settlements, and businesses. Insufficient troop strength forced Sherman to execute his responsibilities in a purely defensive manner. "I regret to say that . . . we do not now possess a force adequate to the wants of this extensive region of country," Sherman notified General D. B. Sackett, whom the War Department dispatched to assess western routes, posts, and settlements, "but you may assure the people . . . that their safety and the protection of their interests will command our attention as soon as Congress increases the regular army." High on General Sherman's list of priorities was protection of the lines of communication on the Great Plains: telegraph lines, railroads and their construction crews, and, above all, the overland trails. One of the newest and hence least secure trails was the Bozeman or Powder River Trail on the northern plains. Sherman, in the spring of 1866, therefore turned to building a chain of forts to protect the trail and the Americans who travelled over it.

The Bozeman Trail, originating seventy-five miles to the west of Fort Laramie, veered off the Oregon Trail and ran northwestwardly through the mining country of northern Wyoming and southern Montana, eventually ending at Virginia City, Montana. Bisecting the Powder River country, the Bozeman Trail proved a major source of irritation to the Sioux: partly because it violated the Fort Laramie Treaty of 1851; mainly since it ran directly through some of their best buffalo-hunting lands. In the early 1860s the Sioux had made several half-hearted attempts to prevent the trail from going through their western lands. Later they made some equally half-hearted attacks on the early travellers—generally miners and hunters, not immigrants—who dared to use the risky route. In the middle of that decade, following the Sand Creek massacre, a num-

ber of Southern Cheyennes and Arapahoes arrived in the Powder River country to take refuge among the Sioux. Even more
recently, the region had been the site of military action. A large
army contingent under General Patrick Connor had been
turned back in the spring of 1865 by the Sioux, with the aid
of the Cheyennes and Arapahoes. Connor's defeat increased
General Sherman's determination to complete construction of
forts along the Bozeman Trail to secure the area.

In June 1866, the Powder River Sioux, many of whom
had defeated Connor's force, received a request to come to
Fort Laramie to meet with federal commissioners. Although
he was not a chief, the esteemed war leader Red Cloud served
as the principal spokesman. Always distrustful of whites, he
was deeply suspicious of the negotiators and adamant against
relinquishing any further territorial rights of the Sioux to the
United States. The Americans reassured him that they respected both him and his convictions. They wished only to
negotiate a treaty guaranteeing the Sioux their lands while al-
lowing whites the right of passage through them, including use
of the Bozeman. In payment the Sioux would receive presents
and $70,000 a year in annuity issues. Red Cloud, believing
that the Americans dealt with him honestly, did not dismiss
their requests but decided to take council with other tribal
leaders.

While the Sioux deliberated and the Americans waited, a
substantial contingent of civilian workers and regular infantry
and cavalry under the command of Colonel Henry B. Carrington arrived at Fort Laramie. Carrington travelled under
orders to march to the Powder River country and erect three
forts along the Bozeman Trail, with or without the permission
of the Sioux. This action outraged the assembled Indians. They
bitterly denounced the treachery and betrayal of the Americans. "The Great Fathers [the commissioners] sends us presents and wants us to sell him the road," Red Cloud decried,
"but White Chief [Carrington] goes with soldiers to steal the
road before Indians say Yes or No." The Powder River party
stormed out of the fort, refusing to offer any guarantees of

safety to either travellers or construction crews on the Bozeman Trail.

The troops and work crews soon left Fort Laramie, journeyed westward along the Oregon Trail, and then moved up
the Bozeman Trail into the Powder River country. There they
began their assignment of building three forts to guard the 545-
mile trail from Bridger's Ferry, on the North Platte, to Virginia
City, Montana. During July and August they enlarged Camp
Connor, renaming it Fort Reno, and began erecting Fort Phil
Kearny and Fort C. F. Smith. Throughout that summer Sioux
warriors, resolved to stop construction of the forts, harassed
the soldiers, suppliers, and builders. The Sioux realized that
once the Bozeman Trail became a popular route to Americans,
they would settle near it. The recent occurrences in Colorado
buttressed their resolve. The Cheyenne and Arapahoes living
with them told of their people's experiences earlier in the decade: The gold rush and subsequent development of the Smokey
Hill Trail through lands that the United States guaranteed
them in the 1850s, their displacement by Coloradans, the newest Concentration treaty at Fort Wise that ratified these acts,
and the clashes with the Colorado militia. The Powder River
Sioux agreed that they must insure that the Bozeman Trail did
not produce a similar outcome for them. Before the end of
August they had killed thirty-three whites involved in work
on the forts.

Soldiers and civilians worked desperately through the fall
to complete construction of the forts before the bitter mountain winter set in. The Sioux worked with the same intensity
to impede the work. In a skirmish on December 6, 1866, the
Sioux discovered an especially effective tactic. If warriors fired
upon soldiers as they went to and from the forts, the soldiers
would give chase and could be led into ambush. Red Cloud
decided that since the tactic had worked on a small scale, a
large ambush might wipe out the garrison at each of the forts.
He targeted the initial effort at the biggest fort along the trail,
Fort Kearny. High-Back-Bone, a Miniconjou, crafted the plan.
Warriors would attack the wagons as the whites returned to

Fort Kearny from cutting wood a half-dozen miles away. The assault on the wagons promised to bring reinforcements from the fort. Then, as the soldiers rode toward the besieged wagons, decoys would lure them away from the main fight and into deadly ambush.

The Sioux, accompanied by Cheyennes and Arapahoes, moved southward from their camps on the Tongue River ten miles north of the fort, and on December 19 they made the first attempt to execute the large-scale ambush. Their attack, however, failed to bring reinforcements from Fort Kearny. Snow postponed the ambush the following day. Then, one day later, the army's agenda for the Powder River Indians played into the hands of Red Cloud purely by accident. A month earlier Colonel Carrington had received orders from General Philip St. George Cooke, his departmental commander, to strike at the "hostiles." Although promising "to make the winter one of active operations," Carrington until now had tarried.

At about 10:00 in the morning on December 21, 1866, warriors led by the Oglala Crazy Horse, a young protégé of High-Back-Bone and soon to be the heir to Red Cloud's military leadership in the region, attacked the wagons of the fort's wood train and its military escort as it moved away from Fort Kearny. Whether Red Cloud participated in the engagement is undetermined. Between fifteen hundred and two thousand warriors concealed themselves in nearby ravines. As quickly as he could, Colonel Carrington, seizing the opportunity to execute General Cooke's directive, ordered out a column of eighty men led by Captain William Fetterman. They anticipated inflicting heavy casualties on the Sioux. But on that cold December morning, the troopers rode behind Fetterman to their deaths. The Sioux could not have hoped for a better man for their designs. Recklessly disobeying Carrington's orders to relieve the train and battle the attackers, but not pursue them, Fetterman gave chase to the decoys and led his men straight into an immense ambush. After less than an hour of intense fighting, William Fetterman and all of his command were dead. Post physician C. M. Hines, after seeing the scalped and mutilated bodies of the soldiers brought back to Fort Kearny, described them with horror as looking "like . . . hogs brought to market." Carrington's report graphically described how his troops' bodies had their eyes, noses, ears, arms, legs, fingers, genitals, entrails, teeth, brains, skulls, and chins cleaved; "eyes, ears, mouth, and arms penetrated with spearheads, sticks and arrows; ribs slashed to separation with knives; [and] muscles of calves, thighs, stomach, breast, back, arms, and cheek taken out."

The remaining soldiers and civilians inside Fort Kearny readied themselves for the impending Indian attack, but Red Cloud did not follow up the Fetterman ambush for the remainder of the winter. Since the men inside the fort could not have known this would happen, the level of anxiety ran extremely high throughout these months. That was exactly Red Cloud's objective—psychological warfare. No further Sioux assaults, either at Fort Kearny or on the other two Bozeman Trail forts, came until the following spring.

Word of the Sioux's victory in the Powder River country reached the East early in 1867, prompting mixed reactions from whites. Some Americans, surprisingly sympathetic to the Sioux, openly expressed indignation at the government's Concentration policy, which had brought about the catastrophe. They called for an immediate investigation into the government's conduct toward the Indians. The Indian Bureau agreed, placing blame for the recent difficulties in the army's lap. Commissioner Lewis V. Bogy's initial, albeit imaginative, explanation was that the Sioux were on a "friendly visit" to Fort Kearny when assaulted by Fetterman's troops. Bogy concluded that given this explanation, it was now the duty of the Interior Department, "with a view of putting the blame where it properly belongs, to have an investigation."

The War Department disagreed emphatically with both the Indian Bureau's charges and the proposed solution. General Cooke, Carrington's superior, whom General Grant relieved of his duties on January 9, 1867, laid the full blame on the Interior Department for failing to check the sale of weapons to the Sioux. Secretary of War Edwin Stanton minced no words in strenuously demanding immediate military retaliation. General Sherman, fully supporting Stanton's recommendation, thundered: "We must act with vindictive earnestness against the Sioux, even to their extermination, men, women, and children. Nothing else will reach the root of this case." Unhesitatingly most Americans, shocked and angered by Fetterman's defeat, concurred with Stanton and Sherman.

President Andrew Johnson, at the urging of Interior Secretary Orville H. Browning and most other members of the cabinet, reined in Stanton and Sherman. Still hoping to find some peaceful means for resolving problems with the Plains Indians, the president, in February 1867, appointed a fact-finding commission chaired by General Alfred Sully. Johnson wanted to know what method short of war would convince these tribes to accept Concentration. He charged the Sully commission with investigating the Fetterman incident and with assessing the mood of Indians on the northern plains, especially ascertaining whether they would still negotiate with the United States.

Hostilities in the Powder River country, and especially Fetterman's defeat, prompted Force Policy proponents in Congress to increase efforts to transfer Indian Affairs from the Interior Department to the War Department. Only the military could deal with the Indians effectively and realize the Concentration policy, they contended. Several senators, including Nevada's W. M. Stewart and Ohio's John Sherman, the general's brother, introduced transfer bills, arguing that the system of divided jurisdiction in administering Indian affairs caused the recent troubles. Wisconsin's Senator James R. Doolittle's Joint Special Committee on the Condition of the Indian Tribes countered these charges in its report of January 26, 1867. Chronicling the worsening state of western Indians' lives and stressing "the aggression of lawless whites" as the cause of recent interracial conflict, the report rebutted the transfer advocates:

The inconveniences arising from the occasional conflicts and jealousies between officers appointed under the Interior and War Departments are not without some benefits also; neither are slow to point to the mistakes and abuses of the other. It is therefore proper that they should be independent of each other, receive the appointments from and report to different heads of departments. Weighing this matter and all the arguments for and against the proposed change, your committee are unanimously of the opinion that the Indian Bureau should remain where it is.

After heated debate the transfer measure carried in the House but failed to pass in the Senate, due to the Doolittle Report. General Sherman, in correspondence with his brother Senator Sherman, expressed disappointment and reaffirmed his answer for ending the Indian question: Soldiers "must get among them, and must kill enough of them to inspire fear, and then conduct the remainder to places where Indian agents can and will reside among them, and be held responsible for their conduct."

Helping block the transfer of the Indian Bureau to the War Department was the immediate effect of the Doolittle Report. Its greater result was to prick the conscience of various groups of Americans, supportive of the Indians or at least concerned with their fate, agitating them to pressure the federal government into reevaluating its Indian policy. The best recounting of their attitudes and activities is Francis Paul Prucha's *American Indian Policy in Crisis: Christian Reformers and the Indian, 1865–1900*. As Americans of their time and place, these eastern humanitarians believed deeply in progress, and they especially believed in it for the Indian. They recognized that the nation was in a dynamic, rather than a static situation, and that Americans felt compelled to expand rapidly and continually. They conceded that the compulsion to engulf more and more land of the western Indians, with little regard to the consequences for these people, was a force that drove the United States government and the American people in this era as remorselessly as any other agent of modernization. These men and women who throughout the remaining decades of this century generously responded to the plight of the Indians, and who made strong appeal against specific iniquities, neither denigrated the steady march forward of progress nor denied an unshakable conviction in the necessity for the Indians to accept and adopt their vision of progress. Most individuals deeply concerned with the ultimate fate of the Indians could not acknowledge sufficient merit in the values, culture, and life-style of this minority not to press for acculturation as the best method of solving the Indian question. That most Indians disagreed with their well-intentioned paternalism failed to sway them.

Meanwhile, the military, blocked by President Johnson from retaliatory measures against the Sioux, sought to redress the humiliation that Captain Fetterman brought upon them. By spring they had selected the target. These events rekindled warfare on the central and southern plains, strained relations between the War and Interior Departments, and further fueled the disagreement between Force Policy and Peace Policy advocates.

By 1865 the Southern Cheyennes had experienced the depth of tragedy. Their lands had been forfeited to the United States. The bitter year-old memory of Sand Creek still burned deeply. It was hard for them to imagine that more could fall on them. After the fighting that followed the Sand Creek massacre, the Southern Cheyennes broke into two principal groups. The smaller migrated to the Sioux's Powder River country, while the larger, led by peace chiefs such as Black Kettle, moved southward in accordance with the terms of the Little Arkansas Treaty until they crossed the Arkansas River into southern Kansas, relocating near Fort Larned on the Santa Fe Trail. Here Colonel Edward W. Wynkoop, a welcome friend, joined them. "Tall Chief," as they called Wynkoop, had attempted to prevent the tragic events of the previous year in Colorado, especially by his heroic but unsuccessful effort to prevent Chivington's attack at Sand Creek. No longer in the army, Wynkoop now served as the Indian Affairs Office's civilian agent to the Southern Cheyennes and Arapahoes. He felt deeply the burden of the Sand Creek tragedy on his own conscience, although he was not to blame, and he vowed to help the remnants of these tribes to find peace. By 1866 Wynkoop was making progress in winning back their trust.

At the same time, more than a thousand Southern Cheyennes who had sought refuge in the Powder River area returned to Kansas. It was then that they learned of the Little Arkansas Treaty and of how Black Kettle and other tribal leaders signed away their land in Colorado and their hunting grounds in western Kansas. Some bowed, albeit ungraciously, to the reality of the situation. Others, embittered by the deed, rejected the peace chiefs and the treaty they signed. They made a fateful decision to remain along the Republican and Smokey Hill rivers on their former Kansas hunting ranges, where they harassed settlers and commerce in the area.

Their decision was less an act of overt aggression than of laying claim to lands that they still considered rightfully theirs. It also underscored crucial differences in political organization between the plains tribes and the government of the United States. None of these tribes had the type of unitary state capable of coercing the obedience of its members. Plains Indians gave their overriding loyalty to the family first, followed by the war society, band, tribal division, and then, finally, the tribe itself. They gave little, if any, consideration to how a given action or strategy—such as remaining in Kansas—affected the interest of the tribe as a whole.

Another important difference was that tribal leaders served as the agents of their people and the executors of their wishes, not their unilateral rulers. Chiefs could not compel, nor would they have tried to compel, adherence by all tribal members to the terms of a treaty. Ultimately, only individuals could determine whether to bind themselves by the actions of their chiefs. Neither Black Kettle nor the other chiefs who signed the Little Arkansas Treaty could compel adherence from the tribe, unless, of course, all tribal members concurred with their actions. And in this instance they did not. Much of what whites considered inconsistent, even treacherous, conduct in Indians often could be explained by these differences. Thus military authorities viewed with the deepest suspicion the reports detailing how the tough warrior Roman Nose led his followers back to their hunting grounds in western Kansas in violation of the Little Arkansas Treaty.

Responding to complaints from settlers and military officers about the presence of armed Indians in the path of Kansas Pacific construction crews, General Sherman made his move in the late winter of 1867. He ordered General Winfield Scott Hancock to lead a large army expedition into Kansas to intimidate the Southern Cheyennes with a show of force. Hancock was not to attack the Cheyennes, but merely march his command around their encampments as a demonstration of American martial superiority in the hope of convincing them to move below the Arkansas River. Yet Hancock made clear that if the Indians provided any cause, he would attack without mercy. He stated to his officer corps in his general field order: "We go prepared for war and will make it if a proper occasion presents. . . . No insolence will be tolerated."

Agent Edward Wynkoop received advance notification of the operation. It alarmed him sufficiently to ride out to meet with Roman Nose and other recalcitrants. He tried to persuade them not to continue their provocative and potentially disastrous course. Wynkoop explained that Sherman, after hearing of Roman Nose's "occupation," was about to order the army out to bully them. Even more frightening to Wynkoop was the clear possibility that General Sherman might launch an indiscriminate attack on the peaceful Cheyennes, too. Wynkoop, well aware of what such an attack would mean, desperately hoped to prevent it. But Roman Nose firmly rejected all pleas to evacuate western Kansas. He was quite willing, he informed Wynkoop, to fight the whites if it came to that.

General Hancock left Fort Leavenworth and headed into central Kansas, picking up along the way the newly formed United States Seventh Cavalry led by Lieutenant Colonel George Armstrong Custer. The addition of the Seventh swelled Hancock's ranks to over fourteen hundred men. Their initial destination was a substantial Cheyenne and Sioux camp on Pawnee Fork, thirty-five miles upstream from Fort Larned. Wynkoop warned Hancock of the highly explosive situation he would run into if he persisted in marching on this camp. He reminded the general of Sand Creek, and of how warriors might be sent out to block him before the troops could come close enough to the camp to state their business. The likely result, as Wynkoop knew, would be another massacre. Hancock, dismissing the warnings, ordered his troops forward. The Indians, not waiting to see what the army wanted, abandoned camp, leaving behind most of their possessions, and put distance between themselves and the federal troops. The women and children left first while warriors covered their retreat. The following day the warriors also withdrew. The peace element eventually relocated further to the south below the Arkansas in the panhandle region of Indian Territory (present-day Oklahoma). The confrontational faction, led by Roman Nose, chose to strike back immediately. They remained north of the river and lashed out at whites, assaulting railroad work crews, stagecoach stations, settlers, and travellers on the overland routes. Soon they had halted all traffic in western Kansas.

Hancock, after arriving at the abandoned camp, hesitated to burn it. Three days later he received word of the attacks by those who remained in Kansas. Hancock concluded that it "was a nest of conspirators" and so, over Wynkoop's strong protests, ordered the camp, containing 111 Cheyenne lodges and 140 Sioux lodges and their contents, burned. Then he sent Custer to pursue the Indians, who led him on a frustrating and largely unsuccessful chase through western Kansas that summer.

Edward Wynkoop assessed General Hancock's actions a "disaster," and two days after the village burning bitterly wrote Indian Commissioner Nathaniel G. Taylor that "I know of no overt act that the Cheyennes had committed to cause them to be thus punished." General Sherman reacted initially to the news of Indian attacks in his accustomed style by calling for the destruction of all natives who might be found between the

Arkansas and Platte rivers. Once he had calmed down, he asked civil authorities to define hostile from peaceful Indians so that the army might direct its efforts only at the guilty party, thus avoiding an assault on innocents. "We, the military," Sherman wrote Secretary of Interior Browning, "do not wish this result, because it would be a national disgrace." Officials in Washington realized they could little afford the bad publicity of another Sand Creek, especially as the national mood was one of general sympathy for the Indians because of the recent report by the Sully commission, whom President Johnson charged with investigating western Indian affairs following the Fetterman fight. General Alfred Sully's probe chronicled a string of flagrant violations of treaty guarantees by whites, accompanied by an unwillingness of the federal government to meet its treaty obligations to the Indians. The Sully commission called for direct action by the government to establish peace on equitable terms with the Plains Indians, particularly with Red Cloud and his Sioux as well as with the Cheyennes and other warring southern tribes. Secretary Browning conveyed the proposal to Congress for its approval. After intense debate, both houses consented on July 20, 1867.

Quickly, President Johnson ordered a federal peace commission to meet with the Indians. He charged them with removing the causes for further hostility, and, as far as possible, concentrating the western Indians on one of three reservations: the Plains tribes on either a large northern reserve west of the Missouri and north of Nebraska or a large southern reserve west of the Arkansas and south of Kansas; and those living west of the Rockies on one in the Southwest. General Sherman had offered the idea the previous year in his annual report. Indian Commissioner Nathaniel G. Taylor, Methodist minister, attorney, and close friend of the president, headed the United States Indian Peace Commission. "In my judgment," stated Taylor, assessing his mission, "the Indians can only be saved from extinction by consolidating them as rapidly as it can be peacefully done on larger reservations, from which all whites except Government employees shall be excluded." Taylor also boasted that his commission could achieve peace in one hundred days at the cost of $250,000; far less than the $5 million expended on Hancock's recent efforts in Kansas. Civilian officials and high-ranking army officers rounded out the commission's membership: Kansas Senator Edmund G. Ross; Samuel F. Tappan, reformer and former Abolitionist; and Generals William S. Harney, Alfred H. Terry, and William T. Sherman. Sherman, with his typical bluntness, commented about Commissioner Taylor's goals of securing peace, clearing the central plains of free-roaming Indians, and concentrating the tribes. "Get them out as soon as possible," the general remarked caustically, "and it makes little difference whether they be coaxed out by Indian commissioners or killed."

The Myth of Peace

Concurrently with events in Kansas and in Washington, Red Cloud resumed his assaults against the forts along the Bozeman Trail. That summer the Sioux and their Northern Cheyenne and Arapahoe allies terrorized whites along the Upper Missouri; assaulted their hereditary enemies, the Mandans, Gros Ventres, and Arikaras; and paralyzed travel in the Powder River country. In late July 1867, Red Cloud ordered two decisive actions. Unable to decide which fort to target first, the Indians divided their ranks and moved to strike two separate objectives. On August 1, a large force mainly of Cheyennes, led by Two Moon, assaulted the Americans at Fort Smith. The battle, called the "Hayfield Fight," was fought to a stalemate, with each side sustaining heavy losses. Two days later on August 3, one thousand warriors under Red Cloud, chiefly Sioux, attacked Fort Kearny. However, the Sioux's deficiency in improvising tactics during the battle, coupled with the effectiveness of the soldiers' new breech-loading Springfield rifles in repelling the attackers, resulted in another indecisive battle, known as the "Wagon-Box Fight." Both sides sustained heavy losses, but casualties among Red Cloud's warriors were particularly high. He would later say that on that day he lost the flower of his young men. The army accepted its tenuous victory and applauded its success in holding onto the Bozeman Trail forts.

A month later, in September 1867, the United States Indian Peace Commission arrived on the Great Plains and initiated talks with tribes. Unfortunately, these councils failed to resolve many of the Indians' complaints about whites. A delegation of Brule and Oglala Sioux, along with some Cheyennes, met with the commissioners in mid-September at North Platte, Nebraska, to receive powder and lead and to complain about Americans in their Nebraska lands. They were particularly incensed by the white hunters who were working for railroad crews and destroying their buffalo supply by mass-kill methods. The commissioners only advised that the Sioux should as quickly as possible select a suitable area within their present territory as the site for a future reservation, before white settlers took it all. There, with the assistance of government agents and white missionaries and educators, the Sioux could convert to farming and learn the culture of the white man. "The President desires to see you prosperous and happy and has sent us here to devise means to secure this end," one commission member told the frustrated Indians. "We have exercised our best judgment and adopted the best plan to improve your condition and save your people. Accept it and be happy." This was hardly the solution the Sioux had expected from a federal commission charged with achieving an equitable peace settlement.

The commission hoped to talk next with Red Cloud, but scouts reported his refusal to come in for a conference. Promising to meet again with the Sioux in November, the commissioners headed for Kansas to meet with the tribes of the southern plains. The Southern Cheyennes were wary and required much coaxing before agreeing to meet in a peace council. In a further attempt to bring lasting peace to the southern Great Plains, the commissioners invited the Kiowas, Comanches, Southern Arapahoes, and Plains Apaches, as well. The council convened in October of 1867 at Medicine Lodge Creek, a popular Sun Dance ground, seventy miles south of Fort Larned in southwestern Kansas and just north of the Indian Territory. Five thousand Indians arrived to observe the momentous discussions between their chiefs and the United States Indian Peace Commission.

The commissioners offered a plan of peace establishing two reserves in the western half of the Indian Territory. They would be fashioned from lands once belonging to the Five Civilized Tribes: the Cherokees, Chickasaws, Choctaws, Creeks, and Seminoles. Virtually charged with treason by the United States for their alliances with the Confederacy during the Civil War, these Indian republics—"Great Father's erring children"—were required to sign Reconstruction treaties in 1866, which, among other stipulations, drastically reduced the landholdings of each tribe. The commission proposed assigning the Cheyennes and Arapahoes to about three million acres between the thirty-seventh parallel and the Cimarron and Arkansas rivers in the Indian Territory. Directly to the south, the Kiowas and Comanches would be concentrated on a comparably large area between the Washita and Red rivers. The Plains Apaches would reside there, too. The commissioners promised honorable terms to the assembled chiefs: an assortment of trinkets, food, clothing, weapons and ammunition for hunting, blankets, as well as farming tools, seeds, and other necessities to begin their new way of life, and, finally, peace with the United States. All would be theirs if they signed the treaty. War and the further destruction of their people would be their lot if they refused. On October 21, 1867, the Kiowas, Comanches, and Plains Apaches signed the Medicine Lodge Creek Treaty. On October 28, the Cheyennes and Arapahoes resigned themselves to their fate and acquiesced.

But the Cheyenne warrior Roman Nose and the volatile Kiowa chief Satanta, two influential leaders, rejected the treaty. During the peace talks Satanta made his position on the Concentration policy absolutely clear to the commissioners:

All the land south of the Arkansas belongs to the Kiowas and the Comanches, and I don't want to give it away. I love the land and the buffalo and I will not part with any. . . . I have heard you intend to settle us on a reservation near the mountains. I don't want to settle there. I love to roam over the wide prairie, and when I do, I feel free and happy, but when we settle down we grow pale and die. . . . My heart feels like bursting with sorrow.

The peace commissioners granted permission to any of the five signatory tribes who preferred not to travel to their reserved land in Indian Territory until the following spring to stay near Fort Larned. While Black Kettle settled most of the Southern Cheyennes into their winter camp near that fort, and leaders of other southern plains tribes did the same, Roman Nose and his followers rode north into the forbidden central Kansas area and Satanta led his people away to Texas. The intransigence of two of the most aggressive Indian leaders boded poorly for residents of the Great Plains, Indians and whites alike.

As for the commissioners, they were heartened by the treaty. Half of the Concentration policy's agenda for the plains tribes was in place. The Medicine Lodge Creek Treaty had reserved land below Kansas where the tribes of the southern plains would reside. The commission's next task was winning agreement from the northern plains tribes for a comparable arrangement above Nebraska. To complete the policy, the United States Indian Peace Commission moved on to Fort Laramie, sending messengers ahead into the Powder River country requesting that Red Cloud meet them at the fort for talks. Red Cloud again refused, explaining that he and his followers were too busy to come to the fort. They were preparing for their fall buffalo hunt. Red Cloud also sent a message back to the commissioners specifying his terms to end hostilities: The Bozeman forts had to be evacuated; only this would bring him down to Fort Laramie. During the winter of 1867–1868 the United States government reached the same conclusion. On March 2, 1868, General Grant wrote to General Sherman, "I think it will be well to prepare at once for the abandonment of the posts . . . and to make all the capital with the Indians that can be made out of the change."

The peace commissioners had to wait until the following spring before meeting with the dominant northern plains tribes. The result was a major federal treaty between these Indians and the United States. On April 29, 1868, chiefs of the Yanktonai Sioux and Brule, Miniconjou, and Oglala bands of the Teton Sioux, signed the Fort Laramie Treaty. The agreement included important concessions and guarantees. The United States guaranteed the area comprising the western half of the present state of South Dakota to the signatory tribes as a permanent home to be designated "The Great Sioux Reservation." The United States also guaranteed these tribes the right to inhabit the Powder River country to the west of the Great Sioux Reservation. This land, defined as "north of the North Platte River and east of the summits of the Big Horn Mountains," was designated "unceded Indian territory," and it was closed to all whites henceforth. The Fort Laramie Treaty also secured for the Indians the right to hunt within this area "so long as buffalo may range there in numbers sufficient to justify the chase." Members of the signatory tribes could reside either on the reserve or in the unceded territory, or they could shuttle back and forth. The newest Fort Laramie Treaty also contained acculturation measures similar to those in the Medicine Lodge Creek Treaty. Finally, the United States agreed to abandon the three forts along the Bozeman Trail.

A week after the Sioux signing, the other major tribes came around. On May 7, 1868, the Crows met with the peace commissioners at Fort Laramie and accepted a reserve in Montana, relinquishing all claim to other territory in Montana and Wyoming guaranteed to them by their first Concentration treaty, the Fort Laramie Treaty of 1851. Three days later the Northern Cheyennes and Arapahoes also signed the accord. They agreed to live either on the Southern Cheyenne and Arapahoe reserve in Indian Territory or on the Great Sioux Reservation.

The following month negotiators in the Southwest realized another major goal of the Concentration policy, in this case with the Navahos. The previous five years had been traumatic for this tribe. During the Civil War, Union forces expelled the

Confederate "Army of New Mexico" from the Territory of New Mexico (which included the present-day states of New Mexico, Arizona, and southern Nevada). With the Confederate threat to this area ended, they turned, in 1862, to ending the 250-year-old white struggle with the Navahos and the Apaches. Colonel James H. Carleton directed Colonel Christopher "Kit" Carson and the New Mexico volunteer militia to break the Indians' power in the area, ordering that there "be no council held with the Indians, nor any talks. The men are to be slain whenever and wherever they can be found. The women and children may be taken as prisoners, but, of course, they are not to be killed." A campaign without quarter during 1863 accomplished the objective of subjugation. Following capitulation, Carleton directed that the approximately nine thousand Navaho survivors be held along with the Apaches at Bosque Redondo near Fort Sumner, New Mexico Territory, on the Pecos River. Disease, coupled with lack of water, food, and the most basic essentials needed to sustain a minimal existence, caused the death of an estimated one-quarter of the Indians there. The government ended the disastrous Bosque Redondo experiment in 1868. On June 1 of that year the Navaho relinquished all claim to their territory and agreed to a fourteen-million-acre reserve encompassing parts of Utah, Arizona, and New Mexico.

Meanwhile, Red Cloud still refused to come to Fort Laramie and discuss signing the treaty. His refusal was not an objection to the treaty itself, but a determination not to sign anything until the United States evacuated the Bozeman Trail forts. "We are on the mountains looking down on the soldiers and the forts," he notified the commissioners through a messenger in May. "When we see the soldiers moving away and the forts abandoned, then I will come down and talk." On May 19, 1868, Washington issued orders to abandon the forts along the Bozeman Trail. During August the orders were executed. All soldiers and civilians at Fort Smith, then Kearny, and finally Reno, vacated their posts. The Sioux then burned each installation to the ground. With these victories accomplished, and with meat stored for winter, Red Cloud and his followers journeyed to Fort Laramie. On November 6, 1868, he, too, signed the Fort Laramie Treaty.

Indian Commissioner Taylor had asserted in 1867 that peace could only be secured, and the extinction of Indians prevented, by realizing the policy of Concentration: "consolidating them as rapidly as it can be peacefully done on larger reservations." The United States Indian Peace Commission then labored throughout much of 1867 and 1868 to accomplish this goal. While the peace they secured at Fort Laramie for the northern plains lasted for almost a decade, the time of amity on the southern plains was short-lived. Civil and military officials disagreed about what caused it to shatter. Taylor suggested that a "spirit of revenge" over the failure of the government to supply the food, guns, and ammunition promised at Medicine Lodge Creek provided the cause. General Sherman was convinced that the government's concessions to the Sioux on the Bozeman Trail issue led some members of the southern tribes to emulate in the hope that Washington would give in. There was truth in both explanations.

The southern tribes, throughout the winter of 1867–1868, had waited in vain for their provisions. During those months Commissioner Taylor had repeatedly warned of the "grave importance" of supplying the southern tribes "in order that the faith of the Government and the promises of the Indian Peace Commission, may be kept good." Congress, however, preoccupied with the impeachment of President Andrew Johnson, failed to appropriate funds to fulfill the commissioners' promises until July 1868, nine months after the peace council at Medicine Lodge Creek. As the Indians' disillusionment and frustration mounted, a growing number of the young men left camp to follow the trail north into the forbidden Smokey Hill hunting grounds of Kansas, acknowledging they did not want to be restricted to living on lands dictated to them by the white man. Recalcitrants like Roman Nose and Medicine Arrows, who had resided in that region since repudiating the peace commission, seized the opportunity to persuade them to emulate the resistance of Red Cloud.

Hints of trouble came when the Cheyennes and Arapahoes in Kansas launched strikes against their old enemies, the Kaws and Pawnees. More serious trouble did not arise until early August. On August 9, 1868, Agent Edward Wynkoop finally delivered weapons and ammunition to the Southern Cheyennes in accordance with the Medicine Lodge Creek Treaty. The supplies were intended for use in securing winter meat. Before a week had elapsed, a party of about two hundred Cheyennes, with a few Arapahoes and Sioux, rampaged against white settlers residing on the Saline and Solomon rivers in Kansas, killing fifteen men, raping women, capturing children, and looting and destroying property. More depredations followed in September. It is unlikely that these men intended to start a full-scale war. Revenge, anger, and the easy availability of liquor from white traders seems to have been at the root of their behavior. That starting a full-scale war was not their intent did not mitigate their actions, which precipitated one.

General Sherman, concluding that there was "open war, all the way from Fort Wallace to Denver," moved quickly. In early August 1868, he issued orders directing his field commanders to bring all Indians into their new reservations in the Indian Territory, peaceful and hostile factions alike. While most complied, some clung tenaciously to their old hunting grounds. Predictably, when the army moved in to round up the hostiles, severe clashes ensued. One of the more famous collisions occurred when troops commanded by Major George A. Forsyth moved against the Southern Cheyennes. The fight became known as "The Battle of Beecher's Island." On September 17, 1868, massed Cheyenne, accompanied by Sioux warriors, engaged Forsyth and his men, trapping them on an island of the Arickaree River, a fork of the Republican River, in northeastern Colorado just over the western border of Kansas. The Indians besieged the island for nine days, nearly eradicating the contingent of Americans. Only after the arrival of a column of the Tenth Cavalry were the survivors rescued.

Realizing that more troops surely would be ordered out to subdue them, many Indians fled toward the Indian Territory to seek haven among the peaceful faction. The reaction of white authorities, however, was far greater than they ever anticipated.

General Sherman was furious when word reached him of Indian resistance to his orders to retire immediately to their reservations. "These Indians require to be soundly whipped," Sherman harangued, "and the ringleaders in the present trouble hung, their ponies killed, and such destruction of their property as will make them very poor." Now with treaties signed and the Concentration policy apparently realized, Sherman was more determined than ever to use military force to keep tribes on their reservations. All Indians, he now directed, who continued to reside off their reservations were to be considered "hostile" and, as such, could be attacked in whatever way military assessment dictated. "We have now selected and provided reservations for all," stormed Sherman. "All who cling to their old hunting grounds are hostile and will remain so till killed off."

Sherman's decision received the support of General of the Army Ulysses S. Grant, the Republican nominee for president and the man whom almost everyone expected would occupy the White House after the fall elections. Although Grant showed some understanding of the problems of the Indians (he would later as president appoint the Seneca Ely Parker to head the Indian Bureau), in this case he supported his old comrade's determination to attack the hostiles without mercy. Grant, with uncharacteristic bombast, asserted to newspapermen: We must "clear the plains for the immigrants even if extermination of every Indian tribe is necessary." Edward Wynkoop, the Southern Cheyennes and Arapahoes' agent, vehemently disagreed with Sherman and Grant and the course they approved. He resigned his post and left for Philadelphia, declaring in a widely published letter condemning the army that he feared the military would use him as "a decoy to lure Indians into a trap."

The forthcoming campaign had three principal objectives, all aimed at enforcing the Concentration policy: first, to permanently remove the southern plains tribes from the land north of the Arkansas River; second, to confine the signatory tribes of the Medicine Lodge Creek Treaty to their reservations in the Indian Territory; and third, to punish those involved in the August and September 1868 outbreak of violence in Kansas. Responsibility for the campaign fell to General Philip H. Sheridan, commander of the Department of the Missouri, which included Kansas, New Mexico, Colorado, and the Indian Territory. Soon he received instructions from Sherman: "Go ahead in your own way, and I will back you with my authority. If it results in the utter annihilation of these Indians, it is but the result of what they have been warned again and again."

Armed thus with specific approval from his superior, Philip Sheridan readied plans for a war of extermination. He resolved to conduct it by means of a new strategy in fighting the Plains Indians: a winter campaign. The people of the plains had no experience with such warfare. Because theirs was largely a food-gathering economy, they obtained no profit from waging war in winter, which would diminish their store of food even more rapidly. Sheridan concluded that the Indians' horses, extremely weakened from foraging on a few tufts of frozen grass during the winter months, could only poorly carry the fighting warriors and escaping tribespeople. He also realized that since the military had usually left Indians alone during the winter, their camps probably would be caught off guard by his troops. As he explained in a letter to William Sherman: "In taking the offensive, I have to select the season when I can catch the fiends." Sheridan also acknowledged the likelihood of casualties among the Indian women and children, and he rationalized, "If a village is attacked and women and children killed, the responsibility is not with the soldiers but with the people whose crimes necessitated the attack." Reminding Sherman of their tactics while campaigning in the Civil War, Philip Sheridan continued, "During the war did any one hesitate to attack a village or town occupied by the enemy because women and children were within its limits? Did we cease to throw shells into Vicksburg or Atlanta because women and children were there?"

Black Kettle, as always a believer in peace and compromise with the white men, had scrupulously obeyed the provisions of the Medicine Lodge Creek Treaty. In the spring of 1868 he had moved his people to the Indian Territory, settling them along the Washita River at the far western edge of the Cheyenne-Arapahoe reserve. In early November the renegades reached his encampment. As he listened to their tale of the recent fighting and learned that soldiers were still in pursuit, he could think of nothing but another assault like Sand Creek on his peaceful village. Black Kettle quickly resolved to journey southward to Fort Cobb on the northern perimeter of the Kiowa-Comanche reservation. There he would seek help from the military authorities. Upon his arrival, he explained his fear to the fort's commander, General William B. Hazen. Black Kettle asked Hazen for permission to move his people to this reservation where they would be under the general's protection. Black Kettle made clear that he spoke only for his band, who wanted peace, not for hostiles who were the target of Sheridan's campaign. Hazen, as he stated in his report of the incident, "followed the book" and suggested that Black Kettle return to his camp on the Washita, contact General Philip Sheridan, and surrender. Uneasy about his decision and worried about the fate of Black Kettle's band, he sent word of the meeting to General Sherman. Hazen was too late to help. Black Kettle, meanwhile, hurried back to his Washita River camp.

By November, Sheridan's scouts had informed him of the whereabouts of the hostile Cheyennes, Arapahoes, Comanches, and Kiowas in the Canadian and Washita valleys in western Indian Territory and northern Texas. With this information, he decided on a three-columned encircling movement to trap and destroy them. He ordered one column, commanded by Major Eugene A. Carr with seven companies of his Fifth Cavalry, to move southward from Fort Lyon, Colorado, toward those Indians wintering near Antelope Hill in western Indian Territory. A second column under Major Andrew W. Evans simultaneously would push eastward from Fort Bascum, New Mexico Territory, toward the Indians along the Canadian River in the Texas panhandle. The third column would be the main strike force, engaging those Indians pushed toward it by Carr's and Evans's troops. It would embark from Camp Supply along the North Canadian River in northwestern Indian Territory. Commanded by Sheridan himself and General Alfred Sully, it consisted of eleven companies of the Seventh Cavalry under Colonel George A. Custer, the Nineteenth Kansas Volunteer Cavalry under Colonel Samuel J. Crawford, and five companies of infantry under Captain J. H. Page. Together the three columns comprised fifteen hundred troops. Sheridan's orders to his commanders left no doubt about how the campaign should be conducted: "To destroy their villages and ponies, to kill and hang all warriors, and bring back all women and children."

The assaults began during the snowy days of late November 1868. The first took place in the early morning hours of November 27 against Black Kettle's village. The hostile Cheyennes had been successfully tracked as they fled across the snow-covered plains. Without a doubt, scouts reported, they presently resided at the peace chief's village along the Washita River on the Cheyenne-Arapahoe reservation. Only a few hours after Black Kettle returned from his unsuccessful trip to Fort Cobb, the Seventh Cavalry attacked his village. The scene was all too reminiscent of Sand Creek, almost four years ago to the day. The soldiers charged from all four sides while a military band, one of Colonel Custer's inspirations, enthusiastically thumped out the marching tune "Garry Owen." Custer reported that his men killed 103 warriors and captured fifty-three women and children. Almost incidentally, he also mentioned that "in the excitement of the fight, as well as in self-defense, it so happened that some of the squaws and a few children were killed and wounded." Additionally, his troops seized or destroyed 875 horses, ponies, and mules; a vast amount of robes, equipment and clothing; and a "whole sup-ply" of meat and food.

Black Kettle, who had twice before missed death in similar circumstances, was killed as he tried to lead his people away from the rampaging soldiers. With a bullet in his back, he toppled from his horse into the cold waters of the Washita. Sheridan, in his official report to General Sherman, expressed jubilation that his troops finally had "wiped out old Black Kettle, . . . a worn-out and worthless old cypher." Far to the east in Philadelphia, Edward Wynkoop anguished over the accounts of the Battle of the Washita and of the death of his old friend. The Cheyennes' former agent bitterly denounced the betrayal by white authorities of this tribe, whom he had labored so diligently to protect from yet another catastrophe of this sort. Black Kettle "met his death at the hands of white men in whom he had too often fatally trusted," lamented Wyn-koop, "and who triumphantly report the fact of his scalp in their possession."

Sheridan's campaign pressed ahead relentlessly through-out the winter of 1868–1869, crushing the Indians found off the reservation. A month after the Washita fight, on Christmas Day, 1868, Major Evans struck the Comanches and Kiowas hard at their village on Soldier Spring, routing them and de-stroying large stores of food and supplies. His victory broke their resistance and forced the two tribes back onto their reservation. Colonel Custer likewise remained in the field throughout the first months of 1869, searching the Texas pan-handle and harrying back to the reservation those Cheyennes and Arapahoes who had yet to surrender. The Indians who had not perished from the soldiers' onslaught were overwhelm-ingly residing at their assigned reserve in the Indian Territory by spring. During the winter campaign of 1868–1869 one of America's most famous aphorisms was coined. Tosawi, the Comanche chief who brought in the first group of his people to surrender, confronted Philip Sheridan while on a stopover at Fort Cobb. Tosawi plaintively asked the general, "Why am I and my people being tormented by you? I am a good Indian."

Sheridan replied with one of the Plains Wars' most infamous and most memorable statements: "The only good Indians I ever saw were dead." Lieutenant Charles Nordstrom, who was present, reported and retold the epigram, although General Sheridan, in his *Personal Memoirs*, denied ever uttering it.

By the spring of 1869, Sheridan had realized the three main objectives of his winter campaign. Indians had been evicted from the land north of the Arkansas River. The signatory tribes of the Medicine Lodge Creek Treaty had been confined to their reservations in the Indian Territory. And, those who had been involved in the August and September 1868 outbreak of violence in Kansas, and quite a few others as well, had been punished by the military.

Some Americans were heartsick over Sheridan's winter campaign. The Quakers, in a memorial to Congress, asked the government to alter its course toward the Indians and prayed "that the effusion of blood may cease, and that such just and humane measures may be pursued as will secure a lasting peace, and tend to the preservation and enlightenment of those afflicted people, whom we regard as the wards of the nation." Eastern humanitarians, stirred to action on behalf of the Indians, bitterly denounced the army's actions and declaimed the Washita River attack as another Sand Creek. Samuel Tappan, a member of the now defunct United States Indian Peace Commission that had secured the Medicine Lodge Creek Treaty in the hope of bringing peace to the southern plains, condemned the campaign as "stupid and criminal blundering." Tappan, Edward Wynkoop, and reformers who promoted the Indians' welfare, such as John Beeson, Lydia Maria Child, and Peter Cooper, demanded that the federal government henceforth permit Christian denominations and humanitarian groups to assume a major role in guiding Indian policy. Indian Commissioner Nathaniel Taylor concurred with the reformers, recommending in his final annual report that "the government should invite the cooperation . . . of all Christian societies or individuals who may be disposed to take part in the work." The new Grant administration soon acted upon these calls.

On the other hand, many Americans, and most especially those residing in the West, were gratified by the winter campaign, and with Philip Sheridan in particular. "Shall we Williampennize or Sheridanize the Indians?" asked the Columbus, Nebraska, *Platte Journal*. The answer was no doubt obvious to the editor who posed the question, and to many readers who paused to ponder it.

Federal officials hoped that the winter campaign of 1868–1869 was decisive, and that they had advanced far in solving the Indian question. Certainly peace in the West appeared to have come at last, secured by the policy of Concentration with the federal authority holding, as William Sherman pointed out to Philip Sheridan, "the olive branch with one hand and the sword in the other."

When I was a boy the Sioux owned the world; the sun rose and set on their land; they sent ten thousand men to battle. Where are the warriors today? Who slew them? Where are our lands? Who owns them? . . . Is it wrong for me to love my own? Is it wicked for me because my skin is red? Because I am a Sioux; because I was born where my father lived; because I would die for my people and my country?

SITTING BULL, HUNKPAPA SIOUX

CHAPTER FIVE

The Plains Wars, Phase II: The Struggle to Enforce the Policy of Concentration

Hostilities between the United States and the Plains Indians decreased sharply following Philip Sheridan's winter campaign of 1868–1869, as Washington realized the policy of Concentration. While the West enjoyed a period of relative calm, the East stirred with controversy over Indian affairs. The violent events of the preceding fall and winter had produced two immediate consequences. First, they revived the Transfer Issue and the controversy over the government's system of jurisdiction in Indian administration. Second, they heightened demands by humanitarian reformers for a greater role in shaping the government's Indian policy. President-elect Ulysses S. Grant, soon to face the task of enforcing the Concentration policy, had to decide which side he would support in each controversy to administer effectively the nation's Indian affairs.

Grant's "Peace Policy"

Captain William Fetterman's defeat in December 1866 during the Powder River War had infused the Transfer Issue. But

Congress, following intense wrangling between proponents and opponents of transfer, early in 1867 voted against moving the Indian service to the War Department. With the Indian service remaining under the Interior Department, the military had little choice but to acquiesce, however grudgingly, in the conciliatory measures advanced by the civilians who oversaw the nation's Indian affairs. By late 1868, in light of almost a half decade of hostilities with the plains tribes and the seeming failure of the treaty system in securing peace with Indians, the nation's military leaders again openly expressed their disillusionment with civilian control of the Indian Bureau. "Does not this magnanimity verge on the borders of folly?" General William T. Sherman argued in a letter to his brother John, the senator from Ohio and a staunch supporter of transferring control to the War Department. "It is a waste of life and waste of money to hunt down nomadic Indians like the Sioux to be turned over to the Indian Bureau, and then turned loose well supplied with food and the means of renewing the war."

General Sherman sounded the clarion for change in his annual report of 1868, renewing the military's demand for transfer of jurisdiction over Indian affairs to the War Department. He strenuously suggested that the change was the "only hope" for concluding the "eternal" struggle with the Indians and for ending the Indian question. Ulysses S. Grant supported Sherman fully, and he threw his considerable prestige behind the calls for transfer of the Indian Bureau. "If the present practice is to be continued," concluded Grant, "I do not see that any course is left open to us but to withdraw our troops to the settlements and call upon Congress to provide means and troops to carry on the formidable hostilities against the Indians until all the Indians or all the whites on the great plains and between the settlements on the Missouri and the Pacific slope are exterminated."

The outgoing administrator of the Indian Bureau disagreed emphatically. Commissioner Nathaniel Taylor, in his final annual report, took exception to Sherman's and Grant's conclusions, offering a nine-page rebuttal of the generals. Asserting that his sole motive was to save the "unlettered children of the wilderness" from the "blighting scepter of military despotism," Taylor contended that transferring the Indian Bureau from the Interior Department would be "tantamount ... to perpetual war." His superior, Interior Secretary Orville Browning, found little cause to judge the military's demands any more sympathetically. "Our experience during the period when the Indians were under military care and guardianship," he wrote, "affords no ground for hope that any benefit to them or to the treasury would be secured."

Philip Sheridan's winter campaign of 1868–1869 gave impetus to humanitarian reformers, and, understandably, they threw their support behind the civilian authorities during the transfer dispute. Appalled by the bloodshed on the western prairies in recent years, their calls for a more humane and enlightened Indian policy had mounted steadily during the Johnson presidency. They charged the military with brutal treatment and indiscriminate aggression against western tribes. They suggested that the Indians' well-being could only be safeguarded, and progress in civilizing the Indians would only be realized, through the efforts of conscientious, concerned, benevolent civilians. The Religious Society of Friends, a Quaker group advocating a Christian approach to solving the Indian question, characterized the goals of the various and proliferating Indian reform groups: To "endeavor to treat them with kindness and justice, to guard them against the imposition and fraud to which their ignorance exposed them; to meliorate and improve their condition; and to commend the benign and heavenly principles of the Christian religion to their approval and acceptance by an upright example consistent therewith."

Congress soon undertook to resolve the controversy. In early December 1868, Congressman James A. Garfield of Ohio, chairman of the House Military Committee, introduced legislation to return the Indian Bureau to the War Department as of January 1, 1869. Garfield noted that "General Grant, General Sherman, and General Sheridan, and nearly all of the leading officers of the Army connected with the Indian service recommend this." Congressman William Windom of Minnesota, chairman of the House Committee on Indian Affairs, led opposition to the proposed legislation. Asserting that transfer would mean all-out war on the Indians, Windom argued that "if there is any Department of this government in which we find the great maelstrom of the treasury, where money is sunk by millions and never accounted for, it is the War Department." His argument failed to sway most colleagues, and the House passed the Garfield bill by a commanding margin of 116 to 33. The final determination of the Transfer Issue now rested with the Senate. "It has cost this government much more to fight the Indians than to feed them—very much more," Senator Thomas Hendricks of Indiana contended, summing up the position of the anti-transfer forces in the upper house, "and I think this a question of whether they shall be . . . fed or fought." The Senate ended the debate by voting to refer the Garfield bill to the Indian Committee, where it died. Other attempts were made in the House that winter to effect transfer. The Senate rejected each effort. Still, those who advocated military control of Indian affairs were confident. General Grant would be inaugurated in March. With him in the White House, they anticipated changes in the administration of Indian affairs. The changes, however, shocked them at first.

Ulysses S. Grant's first inaugural address on March 4, 1869, heartened reformers and distressed many former comrades in the army. "The proper treatment of the original occupants of this land—the Indians—is one deserving of careful study," declared President Grant. "I will favor any course toward them which tends to their civilization and ultimate citizenship." William T. Sherman, whom Grant appointed general-in-chief of the army, a post he held for the next fourteen and a half years, could not believe the turn of events. Sherman, six weeks after the inauguration, wrote General Philip Sheridan expressing dismay and complete disbelief that their old commander apparently had dramatically altered his approach to dealing with the Indian question.

In calling for the "civilization and ultimate citizenship" of the Indians, President Grant seemed to place his administration squarely on the side of the reformers, for they believed fervently that to civilize the Indians was to safeguard them—from the "deleterious" effects of the customs and values of their native cultures and, equally, from aggression from whites. Was it possible, reformers wondered, that of all people the former commanding general of the United States Army might eschew the sword for benevolent methods to manage Indian affairs and solve the Indian question? Certainly the president's statement seemed to affirm a conviction held by only a minority of his fellow citizens: that Indians were not hopeless unregenerate savages; not unchangeable impediments to American pioneer progress whose extinction was a tragic but inevitable fate. Perhaps Grant, after all, agreed with the reformers, that with time and diligent effort the Indians could be "civilized." Was a more humane administration beginning in the federal government's dealings with Indians? In 1869, many reformers thought so.

The genesis of the so-called "Grant Peace Policy" occurred roughly six weeks prior to the general's first inauguration. In late January of 1869 a delegation of Quakers, one of the most active sects in the field of Indian reform, called on the president-elect urging him to embrace an Indian policy grounded on Christian benevolence. "Gentlemen, your advice is good. I accept it," Grant replied to his visitors. "If you can make Quakers out of the Indians it will take the fight out of them. Let us have peace." The delegation was jubilant. After years of tortuous relations with tribes as the government attempted to solve the Indian question, here now was a national hero and the republic's next chief executive promising that "all Indians disposed to peace will find the new policy a peace-policy." Yet Grant, maybe as an instinctive afterthought, also made it clear to the Quakers that "those [Indians] who do not accept this policy will find the new administration ready for a sharp and severe war policy." Perhaps the delegation in its exaltation failed to weigh this statement as carefully as others made that day by Grant. Maybe their lack of apprehension sprang, too, from a supreme confidence in the ability of humanitarians to transform the hearts and ways of the Indians through philanthropic means, thus making enforcement of the Concentration policy through military means unnecessary.

Shortly after inauguration day, on March 20, 1869, Christian reformers met at Philadelphia. Led by William Welsh, Episcopal layman and Philadelphia businessman, the group appointed a committee to press further the humanitarians' demands with the new president. On March 24, President Grant and Interior Secretary Jacob D. Cox welcomed to the White House a delegation of prosperous and influential Pennsylvania reformers, including Welsh; William Strong, judge on the Pennsylvania Supreme Court; and George H. Stuart, Presbyterian layman and merchant from Philadelphia. Like the Quakers they stressed the need for a benevolent policy to solve the Indian question. They also requested that the president let Protestant denominations and humanitarian groups assume a major role in supervising the Indian service and in guiding federal Indian policy, stressing that "without the co-operation of Christian philanthropists the waste of money would be great, and the result unsatisfactory." The Philadelphia delegation urged Grant to establish an autonomous commission to achieve these ends. The president agreed that the idea had merit. On April 10, 1869, Congress passed legislation authorizing Grant to "organize a board of Commissioners, to consist of not more than ten persons, to be selected by him from men eminent for their intelligence and philanthropy, to serve without pecuniary compensation." Accordingly, on June 3, the president issued an executive order establishing the Board of Indian Commissioners. It was assigned a number of important duties: advising the secretary of the Interior and the commissioner of Indian Affairs regarding Indian policy and reform initiatives, serving as a watchdog over the disbursement of funds appropriated by Congress for the Indians and the Indian service's work among them, and supervising the appointment of all agency personnel by Protestant denominations.

President Grant, by creating the Board of Indian Commissioners and by relying on it and Protestant denominations to advise Indian administrators and nominate Indian agents, advocated major changes in the management of Indian affairs in the hope of maintaining peace with tribes and improving their conditions. Grant's agenda did not end here, though. In an effort to reduce fraud and fashion an efficient and honest management system by which to ensure Indian adherence to Concentration policy, the president, now acting more in character, wanted to involve the military heavily: first by appointing army officers to civil posts in the Indian service, and second by placing the Indian Bureau under the War Department, thus striking doubly "at the heart of the old Indian system—the patronage prerogatives of members of Congress." To federal legislators, permitting sweeping denominational influence was one thing, but to relinquish this sizeable share of the lucrative spoils system without a fight was a completely different matter. Consequently, Congress retaliated against Grant's military agenda by striking down another transfer bill and interdicting the appointment of army officers to civil posts within the Indian service. The furious president, thereafter throwing his support ever more behind Christian reformers, chided Congress: "Gentlemen, you have defeated my plan of Indian management; but you shall not succeed in *your* purpose, for I will divide these appointments up among the religious churches, with which you dare not contend."

While denominational control of the Indian service became the principal characteristic of Grant's Peace Policy, two additional provisions were eventually embodied in it as well. First, the United States would discontinue negotiating treaties with Indian tribes. The government under the Concentration policy would no longer regard them and deal with them legally as sovereign polities. To Grant, the Board of Indian Commissioners, and most reformers, treaties perpetuated a fiction. "We recognize a wandering tribe as an independent and sovereign nation. We send ambassadors to make a treaty as with our equals," criticized one principal reformer, Episcopal

Bishop Henry B. Whipple. It is "impolitic for our Government to treat a heathen community living within our borders as an independent nation, instead of regarding them as wards." By an act of Congress in 1871 the United States government ended the treaty-making process with Indians. Second, the government would move to extinguish tribal identification among Indians, ending their reliance on that community for well-being and hopefully replacing it with the ethic of individual responsibility for personal welfare. Grant saw the reformers as the agents for realizing these changes.

To his credit, Ulysses S. Grant was willing to take a relatively open-minded position for that era regarding the Indians, an open-mindedness shaped in no small measure by his newly appointed commissioner of Indian Affairs, Brigadier General Ely S. Parker. Certainly the new commissioner influenced Grant's faith in the potential of civilizing the Indians. As William H. Armstrong skillfully described in *Warrior in Two Camps: Ely S. Parker, Union General and Seneca Chief*, Parker, or Ha-Sa-No-An-Da, an Americanized Seneca from New York State, had enjoyed prominence in both the Indian and white worlds. Not only was he chief of the Senecas and Grand Sachem of the Iroquois Confederation, Parker also was a lawyer, an engineer, a Worshipful Master in the Masons, and a Union Civil War veteran. Only with the greatest of difficulty had he secured a commission as captain of volunteers during the late war, but from that point onward his military career advanced rapidly. Parker joined General Grant's staff during the Vicksburg campaign of 1862 and 1863, and he served on it throughout the remainder of the war. General Parker was one among an intimate circle of trusted lieutenants who accompanied the commanding general to the parlor of Wilbur McLean's farmhouse at Appomattox, Virginia, where Robert E. Lee surrendered.

Following the war, Ely Parker remained as Grant's aide-de-camp until resigning to accept the post of Indian commissioner. Parker directed the Indian Bureau for two years, backing Grant on using the military to control the Indian service, fighting successfully for the abandonment of the treaty system, and supporting both increased denominational influence in the selection of Indian agents and the reforms recommended by humanitarians and by the Board of Indian Commissioners. Like an increasing number of Grant administration appointees, Parker's record was eventually called into question by a House investigating committee. Its report censored the Bureau's awarding of private contracts to some Sioux agencies, although Parker himself was exonerated of fraud or corruption. He resigned as commissioner in July 1871, declaring angrily that it was "no longer a pleasure to discharge patriotic duties." Parker returned to New York where he suffered a series of major financial, professional, and physical difficulties. He died in 1895. At that time Ely Parker held a minor position on the New York police force.

To Grant, Ely Parker personified all that Indians might become in the United States. The president, in his own way, stood ready to help and support the struggle to bring all Indians into the American mainstream. Yet Ulysses S. Grant's Indian policy, as expressed either to the Quakers, other reform groups, or in his first inaugural, actually deviated little from the guideline set by the Concentration policy of the post–Civil War period: force should not be employed until peaceful means first failed. The Grant administration demanded the absolute concentration of Indians on reservations where missionaries of various religious denominations could then labor at transforming the Indians (after 1871, no longer officially dealt with as members of sovereign nations, but as wards of the United States) into Americans. Peace could indeed be secured by tribes and the Indian question solved, but *only* in this manner. This administration, as Grant himself had promised bluntly, was fully prepared to employ the military to ensure that the Indians obeyed its first dictum absolutely. The occasion arose twice, as the Plains Wars erupted again during the Grant presidency. Unlike the campaigns of 1866–1869, these operations left no doubt about their decisiveness. The Red River War of 1874–1875 brought significant conflict on the southern plains to an

end, while the Great Sioux War of 1876–1877 closed belligerencies on the northern plains.

At the Watershed

By 1870 relative peace reigned on the lower Great Plains, less
a peace of reconciliation than of exhaustion. The Kiowas, Comanches, Southern Cheyennes and Arapahoes for the most
part remained on their reserves in the Indian Territory. Although the hostilities of the preceding years had mentally and
physically worn tribal members, they did not view themselves
as conquered peoples, nor did they regard residency on their
reservation as a permanent badge of subjugation by the United
States' Concentration policy or as final defeat. Among many,
the desire to follow their accustomed ways and to eschew the
white man's road burned strong. They were not yet ready to
accept the fate befalling them. What was natural, indeed inevitable, was that they would cling to their old ways and long
to find the means of throwing off the restraints and thwarting
the plans of those who would lead them to a new way of life.
The young men in particular were unable to accept that their
people's days of freedom on the plains had ended, and especially that they would be deprived of opportunities to achieve
cherished societal honors through raiding and warfare.

The attractions that lured the Indians out of the Indian
Territory reservations in the early 1870s were simple. Among
them was the desire to delay the transformation that required
them to abandon the life of migratory hunters and to take up
that of farmers. Few if any of them, at least among the males,
could even imagine their new status as anything but odious.
There is nothing surprising in this attitude, yet much of the
white population seemed to have found it puzzling that the
Indians did not like or welcome what was happening to them.
White males, who remonstrated quite clearly about the division between men's and women's work, apparently took it for
granted there could be no such divisions among "savages."

Forcing Indian males to take up farming, traditionally the job of women, was tantamount to stripping them of their masculinity.

With their background and cultural beliefs, the men readily took advantage of the provisions in the Medicine Lodge Creek Treaty that permitted them to leave the reservations to hunt the buffalo; from time immemorial, so it seemed to them, the traditional and manly way to secure food. Although the federal government required the four tribes to live on their reservations in the Indian Territory, it granted them the right to supplement food allotments by hunting those buffalo grazing on the lands to the south of the Arkansas River, so long as the "buffalo may range thereon in such numbers as to justify the chase." Contained in this seemingly benevolent clause was the legal justification for restraining the southern tribes from all activity on the white settlers' lands and ultimately for permanently restricting them to their reservations. White authorities and Indian leaders alike recognized the implication, and each side manipulated it to their own advantage. Both sides realized the pronounced and obvious potential for violence in this strategy. Yet in light of what was at stake—for the Indians, remaining free of total confinement on the reservations; for the whites, enforcing the Concentration policy, permanently restricting the Indians to the reservation and ending the Indian question—probably little could have been done to prevent the conflict known as the Red River War. Fought in 1874 and 1875, it represented the last significant armed encounter between the United States and the southern plains tribes.

In 1870 buffalo on the southern plains still roamed in plentiful numbers, although nowhere near the size of the herds that covered this region before the 1840s and the onset of American migration across the West. But the situation in 1870 would soon change, paralleling the recent demise of the buffalo on the central plains. In the late 1860s, white buffalo hunters killed off the remaining herds on the central plains in overwhelming numbers. Hunters with new high-powered buffalo rifles spent most of each year in the wholesale slaughter of the lumbering beasts. These men were followed by the skinners, who took only the buffalos' hides, and sometimes just their tongues. The remains of the carcasses were left to rot. White men killed tens of thousands of buffalo per week in this manner. In the face of such slaughter, the central plains became a great charnel house: a buffalo graveyard of decaying, putrid, stinking remains. By 1870 no buffalo could be found on the central plains, a striking testimony to the power of the modern rifle to wipe out animals in numbers now incalculable. In that same year federal officials gave the hunters and hidesmen permission to hunt buffalo on the upper southern plains. The hunters moved to the south and east, nearing the southern plains tribes who resided in western Indian Territory and who continued to journey north and west from their reservation. Since they too were on the move to hunt buffalo, a confrontation became increasingly possible.

There was rising discontent on the reservations in western Indian Territory by the early 1870s. The diminishing buffalo herd provided one source, but there were others as well. One was a combustible group of youthful warriors and older, recalcitrant war leaders. Young Kiowas and Comanches, chafing at the restraints of reservation life and longing to secure war trophies to enhance warrior status on which their culture put such a high premium, in increasing numbers followed firebrands like Satanta, Big Tree, Eagle Heart, and Satank into Texas and Mexico to raid white settlements. They sent overtures to the Cheyennes, many of whom accepted the tempting offer to join them. In an effort to halt the raids in the summer of 1871, General Sherman ordered the arrest of Satanta and Big Tree after learning that they were openly boasting of killing and robbing whites. The two men were imprisoned at the Texas state penitentiary. The government now hoped that the younger warriors, deprived of these influential leaders, would be discouraged from raiding south of the Indian Territory and thus remain on the reservation, but they were not so disposed.

Under pressure from humanitarian groups to release the Kiowa prisoners, the government freed Satanta and Big Tree in October 1873 on the conditions that they remain peaceful and that they convince the young men to end the war against Texas and return to the reservation. An exasperated General Sherman strongly opposed the move and predicted that the raids would not only continue, but would mount. "I have no more faith in their sincerity than I have in the prarie [sic] wolves," he told General Philip Sheridan, "and as I once risked my life to test their sincerity, I do not propose again to expose others to a like danger." As Sherman predicted, Kiowa and Comanche depredations against the Texas frontier escalated.

In those same years white horse thieves, mainly from Kansas, roamed the Indian Territory unchecked, plundering the Indians' herds and antagonizing the southern plains tribes. Cheap whiskey plied by white traders was also plentiful on the Indian Territory reservations, fueling resistance, fraying tempers, and turning more men into besotted, indolent drunks unable to provide minimal food for hungry families. In February 1873 a local observer apprised John D. Miles, the Southern Cheyennes' agent, of the dangerous situation: "The Indians will be hungry and mad very soon and . . . whiskey is more plentiful than good water and all hands in the vicinity are nearly continually drunk." A lack of rations added to the mounting problems. Food allotments that the Medicine Lodge Creek Treaty promised, small as they would have been, were often late, and sometimes never arrived. At times white authorities withheld rations, hoping to force Indians to return captives or stock taken from Texas. And for those Indians who attempted farming, the poor soil of the reservations made it impossible for residents to supplement diets satisfactorily by their own efforts.

These misfortunes came at a time when the mass slaughter of the southern buffalo herd by white hunters drastically decreased the availability of food from that source. Men brought back less and less to their hungry people on the reservation, as their hunting efforts became increasingly ineffective. The killing of the buffalo herds constituted the deadliest threat to these people. The eradication of the southern herd would mean that they would no longer be allowed to leave the reservation. When the buffalo were insufficient to justify the chase, the federal government would take the inevitable next step and confine them to their reserves permanently.

During the early 1870s white hunters continually moved their operations southward. In 1872–1873 they shipped 1,250,000 hides eastward by rail. By the winter of 1873–1874, so many buffalo had been killed on the lands north of the Cimarron River (estimated at seven and a half million) that a new source had to be secured. If other herds were to be exploited, it could only be those in the Texas panhandle between the Cimarron and South Canadian rivers. Lying just to the west of the Cheyenne-Arapahoe reservation, this locale was the Indians' primary buffalo-hunting ground.

With the arrival of spring in 1874, the buffalo hunters moved into northern Texas. There they made their primitive headquarters in the small town of Adobe Walls on the South Canadian River. From this base they fanned out over the prairie where their deeds were soon known to the Indians, who were deeply resentful. But among many it remained only resentment. The quick instinctive response to retaliate was no longer unanimous. While some tribesmen were as ready as ever to defend their hunting grounds, to others this response appeared futile, designed only to bring in soldiers with more repressive punishments. Still, a number of young Kiowas, Comanches, and Southern Cheyennes (the Arapahoes by this time no longer wanted any part in war against the whites) agreed to join in attacking the white buffalo hunters. As historian Donald J. Berthrong summarized in *The Southern Cheyennes*: "Horse thieves, buffalo hunters, poisonous whiskey, lack of rations, restless young men needing trophies and coups for warrior status, and inadequate law enforcement had finally taken their toll." Just before dawn on June 27, 1874, three hundred Cheyenne and Comanche warriors led by Isatai, a Comanche medicine man, assaulted Adobe Walls and the men within. Although repulsed, the warriors sufficiently alarmed the hunters to cause them to abandon Adobe Walls and retire to safer land above the North Canadian River. A number of officials in the Indian Territory urged the army to take action. General John Pope, military commander for the southern Great Plains district, did not agree. Characterizing the white hunters as the basest frontier element who plundered the Indian country in violation of the law while committing "violent and inexcusable outrages upon the Indians," Pope wrote Kansas Governor Thomas A. Osborn: the hunters "have justly earned all that may befall them, and if I were to send troops to the locality of these unlawful establishments, it would be to break them up and not to protect them."

The battle at Adobe Walls stirred the martial ardor of other warriors who had remained in the Indian Territory. With spirits heightened, mounting numbers poured from the reservation to join the fighting. Punitive raids erupted against settlers, travellers, and even army parties, covering a two-hundred-mile radius of the reservations. Making their base in the Staked Plains region of northern Texas, raiders swept into Texas, New Mexico, Kansas, and even faraway Colorado. Yet their security was to last only briefly before disaster overwhelmed them, once again in the form of Philip Sheridan. "This outbreak," Sheridan concluded, "does not look to me, as being originated by the actions of bad white men, or the sale of whiskey to Indians by traders. It is the result of the restless nature of the Indians who has no profession but arms and naturally seeks for war and plunder when the grazing gets high enough to feed his ponies." By mid-summer hostilities were so widespread that civil authorities felt compelled to turn matters over to the military. In July 1874, Interior Secretary Columbus Delano and Indian Commissioner Edward P. Smith gave Secretary of War William W. Belknap full authority to control Indian affairs in and around the Indian Territory. Accordingly, on July 20, General William T. Sherman ordered General Sheridan to enforce the Concentration policy and crush the hostiles.

While the army prepared for this newest mission, several nasty incidents occurred on the Indian Territory reservations. On August 22, for example, troops of the Tenth Cavalry under Lieutenant Colonel John W. Davidson tried to disarm the Comanches and force them to relinquish their white prisoners of war. Gunfire erupted and the two sides battled each other from long-range for two days. The melee produced few casualties, but as a result scores of previously peaceful men moved into northern Texas to join the hostiles. By late August thousands of men, women, and children had bolted from the reservations: eighteen hundred Southern Cheyennes, two thousand Comanches, and one thousand Kiowas. Of these, according to historian Robert M. Utley, perhaps twelve hundred were warriors.

Meanwhile, Sheridan readied his commanders. The general sympathized with the tribes' plight and he understood clearly the principal source of Indian hostility and their resistance to the Concentration policy: "We took away their country and their means of support," he reflected, "broke up their mode of living, their habits of life, introduced disease and decay among them, and it was for this and against this they made war. Could any one expect less?" Sheridan also was convinced that they had "only one profession, that of arms, and every one of them belongs to it, and they never resist the natural desire to join in a fight if it happens to be in their vicinity." Therefore, stamping out this "natural inclination" required that the Indians be punished severely for each breach of the peace.

And so Sheridan again chose a tactic approximating a war of attrition: a total war against the entire population residing off the reservations. Only such a war would convince the hostiles they could not win. It would force proud warriors to consider the welfare of their families and war leaders to think of their bands, however crushing the blows to their pride. Employing the same strategy of convergence used to destroy Indian resistance during the winter campaign of 1868–1869, Sheridan ordered a five-pronged drive aimed at encircling the hostiles in Texas. Although brutal, the strategy was over-whelmingly successful. Wherever the soldiers discovered camps, they put them to the torch. Food, animals, weapons, vast quantities of supplies—all were destroyed, leaving survi-vors to face the bitter winter on the plains. Deprivation and want became the Indians' lot as they struggled against the elements. While the cold and hunger weakened them, troopers relentlessly pursued. The Indians hid or were in constant flight. Sheridan's tactics wore down Chief Lone Wolf and his Kiowas first. The plains were still frozen as the remnants of his band came into Fort Sill in February of 1875. A month later most Southern Cheyennes gave themselves up. Hundreds, however, tried to escape and join the Northern Cheyennes on the upper plains. For some, their efforts were thwarted in a manner that had become all too commonplace. Troops of the Sixth Cavalry under Lieutenant Austin Henely tracked down one group of about sixty and attacked them in their camp on the Sappa River in northwest Kansas. They took no prisoners. Other Southern Cheyennes successfully avoided pursuing patrols and in mid-May 1875 joined the Northern Cheyennes at the Red Cloud agency. By June 1875 the Comanches too faced the reality that further resistance would only result in complete annihilation and so came into Fort Sill and surrendered.

With the Red River War over, military authorities were more determined than ever to prevent a recurrence. They im-prisoned a number of the leading war chiefs. As Philip Sher-idan suggested: "To turn them loose to renew the same old game in the spring seems folly." Among them was the famous—most whites thought infamous—Kiowa war chief Satanta, who was returned to the Texas state penitentiary to serve a life sentence. The absolute confinement proved so loathsome to him that he jumped to his death from an upper window of the prison on March 11, 1878.

A new military policy, proposed by President Grant on March 13, 1875, was implemented. Designed to destroy the southern plains tribes' leadership, and with it those peoples' ability to resist the Concentration policy further, the plan called for exiling the leading warriors and war chiefs from their families and tribes. The government selected seventy-four men, chained and shackled them, and then shipped them under heavy guard to the old Spanish fortress Castillo de San Marcos at St. Augustine, Florida, an installation renamed Fort Marion by the United States. There the men remained imprisoned for three years under the supervision of Lieutenant Richard H. Pratt. A number died—some from disease, others because they could not adjust to the sultry Florida climate, still others from loneliness. The survivors, characterized by reformer Henry B. Whipple as "desperate warriors as ever carried the tomahawk or knife," were treated with kindness and consideration by Pratt, who used the opportunity to educate the captives. Whipple, following a visit to the fortress, tried to meet the familiar charge that Indians could not be "tamed or humanized." From Savannah, Georgia, on March 24, 1876, he wrote of the prisoners:

Their faces are changed. They have all lost that look of savage hate, and the light of a new life is dawning in their hearts. It was my privilege to preach to them every Sunday and upon week-days I told them stories from the Bible. I have never had a more attentive congregation. Captain Pratt's success is due to the fact that he has taught them to labor: he has given them, in the best sense, a Christian school.

The Indians were released on good behavior from Fort Marion in April 1878. Pratt was so exhilarated with this pedagogic calling that in 1879 he founded Carlisle Indian Industrial School in Pennsylvania to educate reservation youths. Carlisle became the model for the government's off-reservation school system, and Pratt himself dominated the Indian education system for nearly two decades.

The Red River War was a watershed for the southern plains tribes. On the one side they had the harsh but satisfying life of freedom on the plains. On the other side they faced adjustment to a life that denied all that they had cherished. No member of these tribes ever again freely roamed the region below the Platte River. Never again did they challenge the policy of Concentration with armed force. With these tribes effectively restricted to their reservations, the army gave full permission to buffalo hunters to move onto the southern Great Plains. The vast area of New Mexico, Texas, and southern Kansas was open for whatever slaughter the buffalo hunters could commit. Only three years later they had all but eradicated the remaining millions there. With the extermination of these great beasts, a way of life passed into darkness.

The Peace That Slipped Away

The Fort Laramie Treaty of 1868 led the dominant tribes of the northern plains to believe they had secured for themselves a right of self-determination under the Concentration policy and the possession of extensive tracts of land in the Dakotas, Montana, and Wyoming. In particular, the Sioux and their Northern Cheyenne and Arapahoe allies had fought grimly for these objectives in the Powder River War. The Fort Laramie Treaty, no scrap of paper but the pledged word of the United States, testified they had won these rights.

After signing the treaty, most of the Sioux moved onto the Great Sioux Reservation, essentially present-day South Dakota west of the Missouri River. There Red Cloud and his rival Spotted Tail continued as the principal sources of authority. In 1868, General William S. Harney, under orders from General Sherman, established a series of agencies along the Missouri where rations and supplies would be distributed to the Indians. Neither of the two Sioux leaders liked the location. Preferring that their agencies be located closer to Fort Laramie and the Sioux's Powder River hunting grounds, for five years both men stubbornly pressed the government to relocate them. Finally Washington, tired of the diplomatic wrangling with Red Cloud and Spotted Tail, gave in and in 1873 established agencies off the reservation in northwestern Nebraska along the White River. According to statistics published by the Bureau of Indian Affairs in 1875, the government supplied approximately eight thousand Brules at Spotted Tail agency, while about nine thousand Oglalas and thirty-five hundred Northern Cheyennes and Arapahoes were served at Red Cloud agency. The Indian Bureau supplied the other reservation Sioux through its Missouri River agencies.

The remainder, rejecting the reservation, preferred to keep away from the whites and live in the more traditional way, hunting the buffalo. They remained on the lands of the Powder River and Bighorn Mountain region, "unceded Indian territory" as the Fort Laramie Treaty designated it, where they were entitled to hunt "so long as the buffalo range thereon in sufficient numbers as to justify the chase." Here the Hunkpapa Sitting Bull and Oglala Crazy Horse emerged as dominant leaders. Sitting Bull had nothing but disdain for the Concentration policy and the agency Sioux who adhered to it. "Look at me—see if I am poor, or my people either," he taunted. "You are fools to make yourselves slaves to a piece of fat bacon, some hard-tack, and a little sugar and coffee." Yet, many off-reservation Sioux were not above seeking free rations at the agencies, and so shuttled back and forth between the Great Sioux Reservation and the unceded territory. Colonel David S. Stanley in 1869 noted that this group spent "half their time at these agencies and half in the hostile camps. They abuse the agents, threaten their lives, kill their cattle at night, and do anything they can to oppose the civilizing movement, but eat all the provisions they can get." By 1871 pressure was mounting from settlers in Kansas and Nebraska and from the War Department for the Interior Department to expunge the buffalo-hunting clause. They argued that this right was the principal source of ongoing friction and possible hostilities. Reformers, such as William Welsh, concurred that the clause should be repealed, but for the reason that continued buffalo hunting by the Sioux promoted "vagrancy" and retarded detribalization efforts.

For four years following the signing of the Fort Laramie Treaty of 1868 relations between the United States and the Sioux and their Cheyenne and Arapahoe allies remained generally harmonious. But by the early 1870s circumstances were

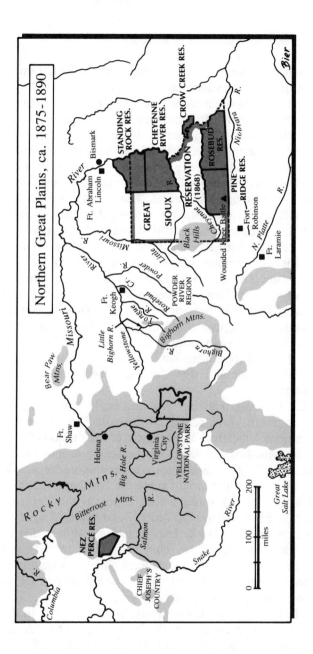

Northern Great Plains, ca. 1875–1890

changing. New tensions on the upper plains would push the government's commitment to its treaty obligations to the limit. The first tremors of disruption occurred in 1872. In that year the Northern Pacific Railroad announced its intention to lay another section of its line across the northern Great Plains.

The Northern Pacific was in the last stages of constructing a rail line from Duluth, Minnesota, to Bismarck on the Missouri River in the Dakota Territory, lying just to the northeast of the Great Sioux Reservation. Then it planned to run the new extension from Bismarck westward, passing above the Great Sioux Reservation until it reached the Yellowstone River valley. There the Northern Pacific intended to build along the Yellowstone. Because of the vague clauses in the Fort Laramie Treaty, it was unclear whether the planned route encroached on the Sioux's unceded western lands and violated the treaty. One thing was clear, however: The off-reservation Sioux adamantly opposed the railroad. Not only would it pass through their buffalo-hunting range and disrupt the remaining herds, it would soon bring white settlers into the region, who would surely demand that the Sioux be confined to their reservation.

The railroad, realizing its action could shatter the fragile peace of recent years, requested the assistance of the federal government. Officials in Washington, equally aware of the possibilities, sent two emissaries to discuss the problem with the Sioux in 1873. They asked for concessions under which the Sioux and their allies would grant the Northern Pacific Railroad a right-of-way through their lands in the Yellowstone Valley. The Sioux answered quickly and firmly. They wanted no whites on their lands. Experience had shown them that more whites would follow. They refused to amend the Fort Laramie Treaty. If they did, they reasoned, it would provide a precedent for other reductions of their promised rights. In the end, any bending would only hurt them.

The Sioux argued persuasively. Still, the Northern Pacific went ahead with its plan to build on the south side of the Yellowstone River. Surveyors for the Northern Pacific arrived in June to map the route. Federal officials made no attempt to stop the railroad, nor did the army. In fact General Sherman, while acknowledging that the Sioux's arguments were correct, assigned a force of over fifteen hundred men under Colonel David S. Stanley to accompany and protect the surveyors. Had they not done so, the surveyors would certainly have been attacked by the Sioux, who knew very well that their rights were being eroded. Protected by the army, the surveyors remained in the Sioux's western territory through the fall. By the time winter arrived, Stanley had quartered his units at Fort Abraham Lincoln, three miles to the south of Bismarck. Meanwhile at Sherman's headquarters in Chicago, plans were drawn for the war that the military confidently expected to erupt in the spring when the railroad began construction. However, the army jettisoned its plans when the financial panic of 1873 threw the Northern Pacific into bankruptcy and obliged it to forego further construction. The Sioux were reprieved, but not for long. Although the thrust of the railroad subsided temporarily, an even more serious situation soon convulsed the Sioux country.

General Philip Sheridan had decided that a new military post must be constructed in the heart of the Great Sioux Reservation to provide protection for future railroad construction and to counter Sioux raids along the frontier. He reasoned, "By holding an interior point in the heart of the Indian country we could threaten the villages and stock of the Indians, if they made raids on our settlements." The military selected the Black Hills as the location for the proposed fort, a place of deep religious significance to the Indians. Even if the Sioux had consented to an army installation somewhere on their reservation, it would most certainly not be located on the land most sacred to them. In the spring of 1874 Sheridan, after receiving permission from President Grant and the secretaries of the Interior and War, ordered Lieutenant Colonel George A. Custer to prepare an expedition into the Black Hills to survey for the new fort. Custer, at the head of ten companies of the Seventh Cavalry plus two companies of infantry, left

Fort Abraham Lincoln in July and headed southwest across the Great Sioux Reservation for his destination, the Black Hills. There he spent the summer conducting the survey for General Sheridan. Red Cloud protested the presence of over a thousand soldiers: "I do not like General Custer and all his soldiers going into the Black Hills, as that is the country of the Oglala Sioux." While there, Custer and his men also made a discovery that produced far wider and deeper tremors than Sheridan's fort ever could have. The Custer expedition confirmed speculations that there was gold in the Black Hills.

Returning to Fort Abraham Lincoln in September 1874, Custer telegraphed word to Denver and Chicago that veins of gold lay in the Black Hills. According to his report, gold was plentiful—veins of it could be found in every hill "from the grass roots down." Exaggerated as it was, his description prompted a resurgence of gold fever. By October the rush to the Black Hills was a stampede. As one miner expressed: "This wealth is hidden away in gorges and is doing the Red Man no good." The Sioux, already provoked by the recent surveying expedition, were enraged when they learned of the large numbers of prospectors digging in their sacred hills. The Sioux dealt with those they caught in a harsh and sometimes deadly manner.

The federal government, faced with a threatening state of affairs on the Great Sioux Reservation, acted quickly. President Grant, by executive proclamation, emphatically directed all miners to leave the reservation. General Philip Sheridan issued orders for troops to intercept and remove, by force if necessary, all whites on the reservation illegally. Commanders promptly dispatched patrols to carry out these orders, but with the lure of gold, however exaggerated, leading them on, violators were not easily deterred. No sooner had the army escorted prospectors off the reservation than they found a different route by which to sneak back to the Black Hills to hunt for gold. The *New York Tribune* summarized the difficulty: "If there is gold in the Black Hills, no army on earth can keep the adventurous men of the west out of them."

Only the onset of winter ended this escapade. But as soon as spring arrived, whites were back again to find gold, dodging army patrols and Indian scouts. The number of prospectors who crossed the Great Sioux Reservation to the Black Hills mounted steadily as spring turned to summer, with no hint that the human flow would diminish. The angry Sioux demanded that the federal government enforce its treaty, remove the white gold hunters, and reimburse them for damage done to their land. "The white man is in the Black Hills just like maggots and I want you to get them out just as quick as you can," Baptiste Good protested vigorously. "The chief of all thieves [George Custer] made a road into the Black Hills last summer, and I want the Great Father to pay the damages for what Custer has done."

It became evident to officials in Washington that they faced a crisis. Army patrols had been ineffective in keeping Americans out of the reservation. On the other hand, the Sioux, Cheyennes, and Arapahoes were becoming increasingly bitter at repeated treaty violations. It appeared only a matter of time before the Indians would take matters into their hands and eradicate the prospectors on their land. As Secretary of War William W. Belknap assessed: Recent reports "foreshadow trouble between the miners and the Indians of the country known as the Black Hills, unless something be done to obtain possession of that section; for the white miners have been strongly attracted there by the reports of rich deposits of the precious metal." The United States government concluded that it could not successfully defend the treaty and territorial rights of the Sioux. Indian Bureau, military, and congressional officials all now agreed that the way to defuse the crisis was to purchase the Black Hills from the Sioux.

In September 1875, a delegation of key congressional and military officials journeyed to the Red Cloud agency to discuss the hoped-for purchase. They also dispatched messengers to request the attendance of Sitting Bull and Crazy Horse, the off-reservation leaders. Sitting Bull and Crazy Horse replied that they would not come to the meeting nor would they authorize the sale of a foot of their land to the United States. "I want you to go and tell the Great Father that I do not want to sell any land to the government," Sitting Bull told the hapless messenger. "Not even this much," he added defiantly, waving a pinch of earth in the man's face. In spite of his intractability, the commissioners confidently believed they could persuade Red Cloud, whom they realized was losing touch and authority with the younger warriors, to sell the Black Hills. After some preliminary discussions, the proposal was placed before the Sioux. The government offered to lease the Black Hills for $400,000 a year or buy the area for $6 million. The Sioux pondered the matter carefully before offering an opinion. Finally they declared the Americans' offer unacceptable. Government officials and Indians alike realized the futility of further conversation. There was nothing either could do but accept an impasse.

The commissioners, as much embarrassed as enraged, since they had been confident of getting their own way, returned to Washington in a vindictive mood. The United States government had no legal right to chastise the Sioux for refusing to sell the Black Hills. The Fort Laramie Treaty as well as general law made that clear. Yet officials strongly believed that the Sioux, especially those residing off the reservation, must be dealt with sternly and brought fully under the Concentration policy. A meeting of key officials convened at the White House on November 3, 1875. It included President Grant, Interior Secretary Zachariah Chandler, Indian Commissioner Edward Smith, Secretary of War William Belknap, and Generals Philip Sheridan and George Crook. The group approved the withdrawal of all troops from the Black Hills, thus effectively recognizing the possessory rights of the fifteen thousand miners there. It also decided to take the necessary steps to break the power of the off-reservation Sioux, forcing them from the unceded territory and onto the reservation. The receipt, within a week, of a report by Inspector E. C. Watkins seemed to verify the wisdom of the group's decisions. Watkins, after scrutinizing the Sioux country, noted that warriors under Sitting Bull and Crazy Horse terrorized white settlers and Indian tribes along the frontier and now seemed on the verge of a major outbreak of violence. "The true policy, in my judgment," Watkins stated, "is to send troops against them in the winter, the sooner the better, and *whip* them into subjection." The Interior Department agreed and acted immediately. Commissioner Smith issued an ultimatum to all Indians residing in the Sioux's western territory. It required them to come into the Great Sioux Reservation and report to their assigned agency by January 31, 1876. To fail to do so would expose them to military retaliation.

The commissioner's ultimatum was not only illegal, it was also impossible to comply with. By the terms of the Fort Laramie Treaty, neither the Sioux nor the Northern Cheyennes and Arapahoes were confined to the Great Sioux Reservation. Since all the unceded territory was unqualifiedly theirs, they could reside without restriction in any part of it. The demand to come into the reservation was, moreover, a near impossibility because of the desperately harsh winters in the area. Even if the off-reservation bands had desired to comply with the ultimatum, which none did, only the most foolhardy would have braved the elements to make the journey at that time of year. The deadline of January 31, 1876, came and went without compliance. No one in the unceded territory moved. Some consciously refused, others never heard of the ultimatum until the deadline had passed, still others never received word of it at all. On February 1, 1876, the War Department, upon the recommendation of the Interior Department, proclaimed that henceforth they considered all Sioux, Northern Cheyennes and Arapahoes not residing on the Great Sioux Reservation as hostile and in a state of war against the United States. It thus turned matters over to General Philip Sheridan and the United States Army on February 7. The "Great Sioux War," the final major engagement of the Plains Wars, was underway.

The Last Great Struggle

To defeat the Sioux and concentrate them permanently on the Great Sioux Reservation, General Sheridan again elected the tactic of convergence. William T. Sherman summarized the operation: "General Sheridan determined to proceed . . . systematically, by concentric movements, similar to those which in 1874–1875 [in the Red River War] had proved so successful at the south against the hostile Comanches, Kiowas, and Cheyennes." Sheridan planned a three-pronged encircling offensive against the people residing in the Bighorn Mountain area. General Alfred Terry was to move west from Fort Abraham Lincoln along the Yellowstone River, continuing through the northern part of the Sioux's western territory until reaching Rosebud Creek. Colonel John Gibbon at the same time was to move southward from Fort Ellis, Montana. His march would intercept the Yellowstone, and from there he was to push eastward along that river until his forces met Terry's at the mouth of Rosebud Creek. Finally, General George Crook was to start at Fort Fetterman on the North Platte River and thrust northward up the old Bozeman Trail until his troops joined with the other two wings of the assault. If Sheridan's strategy succeeded, all the "hostiles" would be trapped among the converging prongs and systematically destroyed.

Sheridan hoped to invade the Sioux country immediately, again using winter as his ally. "Unless they are caught before early spring," he assessed, "they cannot be caught at all." But his winter campaign failed to develop satisfactorily. Of the three columns of the invasion force, only Crook's engaged the off-reservation Indians before spring. Deep snows prevented Terry's forces from leaving Fort Lincoln on schedule, while it took Gibbon until early April to establish a supply depot at the junction of the Bighorn and Yellowstone rivers, and then his troops were unable to find any Indians in the vicinity.

In March, General George Crook led a large expedition into the Powder River country. On March 17, three companies of cavalry under Colonel Joseph J. Reynolds assaulted a Cheyenne and Sioux camp of one hundred lodges, situated on the Powder River directly east of the Bighorn Mountains and just to the northeast of the former Fort Kearny. Two Moon, Old Bear, Little Wolf, Maple Tree, and White Bull were the Cheyenne leaders. The Oglala chief He Dog led the Sioux. Reynolds's onslaught took the camp absolutely by surprise. As one old man sounded the alarm, "The soldiers are right here! The soldiers are right here!" Reynolds's men charged through the line of tepees. Warriors frantically grabbed their weapons and rallied to defend the women, children, and elders. Although driven from their camp, the Indians counterattacked and after a pitched battle repelled the soldiers. But the fight destroyed the camp and left its inhabitants with little else than what they had on their backs. "Our tepees were burned with everything in them," Wooden Leg lamented, describing the plight he shared with all others of the camp. "I had nothing left but the clothing I had on." With the temperature well below freezing, Two Moon and the other chiefs sought refuge with Crazy Horse and his Sioux, encamped three days ride to the northeast. "I'm glad you are come," Crazy Horse declared, welcoming Two Moon upon his arrival. "We are going to fight the white men again." "All right, I am ready to fight," the Cheyenne chief replied. "I have fought already. My people have been killed, my horses stolen. I am satisfied to fight." An acute uneasiness over another attack by the army prompted Crazy Horse, within a week, to move the group further north to Sitting Bull's camp alongside the Little Bighorn River, where they were generously received.

News of Reynolds's attack spread quickly throughout the Bighorn Mountain region, and from there to the Great Sioux Reservation where the Sioux greeted it with an increased resolve to defend their territory against American incursion. The events of the past months had renewed old fears and old animosities. The United States government was acting with such obvious duplicity that men who had wanted to believe peace possible now joined the off-reservation Indians. Meanwhile, Sheridan ordered his forces into the field for a summer campaign, permitting his department commanders wide discretionary powers in developing field strategy for the operation. "I have given no instructions to Gens. Crook or Terry," Sheridan reported to Sherman, "as I think it would be unwise to make any combinations in such a country as they will have to operate in. As hostile Indians, in any great number, cannot keep the field as a body for a week or at most ten days, I therefore consider—and so do Terry and Crook—that each column will be able to take care of itself, and of chastising the Indians should it have the opportunity." General Alfred Terry and his twelve hundred soldiers set out on May 17 from Fort Abraham Lincoln, Dakota Territory. The main attack force consisted of the Seventh Cavalry under George Armstrong Custer. At the same time, Colonel John Gibbon's columns, equal in size to Terry's, were patrolling the Yellowstone River waiting to rendezvous with Terry. By early June the two columns met according to plan at the mouth of Rosebud Creek on the Yellowstone. Their responsibility was to intercept the fleeing Indians whom General Crook pressured northward.

Crook moved first. Since the battle at the Powder River he had remained immobilized for almost two months at his supply base in northern Wyoming. In May the general again ordered his troops up the old Bozeman Trail to engage the Sioux and their allies. Arriving in the Bighorn Mountain country, Crook sent out Crow and Shoshoni scouts to locate the camp of the "hostiles." The Crows and Shoshonis were willing to assist the army in this operation against the Sioux, their long-standing enemy. Unable to retaliate successfully against the powerful Sioux for conquering their lands in the Bighorn region and elsewhere earlier in the century, the Crows and Shoshonis eagerly looked forward to the Americans exacting the measure of revenge that the two tribes could not inflict. The scouts brought back a report in early June. A large camp of Sioux and Cheyennes lay a day and a half to the north. Crook made immediate plans to attack. On the morning of June 16 he moved his troops forward, anticipating an assault on the camp within two days.

If Crook expected to profit by surprise, he was to be disappointed—Sitting Bull's scouts had the troops under continuous surveillance. The Hunkpapa chief and spiritual leader was determined to keep the soldiers far enough away to preclude an attack on his camp. When Crook reached the Rosebud, Crazy Horse took the offensive. Just after dawn on June 17, 1876, Sioux and Cheyenne warriors directed a massive assault against Crook. A savage fight raged throughout the entire day. At times the fighting was in scattered areas where hand-to-hand combat prevailed; at other times the adversaries locked together in frontal assaults. Neither side obtained a decisive advantage. Many times Crazy Horse rushed to the front of his warriors, exhorting them with the cry, "Come on Lakota [Teton Sioux], it's a good day to die!" At one critical juncture in the fight, Crow and Shoshoni auxiliaries of the U.S. Army prevented Crook's troops from being overrun by the Sioux and Cheyenne warriors. By dusk, the combatants ceased fighting. Although Crook possessed the battlefield and would claim victory in the engagement, the Sioux and the Cheyennes emerged as the emotional victors of the Battle of the Rosebud by having prevented an American assault on their camp. The next morning General Crook, recognizing that he needed reinforcements before again engaging the determined Indians, retreated to his supply base. The Indians, meanwhile, returned to their camp on the Little Bighorn to celebrate their victory, unaware of an even stronger American force massed to the north at the mouth of Rosebud Creek.

General Terry, unaware of Crook's setback, sent Major Marcus A. Reno, second in command of the Seventh Cavalry, with six companies to scout for the hostiles. Eight days later they returned with news that Sitting Bull's camp appeared to be located between the Bighorn and Little Bighorn rivers, about fifty miles to the southwest of the army's position. With this information, Terry decided upon a circling tactic to trap the Indians. He and Gibbon would move thirty miles west until they reached the mouth of the Bighorn, then they would march southward down that river to Sitting Bull's camp. At the same time, Colonel Custer would move the Seventh Cavalry in a parallel line along Rosebud Creek before swinging westward around the southern edge of the Wolf Mountains. From there he was to follow the Bighorn River northward until he too reached Sitting Bull's camp. Terry ordered both columns to time their movements to reach their destinations simultaneously and thus assault the Sioux and Cheyennes in force. Custer, after receiving his orders, sent a note to his wife, Elizabeth. "Do not be anxious about me," he comforted, trying to reassure her that he soon would return home to her. "A success will start us all toward [Fort Abraham] Lincoln" (where the Custers resided).

On the evening of June 24, after two days of marching up Rosebud Creek, the Seventh Cavalry made camp. The troopers were at ease, confident in their belief that it would still be a couple of days before they linked up with Terry and Gibbon to initiate the assault aimed at destroying the hostiles. Their repose was cut short. After dusk, Crow and Arikara scouts came to Custer's tent and informed him that a large encampment lay fifteen miles almost directly west of them in the valley of the Little Bighorn. This could only be Sitting Bull's camp, the Seventh Cavalry's target. Custer, fearing that Sioux scouts might already have detected his approach and sounded the warning for the camp's inhabitants to flee, decided to attack his target without delay. Quickly he roused his weary troops for a night march. The cavalry marched half the night until exhaustion and poor visibility forced a halt until daybreak. But the men were up again and on the move as the sun rose on Sunday, June 25, 1876.

George Custer, never lacking in boldness, did not attempt to disguise his movement as the Seventh Cavalry steadily approached Sitting Bull's substantial camp. Instead of approximately one thousand warriors expected by the army, at least double that number, with their families, resided in the camp, which stretched for nearly three miles along the west bank of the Little Bighorn. Within it were the Cheyennes of Two Moon, Lame White Man, Dirty Moccasins and other chiefs, as well as more than a half dozen bands of Sioux under the direction of hardened and skilled war leaders, among them Gall, Lame Dear, Hump, Sitting Bull, and Crazy Horse. A few Arapahoes also were present.

Crossing the Wolf Mountains about noon, the cavalry followed a stream (now named Reno Creek) westward that led directly to Sitting Bull's camp. From a military point of view, Custer's course was questionable: he divided his forces into four parts. Custer's unit of 225 men and Reno's of 112 soldiers with twenty-five Indian scouts and three white scouts constituted the first two battalions. They would strike the encampment. Custer ordered a third battalion of 125 men, under the command of Captain Frederick Benteen, to scout to the south and intercept all fleeing Indians. A fourth group, with the pack train and its accompanying 130 soldiers, contained the extra ammunition and supplies. That day it lagged several miles behind Custer's and Reno's columns.

In the early afternoon, Custer ordered Reno and his men forward to invade the southern end of the camp where the Hunkpapa lodges were located. Marcus Reno, after the attack began, was overcome by intense anxiety, a foreboding shared by his troops and the Indian scouts, many of whom deserted the Americans. Their forebodings were justified as a massive wave of Sioux warriors counterattacked from front and sides. The Sioux leader Gall, who had lost two of his wives and three of his children to Reno's assault, led the attack with vengeance. "It made my heart bad," he recounted a decade later. "After that I killed all my enemies with the hatchet." The soldiers dismounted and took cover as best they could in the nearby trees and sagebrush. From this position they tried desperately to fend off the onslaught. For over an hour the battle raged; half of Reno's men became casualties. Finally the Sioux routed the soldiers, chasing them south and east to the bluffs above the Little Bighorn where they frantically dug in using knives, cups, and spoons. Most of the shovels were with the pack train, an hour's ride behind them. Then suddenly, to the soldiers' amazement, most of the Sioux hurried toward the north, where the sound of heavy gunfire could be heard. Major Reno realized that Custer's forces were in that general direction, but did not know that they faced a situation worse than his own. Soon Captain Benteen arrived after scouting to the south to reinforce Reno. At the sound of intense fighting Benteen and his men had returned to the area. "For God's sake help me, Benteen," the frantic Reno screamed as the reinforcements arrived, "I've lost half my men!" The two groups, unable to withdraw because of continuing enemy fire, remained trapped on the hill the rest of the afternoon and night.

At the same time that Major Reno launched his invasion against the southern end of Sitting Bull's camp, Custer led his men into battle. After ordering Reno forward, Custer and his command trailed behind him for about two miles before turning off to head northward along the towering bluffs overlooking the east bank of the Little Bighorn. On their left and down the steep escarpment they saw ravines leading to the wooded banks of the river. Across it they spied the camp of Sitting Bull, obviously a very large one. As they marched, Custer's units were under careful scrutiny: from the people in the camp, from Cheyenne warriors lying in wait beyond their lodges at the camp's north end, and from Sioux warriors hidden in the ravines past which the Seventh Cavalry rode.

As the soldiers neared a point directly across the river from the camp's northern end, Custer moved his troops into the formation from which they would charge. Before the Seventh Cavalry could advance, the Sioux hidden in the ravines attacked from the rear. As the soldiers wheeled to defend themselves, Sioux and Cheyenne led by Crazy Horse and Two Moon, attacking from the north, overwhelmed them. Now, with the Americans turned to face the assaults, a third wave of Sioux, freed from the fight at the southern end of the camp, broke over them. Gall, who had led the mauling of Reno, was at their head. On that scorching afternoon, as warriors swarmed over Custer's defenses—"like a hurricane," remembered the Sioux chief Kill Eagle, "like bees swarming out of a hive"—the outcome could only be disastrous. Custer and all of his men perished after perhaps an hour of fighting in a dusty, choking cloud. "Where the last stand was made," said Sitting Bull in an interview given in Canada the following year detailing Custer's final moments, "the Long Hair stood like a sheaf of corn with all the ears fallen around him." Black Elk, the Oglala Sioux holy man, recalled how he felt as a thirteen-year-old boy witnessing the defeat of the Seventh Cavalry at the Battle of the Little Bighorn. "I was not sorry at all. I was a happy boy. Those Wasichus [white men] had come to kill our mothers and fathers and us, and it was our country."

Early the next morning the Sioux and Cheyennes pursued their attack against Reno's and Benteen's position; but by noon their assault slackened and, much to the soldiers' relief, the Indians began to dismantle their camp and move off toward the south. By dusk they had completely withdrawn from the area. The reason for their withdrawal soon became clear. Earlier in the day, Sioux scouts had detected a large body of soldiers to the north, moving toward Sitting Bull's camp. The troops spotted were those of Terry and Gibbon, who had waited only nine miles away throughout the Battle of the Little Bighorn for Custer's message telling them of his location and the speed of his movement. When no word arrived by June 26, the columns continued the march toward Sitting Bull's camp, reaching their destination the following morning, Tuesday, June 27. They rescued Reno, Benteen, and the survivors of their companies and found the battlefield where Custer and his command perished. "It is marked by the remains of his officers and men and the bodies of his horses, some of them strewed along the path, others heaped where halts appear to have been made," General Terry recorded that day. The sight appalled both the troops and their commanders: "a scene of sickening, ghastly horror," one soldier recalled after viewing the corpses littering the battlefield, some of whom were stripped and mutilated. Within several days, the entire nation shared their feelings.

Enforcing Concentration: "To Conquer a Lasting Peace"

News of "Custer's Last Stand" shocked a disbelieving American public on July 6, 1876, in the midst of the republic's jubilant celebration of its centennial. Philip Sheridan and many of the military's senior hierarchy learned of the Battle of the Little Bighorn while in Philadelphia attending the centennial exposition dedicated to the theme "A Century of Progress." At first Sheridan refused to believe the initial Associated Press wire story. The arrival of General Alfred Terry's confidential report left no doubt about the annihilation of Custer and his five companies. The nation clamored for revenge against the Indians.

But not everyone exonerated Custer. "We admire the gallantry of General Custer and his men," a commentator editorialized in *The Nation* magazine, "but who shall blame the Sioux for defending themselves?" General Terry's report clearly attributed the fiasco at the Little Bighorn to Custer's egregious conduct. "Custer's action is inexplicable in the case," Terry asserted. That his analysis was overwhelmingly correct was the least of the public's concern. The legend and the mystique of George Armstrong Custer—the martyred American hero, immortality secured through utter defeat—had already been born. "Victory that day on the Little Bighorn would have made Custer the historical equivalent of a Nelson A. Miles: an important frontier officer, certainly, but not a figure to command the popular imagination," wrote scholar Brian W. Dippie about the myth-making process surrounding the Custer legend. The legend is laced with irony, too, as Dippie further noted: "Defeat brought immortality. Custer's Last Stand: the very words still conjure up an unforgettable image of a soldier at bay, surrounded and doomed, winning lasting fame by failing to win a battle."

Tributes were fast in coming. The *New York Tribune*, for example, published Walt Whitman's "A Death Sonnet for Custer" on July 10, four days after news of the battle reached the American public:

There in the far northwest, in struggle, charge, and sabre-smite,
Desperate and glorious—aye, in defeat most desperate, most glorious,
After thy many battles, in which, never yielding up a gun or a color,
Leaving behind thee a memory sweet to soldiers, Thou yieldest up
  thyself.

The Custer legend continued to grow in the years following
his death. Elizabeth Custer, widow of the fallen commander
of the Seventh Cavalry, became a key person responsible for
molding and defending it. Outliving George Custer by almost
fifty-seven years, she published a popular three-volume rem-
iniscence depicting the "Boy General" in the most positive
terms: a gallant and courageous soldier, a caring, faithful, sen-
sitive spouse. *Boots and Saddles, or Life in Dakota with General Custer* appeared in 1885; *Following the Guidon* in 1890;
and her third and concluding volume *Tenting on the Plains,
or Gen'l Custer in Kansas and Texas* in 1893. If popular acceptance is any measure, Elizabeth Custer succeeded in
nurturing and enlarging her husband's legend, as well as defending it against critics both in and out of the military, who
characterized George Custer as an impetuous, ambitious, vain-
glorious officer who recklessly led his troops to annihilation.

Humiliated by the Battle of the Little Bighorn, the army
clamored for swift retaliation. Stunned by the death of his
young protégé, General Sheridan immediately prepared to invade the Sioux country again. First he ordered his soldiers to
dismount and disarm all Indians at the Cheyenne River, Red
Cloud, and Standing Rock agencies. Then dispatching substantial reinforcements to Montana, Sheridan ordered Terry
and Crook into the Bighorn Mountain country to crush the
Indians between their columns. Much to the chagrin of the
invading forces, they were unable to find many. The army
spent the remainder of the fall searching with little success for
the vanished hostiles. The Sioux and Cheyennes, moving in
small bands, successfully eluded the soldiers, anticipating that
if they could sustain themselves until winter, the army might
give up its hunt. They had not counted on the unwavering
resolve of Philip Sheridan. The general, a man not easily de-

terred from his goals nor discouraged by the military's recent lack of success, merely changed his strategy. He selected another of his time-tested tactics: a winter campaign. Two years earlier, in the Red River War, he had destroyed the southern plains tribes' resistance to the Concentration policy with this strategy. Sheridan saw no reason why it should not succeed against the northern plains tribes, too. He realized the campaign would not result in one decisive battlefield victory as much as it would wear down the enemies through relentless pursuit and force them to surrender. "I have never looked on any decisive battle with these Indians as a settlement of the trouble," Sheridan informed Sherman. "Indians do not fight such battles; they only fight boldly when they have the advantage, as in the Custer case, or to cover the movement of their women and children as in the case of Crook on June 17 [the Battle of the Rosebud], but Indians have scarcely ever been severely punished unless by their own mode of warfare or tactics."

The winter campaign began in November of 1876, and it caught the Indians off-guard. Conditions were excruciating for Indians and federal troops, in part because of blizzards, piles of drifting snow, and sub-zero temperatures. One soldier recalled the depravations: "Beards, moustaches, eye-lashes and eye-brows were frozen masses of ice. The keen air was filled with minute crystals, each cutting the tender skin like a razor, while feet and hands ached as if beaten with clubs. Horses and mules shivered while they stood in column, their flanks white with crystals of perspiration congealed on their bodies, and their nostrils bristling with icicles." The winter campaign of 1876–1877 completely wore down the Indians, as Sheridan had anticipated. "What have we done that the white people want us to stop?" Sitting Bull asked in the face of the troops who pursued relentlessly. "We have been running up and down this country, but they follow us from one place to another." The army engaged the Cheyennes first and, as might have been expected, the soldiers were completely victorious. The government sent many of the survivors who turned themselves in south to the Indian Territory and placed them on the

Cheyenne-Arapahoe reservation. The army engaged the Sioux next. Those who escaped the soldiers returned to their reserve by the spring. However, Sitting Bull and Gall avoided capture, and, with a small group of followers, fled to Canada in February 1877. Over the next few years, hunger and loneliness convinced many Sioux to slip back to the reservation and surrender. Sitting Bull did not return to the United States until 1881. On July 19 of that year he surrendered at Fort Buford, Montana. "I wish it to be remembered that I was the last man of my tribe to surrender my rifle," Sitting Bull declared to Major David H. Brotherton, as the Sioux chief handed his Winchester to his son, asking him to present it to the officer, "and this day have given it to you."

Only Crazy Horse escaped defeat in the winter campaign. Starving but proud and unbeaten, he brought his eight hundred followers into Fort Robinson, Nebraska, in May 1877. He perhaps best exemplified those Indians absolutely dedicated to resisting the United States' Concentration policy. Besides being alarmed, even frightened, by the depth and vehemence of his convictions, most whites found his strident demeanor offensive. "This incorrigible wild man," as one agent described Crazy Horse during his tenure at Fort Robinson, was "silent, sullen, lordly and dictatorial." He and his band finally submitted because General George Crook promised to secure them an agency on the Tongue River if they laid down their arms. But again they were to be frustrated. Officials in Washington refused to sanction the agreement. After learning that Washington had backed off of the agreement, Crazy Horse prepared to leave Fort Robinson for the Powder River country. Before he could leave, however, Crook ordered troops from the fort and Indian police to place Crazy Horse under arrest. Protesting their efforts to disarm him and take him into custody, Crazy Horse resisted, and he received a mortal stab wound. It remains a matter of contention whether the perpetrator was a soldier or an Indian. Major H. R. Lemly, witness to the chief's final hours, recorded the scene:

In a weak and tremulous voice, he broke into the weird and now-famous death song of the Sioux. Instantly there were two answering calls from beyond the line of pickets, and Big Bat told me they were from Crazy Horse's old father and mother, who begged to see their dying son. I had no authority to admit them, and resisted their appeal, piteous as it was, until Crazy Horse fell back with the death-gurgle in his throat.

Crazy Horse died that evening, September 5, 1877. "It is good," one Miniconjou chief remarked at the Oglala's passing, "he has looked for death, and it has come." The following day soldiers released the remains to his parents. A horse-drawn travois transported Crazy Horse's body, placed in a wooden box, to Spotted Tail agency where, in the traditional fashion, the Sioux set it upon a burial scaffold.

With the fall of Crazy Horse, the self-imposed exile of Sitting Bull, and the crushing defeat sustained by the Sioux and the Cheyennes, the last possibility for armed resistance to the policy of Concentration by Indians on the northern plains ended. Sheridan's winter campaign had been overwhelmingly successful. One of the first actions of the United States shortly after the defeat of Custer at the Little Bighorn was to seize large portions of the landholdings that the Fort Laramie Treaty of 1868 had safeguarded to the Sioux and Cheyennes. First the government confiscated the Black Hills, with its billions of dollars in mineral wealth, then the Indians' unceded territory: the Bighorn Mountain and Powder River regions. Following the Sioux War and the shattering of the Sioux and Northern Cheyenne nations, the United States altered the western boundary of the Great Sioux Reservation from the 104th to the 103rd meridian and appropriated rich reservation land between the forks of the Cheyenne River, thus reducing the reserve by roughly a third. The United States also evicted the Sioux from Nebraska. In the 1880s, the government divided the Great Sioux Reservation into five smaller ones. Standing Rock reservation straddled the border of North and South Dakota. Directly to its south was Cheyenne River reservation, while to the southeast lay the Crow Creek reserve with the Missouri River flowing through its center. West of the Missouri, nestled along the southern border of South Dakota, sat the Rosebud and Pine Ridge reservations.

The Oglala Red Cloud offered his summation of the policy of Concentration and the efforts of the United States to solve the Indian question by that policy. Most other Indians probably would have shared his sentiment. Tinged with what for him must have been painful irony—for he was the only Plains Indian leader to defeat the United States in war, and his victory had forced the federal authority to offer generous terms in the Fort Laramie Treaty of 1868—Red Cloud concluded ruefully: "They made us many promises, more than I can remember, but they never kept but one. They promised to take our land, and they took it."

The struggle of arms between the United States and the Indians to realize, then enforce, the policy of Concentration effectively ended by 1877, leaving the government in complete control. The wars of Grant's "peace policy," wars conducted "to conquer a lasting peace," had destroyed the last vestige of self-determination of the once powerful tribes who had resisted the Concentration policy and who once dominated the middle of America. Now their lives would be devoted to adapting to a new and alien life-style: one of absolute confinement on a reservation. The army's job became easier following the Red River and the Great Sioux Wars, with nearly all of its former adversaries restricted to reservations and relegated to the status of wards of the United States government. The primary responsibility of soldiers became rounding up those Indians who refused to report to, or remain on, their reservations. Occasional clashes still broke out, but they arose generally between individuals and usually ended quickly. The army clearly had the upper hand.

The final actions concluded in 1886 when Geronimo, the last to resist the policy of Concentration, surrendered to General Nelson A. Miles following brilliant campaigning by General George Crook. Geronimo, with a small following of Chiricahua Apaches, had hidden in the mountains of Arizona and New Mexico. For a while he effectively fought off a much larger federal force. Like a few other Indian groups, the Apaches briefly captured the imagination of the nation, and their leader Geronimo is probably one of a half dozen Indians recognized by name by the American public. As increasing attrition, weariness, and military pressure overcame them, these Apaches could not continue the fight. Following his surrender at Skeleton Canyon, Arizona, on September 4, 1886, federal officials sent Geronimo and nearly five hundred Apache followers to a military prison at Fort Pickens in Pensacola, Florida.

The end of the Indian wars in 1877 concluded one long chapter of United States–Indian relations and began another. Spanning almost three decades, the United States first had fashioned, then implemented and enforced the policy of Concentration to solve the Indian question. The responsibility for inaugurating the new era fell to President Rutherford B. Hayes, who took office in March 1877. Even though the government had realized the Concentration policy, it proved to be neither the panacea nor the permanent solution Americans expected and predicted it to be. The end of the Indian wars raised an issue of great magnitude, too. The president was acutely aware of this: "How best can we aid them [the Indians]?" Hayes pondered in his diary. "How to deal with them is a problem which for nearly three centuries has remained almost unsolved." The answer to his introspective query proved elusive, as his eighteen predecessors had discovered before him. The search for the solution to the Indian question had not ended for the United States.

The Wise Ones said we might have their religion, but when we tried to understand it we found that there were too many kinds of religion among white men for us to understand, and that scarcely any two white men agreed which was the right one to learn. This bothered us a good deal until we saw that the white man did not take his religion any more seriously than he did his laws, and that he kept both of them just behind him, like Helpers, to use when they might do him good in his dealings with strangers. These were not our ways. We kept the laws we made and lived our religion. We have never been able to understand the white man, who fools nobody but himself.

PLENTY-COUPS, CROW

CHAPTER SIX

The Search for a New Order

The year 1877 marked an important juncture in the history of United States–Indian relations. Centuries of struggle and armed conflict between the two races, culminating in the Plains Wars of the 1860s and 1870s, ended shortly after Rutherford B. Hayes's inauguration. The Great Sioux War, the last major conflict to enforce the policy of Concentration, and the mauling of George Armstrong Custer at the Little Bighorn, lay less than a year in the past. The crushing defeat sustained by the Sioux and their allies marked the end of Indian military power, and with it the Indians' ability to defend and sustain their accustomed way of life and resist the Concentration policy through force of arms. By the spring of 1877, as Hayes commenced his duties as the nation's chief executive, the Indians had been humbled. Their military power was broken, never to revive; their lands were drastically reduced; many Indian leaders were confined in federal prison; the remnants of a fiercely independent people were reduced to emotional, cultural, and material bankruptcy on reservations. Although minor conflicts would continue into the early twentieth century, President Hayes correctly notified Congress in his first annual message that "after a series of most deplorable conflicts ... we are now at peace with all Indian tribes within our borders."

The issue of how to govern the Indians in the aftermath of the Indian wars and to provide for their well-being demanded the immediate attention of the government. The challenge was clear: What policy should guide relations between the United States and the Indians in the transition between war and peace? The question excited much interest, both in government and among the general public. In response, Thorndyke Rice, editor of the *North American Review*, requested that General Nelson A. Miles write an article giving his views on the subject. Miles suggested that "the real issue [is to] devise some ways of still improving the practical and judicious system by which we can govern a quarter of a million of our population, secure and maintain their loyalty, raise them from the darkness of barbarism to the light of civilization, and put an end forever to these interminable and expensive Indian wars." Although the challenge was clear, the solution proved elusive and difficult.

The necessity of developing an effective and positive Indian policy in the aftermath of the Indian wars was underscored by a feeling of urgency. Those who were aware of the state of Indian life—the terrible conditions on western reservations, the distressing sense of dislocation among tribes, the near nonexistent means for them to provide for their needs by accustomed methods—feared for their survival. "The civilization or the utter destruction of the Indians is inevitable," surmised John Q. Smith in 1876, U. S. Grant's fourth and last Indian commissioner. "If they cannot be taught, and taught very soon to accept the necessities of their situation and begin in earnest to provide for their own wants by labor in civilized pursuits," he predicted, "they are destined to speedy extinction."

The Hayes administration was the first to grapple with the Indian question following the era of warfare. Hayes characterized the transition period as an era "when old questions are settled, and the new are not yet brought forward." Although the agenda it advanced was not translated into an effective, well-defined program until after Hayes's term of office, it followed a direction that evolved into the Indian policy of the United States for the next half century: the policy of Americanization. It is thus instructive to investigate how the Hayes administration dealt with the management of Indian affairs and the Indian question in the period of transition from war to peace.

Reforms and Jurisdictional Disputes

President Hayes realized that crucial to the success or failure of his administration's handling of Indian affairs was the individual appointed secretary of the Interior, for that official's jurisdiction included supervisory responsibility over the Indian commissioner and the Indian Bureau. Hayes selected Carl Schurz of Missouri to fill the post. Liberal Republican, outspoken critic of the rampant corruption in Grant's administration, and long-time champion of civil service reform, Schurz served with distinction in his cabinet post. With the support of the president, he introduced civil service examinations and initiated conservation of the nation's forest resources. Of all the responsibilities under Schurz's jurisdiction, Indian affairs proved the most frustrating and involved him in the most controversy. The secretary knew almost nothing of the Indians and their problems upon assuming his post, but to his credit he labored diligently to master this area. Henry Adams, writing to Henry Cabot Lodge in December 1877, remarked of Schurz's singleminded determination, that "lumber and Indians are his sole mental food just at the present." Schurz's policies were instrumental in reforming the Indian Bureau, ridding the Indian service of incompetent and corrupt officials, maintaining civilian control of the service, and attending to the substantive problems of the Indian question in the aftermath of the era of warfare.

For years Carl Schurz had preached reform, and now as Interior secretary he had a chance to practice it. Rampant political graft and corruption, combined with the executive irresponsibility of Ulysses S. Grant, had driven the prestige of the presidency to one of its lowest levels in history. President Hayes's insistence upon efficient management and clean government quickly brought the Bureau of Indian Affairs under close scrutiny. Perhaps of all federal departments and bureaus, it was in greatest need of housecleaning. Almost from its inception in 1824 it was notorious for fraud, corruption, and inefficiency. Over the years, as the Bureau fell increasingly under the domain of political patronage, these problems were exacerbated. Agents were partisan appointees, often of unscrupulous character. They, in turn, distributed the spoils associated with their posts, often appointing subordinates who were minimally qualified at best. Patronage seekers clamored for Indian service positions, hoping to satiate their rapacity and lust for "honest graft" through readily available opportunities. General Henry Heth, who served as an inspector in the Indian service, commented about agents: "The Indian Bureau has been made the dumping ground for the sweepings of the political party that is in power." Episcopal Bishop Henry B. Whipple agreed. "They [Indian agents] are often men without any fitness, sometimes a disgrace to a Christian nation; whiskey sellers, barroom loungers, debauchees, selected to guide heathen people," charged this Indian rights advocate whom the Indians called "Straight Tongue." A job in the Indian service, as everyone realized, provided a cornucopia of opportunity for graft. Too many agents, earning an annual salary of a couple thousand dollars, banked outrageous sums of money during their service. One Indian recalled: "When he [the agent] come he bring everything in a little bag, when he leaves it take two steamboats to carry away his things." So riddled with corruption was the Indian service that Secretary Schurz lamented that "a thoroughly competent, honest, and devoted Indian agent is ... so rare a jewel that ... nothing could induce me to part with him."

President Hayes clearly recognized the pressing need to reform the Indian Bureau and to employ trained, honest, and efficient personnel. In his first annual address he affirmed the need for immediate reform and strongly supported Schurz's efforts. The secretary had acted with dispatch after assuming his cabinet post. To study the Indian Bureau in action, he made a six-week tour of the Indian Territory. The trip convinced him that the situation was even worse than expected. Schurz immediately ordered a full investigation of the Bureau, Indian agencies, and the agents' business methods. He appointed a board of three individuals—one each from the Justice, Interior, and War Departments—to investigate. He also ordered Indian Commissioner Smith to assess the Bureau. Smith, in his report to Schurz, assured him that "I know of no custom in the Bureau which can properly be termed an abuse." The Inquiry Board came to a different conclusion. It discovered evidence of widespread inefficiency, manipulation, fraud, and other irregularities, including unethical activities by Commissioner Smith and the chief clerk, S. A. Galpin. The board's report, submitted in January 1878, accused the Indian Bureau of "cupidity, inefficiency, and most barefaced dishonesty," and it concluded that the Bureau was "simply a license to cheat and swindle the Indians in the name of the United States." It confirmed the worst suspicions of Hayes and Schurz. Schurz obtained Smith's resignation and dismissed Galpin, as well as the worst subordinates. The former commissioner appealed first to Secretary Schurz, who responded: "The fact is, you never knew what was going on in the office under your charge, and your clerks were well aware that you did not know it." A month later, in February 1878, Smith wrote a long letter to Hayes protesting the criticism of his management of the Indian Bureau, but his arguments failed to move the president to reverse the firings.

Secretary Schurz immediately reorganized the Bureau. He ordered nepotism to end, long a common Indian service hiring practice. All agents who continued the practice were removed. A stricter system of keeping accounts and greater insistence that agents promptly submit their accounts for review was introduced, reducing fraud during the Hayes presidency. And finally, the Bureau for the first time issued a code of regulations outlining appropriate conduct for agents. As part of his house-cleaning, Schurz sought a person of high integrity to be the new commissioner. He wanted him to be "a man of thorough business training and habits, indefatigable industry, quick judgment and great power of resistance." When the reformer William Welsh declined the post, Schurz turned to Ezra A. Hayt, a wealthy New York businessman, former chairman of the finance committee of the Board of Foreign Missions of the Reformed Church, and former member of the Board of Indian Commissioners. Although Hayt worked well with Schurz on Indian matters, scandal drove him from office in early 1880.

The reforms implemented by the Hayes administration improved the Indian service and its methods, thus decreasing possible agitation, or even open hostility, by the Indians. The changes so impressed General Philip Sheridan, long experienced with western Indians and corrupt Indian agents, that he fairly crowed, "The service of Indian affairs was finally lifted out of the mire of corruption that had long made it a discredit to our civilization." Schurz likewise was pleased: "I do not pretend that the Indian service, as at present organized, is all that it ought to be. But it has been and is my earnest endeavor to make and keep it as honest and efficient as any other branch of the public service, and I have reason to believe that considerable progress has been made in that direction."

Efforts to reform the Indian service soon brought Carl Schurz into bitter conflict with religious reformers, a conflict that undermined the reforms he had realized. From the earliest white settlement of North America onward, various Christian denominations had labored among the Indians. While the Spanish and the French enjoyed moderate success in the vineyard of saving souls, their British, and later American, counterparts lagged considerably behind in the progress of their own missionary efforts among native groups. The establishment of a network of western reservations in the 1850s and

1860s by the United States under the Concentration policy heartened missionaries, for access to Indians en masse would be possible now. Working together with sympathetic officials in Washington and various secular reform groups dedicated to the destruction of tribal ways and beliefs, missionaries could work industriously on reservations, toiling to transform the Indians into self-supporting, productive Christian Americans.

The fortunes of the missionaries received a bigger boost in 1866. In that year the government granted religious bodies permission to work on federal reserves, not only in the capacity of missionaries of their particular denomination, but as civilian agents of the Indian Bureau. At the same time, concern over rampant corruption within the Indian Bureau and the abuses of political patronage in selecting Indian service agents and administrators spurred religious and secular reformers to seek control over the Indian service and Indian policy. Their efforts were realized, and their influence dramatically increased, when in 1869 Congress authorized the ten-member Board of Indian Commissioners, whose members epitomized the evangelical religious attitudes of the nineteenth century.

The Board of Indian Commissioners, in theory, represented all Christian denominations, but trouble quickly arose when no Roman Catholics were appointed to the Board, although that church had been more active in the Indian mission field than any other denomination. The Roman Catholic Church also had contributed more than half of the funds for missions on reservations. The intense anti-Catholic sentiment of the nation also affected the low number of agencies assigned to the Roman Catholic Church, relative to those awarded to Protestant denominations, even though Grant's guidelines recommended that an agency should be assigned to the missionary sect that already worked there among the Indians. The Church pointed out, to little avail, that of the ninety-four initial agency appointments, Catholic missionaries were awarded only seven, or less than eight percent of those available. Consequently, in 1874 a central Catholic agency was established in Washington, D.C., and five years later the Bureau of Catholic Indian Missions emerged in answer to the Protestant-controlled Board of Indian Commissioners. The Bureau of Catholic Indian Missions monitored Catholic missions and acted as agent to the federal government. The best account of Catholic activities and the problems encountered by that church is Peter J. Rahill, *Catholic Indian Missions and Grant's Peace Policy, 1870–1884.* Once Carl Schurz became Secretary of the Interior, the Catholic Church pressed its demands with him for religious freedom on the reservations.

Religious reformers expected the Hayes administration to be as supportive of their efforts as had Grant's. They had badly misjudged Interior Secretary Schurz. "The present system which permits religious societies to nominate candidates for Indian agencies is, in some respects, undoubtedly an improvement upon the former practice of making appointments . . . on political grounds," he declared. Yet, Schurz vigorously disapproved of the heavy denominational influence on the Indian service and on the shaping of Indian policy for three principal reasons. First, his negative assessment was shaped by the rancorous competition among sects for Indians' souls, and by the missionaries' obvious lack of success in their work among the tribes. And, Schurz was not the only one disconcerted by religious reformers. Indians were too. They observed the ferocious discord among sects and the striking contradictions manifested by the sectarians and their work on reservations. The conflicting dogmas advanced by competing Christian denominations confused Indians, who scorned the obvious disparity between sermons advocating brotherly love and the absence of Christ-like deportment among the battling missionaries. The assessment of Chief Joseph of the Nez Percé provides a good example of the reasoning of many tribal leaders who refused to permit missionaries to work among their people. "They will teach us to quarrel about God as the Catholics and Protestants do," warned Joseph. "We may quarrel with men . . . but we never quarrel about God. We do not want to learn that." Indians scorned equally the hypocrisy of the society that had crushed them and now sent religious representatives to offer instruction in "proper" conduct and life-style. "It is your people, who you say have the Great Spirit's book, who bring us the fire-water," a Sioux elder retorted acerbically when missionaries sought his permission to toil among the tribe. "It is your white men who corrupt our daughters. Go teach them to do right, and then come to us and I will believe you."

Schurz based the second criticism on his assessment that religious appointees lacked the appropriate business expertise to manage Indian agencies efficiently. The Inquiry Board that Schurz convened in June 1877 to assess the Indian Bureau and its agents reinforced this evaluation. In addition to detailing evidence of widespread abuses, as indicated earlier, the Board also criticized the appointment of agents "because of a sentiment," rather than because of business knowledge and administrative qualifications. The Board offered Schurz a harsh and sarcastic appraisal of religious reformers: "Pigmies [who undertake] the solution of a problem that has engaged the best efforts of statesmen and philanthropists ever since the days of the republic."

Finally, Schurz considered denominational influence and appointments as an unacceptable impingement upon his jurisdiction. Soon after taking the reins of the Interior Department, he moved purposefully to undercut the influence of Christian denominations in the Indian Bureau, the principal feature of Grant's "peace policy." Although entrenched by 1877, the practice of nominations by religious groups lacked the force of statutory law and thus provided Schurz the necessary latitude to challenge the practice. The secretary moved quickly to undercut the religious reformers. He ordered the Indian office to assume responsibility for appointing agency clerks and physicians. Before the end of Hayes's first year in office, thirty-five of the seventy-four Indian agents had been replaced. The new policy of widespread replacements and central control under the Interior Department struck a blow to the churches from which they never recovered. When the controversy between Protestants and Catholics over exclusive religious jurisdiction on reservations did not subside, Schurz, in

February, 1881, ruled that all reservations would be open equally to missionaries of all denominations.

Late in the Hayes presidency churches increased their efforts to regain control of agent appointments, but it was too late. Christian missionaries steadily abandoned work among Indians in favor of a more "challenging" and, so they judged, equally deserving population: Asians, especially the Chinese. The shift in appointments from religious to government nominees ironically played into the hands of politicians and spoilsmen, who desperately hoped to regain their lost influence in the lucrative Indian service. By passing over religious sects to fill Indian Bureau and agent vacancies, the administration was forced to rely instead on political nominees—the "venerable pool of the spoils system." By 1883 and the passage of the Civil Service, or Pendleton, Act, the spoilsmen had nearly regained complete control of appointments to the Indian service. The conflict between Protestants and Catholics did not end here, and, in fact, the period of severest tension peaked between 1888 and 1912 as the two sides battled over control and apportionment of Indian mission schools, as Francis Paul Prucha details in *The Churches and the Indian School, 1888–1912*.

The Reappraisal of the Concentration Policy

The Hayes administration's conduct toward Indians passed through two stages, paralleling a changing of United States Indian policy and its program for solving the Indian question. The first stage, characterized by further implementation of the Concentration policy, gradually shifted to the policy of Americanization, which emphasized "civilizing," then assimilating, the Indians into the dominant society, while providing them the means for economic security. Hayes suggested that three principal results would accrue eventually from the Americanization policy. First, there no longer would be a need either for the federal government to maintain land reserves for Indians or for it to defend Indians and reservation land from the constant threat of white encroachment. Second, Indians would be productive, self-sufficient members of American society. And third, it would solve the nation's Indian question. At first, however, the Hayes administration followed a well-worn road.

The Concentration policy had served as the bedrock of federal Indian management since the early 1850s. The government's insistence on total compliance by western tribes precipitated a series of conflicts known as the Plains Wars. During the Grant presidency, the consensus of opinion was that it would be in the best interests of both the whites and Indians if Indians were consolidated further on smaller land reserves: zones of protection. The United States would provide a haven in Indian Territory and in an area on the northern plains for tribes displaced by white expansion. Consequently, the government modified the policy of Concentration to reflect a "small reservation approach." By 1877, as Hayes took office, over sixty tribes had been resettled in the Indian Territory, while many more were shifted from their homeland to new locales. Reflecting the frustration caused to tribes by frequent relocation, the Sioux chief Spotted Tail suggested with mock sincerity: "Why does not the Great Father put his red children on wheels, so he can move them as he will?" Yet the small reservation system seemed the best means of minimizing the hostility between Indians and whites, and it was certainly a better alternative to the wars that had reduced the Indians' land and their population. Because of his inexperience in dealing with Indians or in considering the Indian question carefully, Secretary Schurz supported this assumption and built his policy upon it.

Shurz's decision to sustain and further enforce the small reservation approach of the Concentration policy fell hard on Indians, producing another round of armed conflict. "The period of tranquility was not long to continue," lamented General Nelson Miles. "Over the Western Mountains came the rumbling of a coming storm. Another Indian war, or, more strictly speaking, another cruel unjustice, was to be enacted."

Resentment by some tribes upon being relocated to smaller and less desirable reserves led to military conflicts with Chief Joseph and his band of Nez Percé in 1877, then against the Utes and the Apaches in 1879. Of the three conflicts, perhaps the most tragic and certainly the one that stirred the greatest public interest and indignation was that with Chief Joseph. More significantly, it became the first of three events that made the United States government begin to move away from the old answer for solving the Indian question.

The traditional domain of the Chopunnish, or Nez Percé, was the valley of the Clearwater River, which flows through the three northwestern states of Oregon, Washington, and Idaho. Their lands, like those of other western tribes, were reduced and defined in the 1850s when the federal government implemented the policy of Concentration (see Chapter Two). By means of a treaty signed at Camp Stevens, Washington Territory, on June 11, 1855, the Nez Percé surrendered one-half of their lands to the United States. The government organized the remaining half into the Lapwai reservation where it expected the tribe to live and where, by the terms of the treaty, whites were forbidden to enter.

The treaty's provisions were clearly stated; indeed they were much like most Concentration treaties. Also typical was its violation by whites almost immediately after its implementation. Prospectors arrived first after rich gold deposits were discovered on the Lapwai reservation, followed by settlers with their farms and towns. The Nez Percé, a warm and harmonious people who had always been friendly and helpful to whites, remained peaceful toward the Americans residing on their reservation land. The *Oregon Statesman*, on April 28, 1862, remarked about their commitment to peace. "If open hostilities have not commenced with the Nez Percés, it is not because they have not been outraged to that degree when 'forbearance ceases to be a virtue,' " William Purvine noted in the paper. "In return for the continued friendship in time of want, and generous acts of hospitality, always so readily extended towards the whites by these Indians, they now reap an abundant harvest of every species of villainy and insult." The Nez Percé requested that the federal government enforce its own treaty, while the Americans who had moved onto the reservation illegally demanded that Washington remove the Nez Percé from the reservation's best lands. A subsequent treaty in 1863 opened nearly three-quarters of the reservation to white homesteaders. The new accord shattered the unity of the Nez Percé. Many of the chiefs, led by Old Joseph, refused to sign the document, seeing in it nothing but futility; the federal government would no more honor these terms than those of the earlier treaty. As a result, some six hundred Nez Percé, no longer in possession of any treaty at all, remained on the land of their former reservation.

By the 1870s, pressure from whites was building to force those Nez Percé not bound by a treaty onto the sharply constricted Lapwai reservation. In 1873 President Grant tried to forestall trouble by issuing an executive order setting aside for these Nez Percé a part of their old land in the Wallowa Valley where no whites could settle. But the protest from Oregonians swelled to such intensity that he rescinded the order two years later. A federal peace commission came west in November 1876 to convince these Nez Percé to move onto the reservation. The chief with whom they negotiated was Hinmatonyalatkit, or Joseph. Born in 1840, Joseph succeeded his father, Old Joseph, as the leader of those Nez Percé who refused to participate in the renegotiation of the 1855 land cession treaty. Old Joseph died in 1871, but he left his son with a stern admonition: "Always remember that your father never sold his country. You must stop your ears whenever you are asked to sign a treaty selling your home. A few years more, and white men will be all around you. They have their eyes on this land. My son, never forget my dying words. This country holds your father's body. Never sell the bones of your father and your mother." The new Chief Joseph was calm, intelligent, self-assured, and commanding. Although his gentle but egalitarian behavior toward the Americans angered several of the commissioners, they returned to Washington agreeing that his claims were indeed right. Even so, these men were influenced by the ideas of their time, and they accepted Concentration as the best solution to the Indian question. Thus, their report recommended that unless Joseph moved his people to the Lapwai reservation "within a reasonable time," force should be used to relocate them.

Carl Schurz inherited the problem. He realized clearly its source: It springs "from the greedy encroachments of white men upon Indian lands, and that, hostilities being brought about in this manner, in which the Indians uniformly succumbed, old treaties and arrangements were overthrown to be supplanted by new ones of a similar character, which eventually led to the same results." Still the secretary, secure in his decision to sustain and enforce the small reservation approach, decided to settle the issue without further negotiations. All of the Nez Percé were to be forced onto the reservation. General Oliver Otis Howard, the former head of the Freedmen's Bureau who was known as the "Christian General," now commanded the Department of the Columbia and was given the responsibility of enforcing the government's orders. Howard gave Chief Joseph one month to bring his people into the reservation and warned him that if they were late, he would order troops out after them. Joseph tried to reason with Howard. He explained that the deadline would be difficult to meet because of the many newborn animals in his cattle and horse herds. Even nature failed to move Howard to extend his deadline. Some of the cattle and horses had to be left behind, while the rest were rounded up for the journey to the Lapwai reservation.

Along the way trouble ensued when a few young men sought a final measure of revenge on local whites before accepting confinement on the reservation. General Howard immediately sent troops after the Nez Percé, attacking them twice—once in June 1877 at the Clearwater River and again in July in the Big Hole Valley. Even though the Indians repulsed both assaults, Howard's actions convinced the Nez Percé they faced one of two alternatives: war or flight. Following a council, they decided to avoid further conflict, quit the area, and seek haven east of the Rocky Mountains. "I would give up everything," Chief Joseph concluded, "rather than have the blood of my people on my hands." Thus, in late July 1877, 650 Nez Percé embarked on an arduous and dangerous journey over the Rockies.

Joseph expected that once they were outside of Howard's jurisdiction, the general would find no further reason to give chase. The error of this assumption quickly became clear as troopers relentlessly pursued. Throughout the summer of 1877 the Nez Percé travelled over the northern Rockies in an incredible effort to escape the soldiers; under the skilled direction of Looking Glass they eluded and, when necessary, defeated a much larger foe. By mid-September Chief Joseph and his people had swung far enough east to pass through the newly opened Yellowstone National Park. (They almost bumped into General William T. Sherman, who was in the park on a sightseeing tour.) But more troops joined in the hunt and for all the adroitness of the Indians, the murderous pace of their pursuers wore down the Nez Percé. Still, they stumbled on to Montana, where they would turn northward toward the Canadian border. In late September they made camp just above Bear Paw Mountain. These men, women, and children had travelled seventeen hundred miles since June over mountainous terrain, and now the group was only thirty miles from Canada—a long day's ride. Had they stopped briefly and then pushed on, they might have made it. Instead, yielding to exhaustion, they rested. The decision proved fatal. Forces under General Nelson A. Miles caught up with them on September 30, blocking the way to Canada. Even though greatly outnumbered, the Nez Percé for the moment held the soldiers at bay.

A heavy snowfall on the first of October lasted for three days. The federals could not fight, but the Nez Percé were prevented from slipping through the cordon of troops to reach Canada. In the interim, the Nez Percé debated what course to take next. Joseph, unwilling to sacrifice the lives of the surviving Nez Percé, counselled negotiating with the Americans.

Looking Glass, who had directed the armed defense of the Nez Percé during their flight, urged a "do-or-die" dash for Canada. The matter was settled shortly after the meeting concluded, when a sniper's bullet struck Looking Glass in the forehead, killing him instantly. On October 4, 1877, Joseph surrendered conditionally to Generals Miles and Howard, who promised that the Nez Percé would be treated with honor and returned to their homeland. Chief Joseph's words of capitulation, capturing the mood of tracked desperation felt by the Nez Percé, were recorded in their English translation by Lieutenant Charles Erskine Scott Wood. It became one of the most famous speeches by an Indian:

I am tired of fighting. Our chiefs are killed. . . . The old men are dead. . . . It is cold and we have no blankets. The little children are freezing to death. My people, some of them, have run away to the hills, and have no blankets, no food. No one knows where they are— perhaps freezing to death. I want to have time to look for my children and see how many I can find. Maybe I shall find them among the dead. Hear me, my chiefs, I am tired; my heart is sick and sad. From where the sun now stands, I will fight no more forever!

Six hundred and fifty Nez Percé had set out in June. Four hundred were taken prisoner and about fifty were able to escape to Canada where Sitting Bull took them in. The remainder had died on the long trek. Howard characterized their flight as "remarkable for the brilliant leadership of an Indian; . . . a feat that is perhaps without parallel in Indian warfare," while Miles stated in his report to Secretary of War George W. McCrary that "the Nez Percé are the boldest and best marksmen of any Indians I have ever encountered, and Chief Joseph is a man of more sagacity and intelligence than any Indian I have ever met." Regardless of the laudatory comments, General Sherman, fully aware of the administration's decision to sustain and further implement Concentration, overrode Miles's and Howard's pledges to return the Nez Percé to the Lapwai reservation in Idaho and ordered them transported to the Indian Territory where over a quarter of them quickly succumbed to malaria and other effects of the lowland climate.

Commissioner Hayt noted matter-of-factly in his 1878 annual report that "the extinction of Joseph's title to the lands he held in Idaho will be a matter of great gain to the white settlers in that vicinity." An embittered Chief Joseph declared: "General Miles promised that we might return to our own country. I believed General Miles, or *I never would have surrendered.*"

In those same years two other tribes, the Bannocks and the Northern Cheyennes, took desperate action because of reservation conditions. Their discontent, Hayes accurately assessed, "appears to have been caused by an insufficiency of food on the reservation, and this insufficiency to have been owing to the inadequacy of the appropriations made by Congress to the want of the Indians at a time when the Indians were prevented from supplying the deficiency by hunting." In the case of the Northern Cheyennes, their exodus in 1878 from the Southern Cheyennes' reserve in the Indian Territory to return to their homeland on the northern plains had the additional impetus of intense homesickness, coupled with wretched conditions.

Following the Great Sioux War of 1876–1877 Washington relocated the Northern Cheyennes, allies of the Sioux in that conflict, in the Indian Territory at the Southern Cheyenne and Arapahoe agency. Here the government intended to force a consolidation of the two branches of the Cheyenne people, melding the northern wing with the southern. The Northern Cheyennes arrived among their kinfolk in the terrible heat of August 1877. Sickness and death, caused by the hot, damp, malarial climate, ravaged these displaced people during the winter of 1877–1878. Little Chief described his people as "homesick and heartsick in every way." The gall of their wretched existence in Indian Territory was made even more bitter by the contempt of the Southern Cheyennes, who scorned the Northern Cheyennes as "fools" and "Sioux." Desperately homesick and increasingly harried and distraught by conditions in their exile, many were driven to escape, to venture across the prairies in an all-or-nothing gamble to reach their homeland along the Rosebud, Bighorn, Powder, and Tongue rivers on the northern plains. On September 9, 1878, 273 Northern Cheyennes fled the reservation, led by Morning Star (also called Dull Knife) and Little Wolf.

The fugitives crossed the plains with caution, trying to elude both the army patrols searching for them and settlers who were always ready to turn them in. Reaching central Nebraska, they disagreed over their eventual destinations and so separated. Morning Star and his group placed their hopes on reaching their old hunting grounds near the Sioux's Pine Ridge reservation. Little Wolf's band was set on reaching the Yellowstone Valley. After wintering in northern Nebraska, Little Wolf's group resumed its journey homeward. Little Wolf led his people across the Sioux reservation in South Dakota, around the Black Hills, and as far as the southeastern corner of Montana Territory before soldiers captured them. The group was confined at Fort Keough. Its fate would be shaped by the government's response to Morning Star's band, who were already in federal custody. After the bands split, Morning Star's had travelled as far as northwestern Nebraska before running into an army patrol during a heavy snowstorm. They were taken captive on October 23, 1878 and imprisoned at Fort Robinson.

The Northern Cheyennes' flight from the Indian Territory and Chief Joseph's attempt to reach Canada threatened the Concentration policy and shocked the War and Interior Departments. While General Philip Sheridan acknowledged sympathetically that a common condition on reservations was "insufficient food and irregularity in its supply," and that this was a principal source of great Indian discontent, he and Secretary Shurz nevertheless agreed that "unless [the Indians] are sent back to where they came from, the whole reservation system will receive a shock which will endanger its stability." Consequently, both tribes received harsh treatment to set an example for others who might consider the same course, although in both cases public indignation and the lobbying efforts of humanitarians and others eventually forced the government to relent.

On January 3, 1879, the Northern Cheyennes' fate was decided when Shurz ordered them returned to the Indian Territory. Morning Star and his people were anguished by the verdict, bluntly telling Captain Henry W. Wessells, Jr., Fort Robinson's commander, that they would never go back to a slow and agonizing death in the South. "Great Grandfather sends death in that letter [the removal order]. ... You will have to kill us and take our bodies back down that trail," they warned. "We will not go!" Their refusal to be relocated again prompted Wessells to break their will. He cut off rations of food and water first. A few days later he deprived the Northern Cheyennes of fuel. The freezing cold of the plains added to the torture of their hunger, but the prospect of returning to Indian Territory was unbearable. Morning Star and his people resolved it would be better to die fighting on the open prairies than to perish on a reservation in Indian Territory. On January 9, 1879, they shot their way out of Fort Robinson, sustaining heavy casualties in the process. They did not get far. Soldiers tracked them down and, on January 21, captured them after a bloody fight. Their unsuccessful escape had cost them dearly; only seventy-eight of Morning Star's people, half their number, were returned to Fort Robinson.

Widespread condemnation followed the government's handling of this affair. Compounded by strong criticism of the recent episode with Chief Joseph, both incidents jolted the Hayes administration and forced it to reassess the government's Indian policy. Commissioner Hayt wrote Secretary Shurz noting the "impolicy of sending northern Indians to Indian Territory." Shurz did not "hold the Government entirely guiltless of the wrongs inflicted upon the Indians," reflecting on his decision to sustain and enforce the small reservation approach of the policy of Concentration. "Still less would I justify some high-handed proceedings on the part of the Government in moving peaceable Indian tribes from place to place without their consent, trying to rectify old blunders by new acts of injustice." General Nelson A. Miles, who continued to press for the return of Joseph and his Nez Percé to their homeland, published a stinging indictment of the government's Indian policy in the *North American Review* in 1879. "The forcing of strong, hardy mountain Indians from the extreme North to the warmer malarial districts of the South was cruel, and the experiment should never be repeated." Criticism came from Congress, too. "Mr. Shurz made one very unfortunate mistake quite early in the course of his administration of the Interior Department," concluded Senator George F. Hoar of Massachusetts. "He had formed the opinion, I suppose without much practical experience in such matters, that it would be a good plan to get the civilized Indians of the country into the Indian Territory." Secretary Shurz, in his annual report for 1880, conceded that he had supported that policy in the belief "that [it] would be apt to keep the Indians out of hostile collision with their [white] neighbors, and in exclusive and congenial contact with their own." He conceded that it was "a mistaken policy."

One additional event bolstered the government's resolve that the Concentration policy must be eliminated. The event centered on a plan by whites to encroach on the lands of the Indian Territory. The reservation system annoyed westerners. Many refused to acknowledge the validity of federal pledges providing tribes with inalienable areas to live; areas whose integrity Washington solemnly vowed to preserve and defend. Westerners preferred to view reservations as valuable public land they had an indisputable right to settle, but which for the moment was inconveniently encumbered by Indian residents. For the government maintaining the integrity of reservations, the bedrock of the Concentration policy, became a problem of increasing difficulty after the army broke the Indians' military power, which deprived them of the ability to defend their lands. "The settler and miner are beginning, or at least threatening, to invade every Indian reservation that offers any attraction, and it is a well-known fact that the frontiersman almost always looks upon Indian lands as the most valuable in the neighborhood," Carl Schurz observed. "From the articles in the newspapers of those remote Territories, it would sometimes appear as if, in the midst of millions of untouched acres, the white people were deprived of the necessary elbowroom as long as there is an Indian in the country." He concluded: "It is needless to say that the rights of the Indians are a matter of very small consideration in the eyes of those who covet their possessions."

The Indian Territory was critical to the government's plan to concentrate tribes. Established in the 1830s under the policy of Separation for the exclusive use of the removed members of the Five Civilized Tribes, the United States reorganized it in the aftermath of the Civil War to facilitate the Concentration policy. The Reconstruction Treaties of 1866, imposed by the victorious Union government as penalty for the five tribes' involvement in the war, stripped them of substantial territories (virtually the entire western half of the present state of Oklahoma). This area was then divided into reservations for the southern plains Indians, whom the government concentrated in this area after the Plains Wars of the 1860s and 1870s. It was then partitioned further to provide new homelands for dozens of relocated tribes under the small reservation approach.

That territory was a powerful magnet for avaricious whites. Over the winter of 1878–1879, westerners organized an extensive scheme to take forcible possession of lands in Indian Territory. Parties interested in the project published letters and circulated them in the states surrounding the territory. The letters declared that these were public lands, not federal land that the government could reserve for Indian use, thus they were open to settlement by American citizens. A large number of persons from Missouri, Kansas, and Texas entered the Indian Territory in the spring of 1879, carrying their household goods and farming implements with the purpose of settling permanently. "The success of this invasion," declared Carl Schurz, "introducing into the heart of the Indian Territory a reckless, lawless, grasping element of adventurers, sure to grow and spread rapidly after once having gained a foothold, would bring upon the Indian population of that Territory in its present condition the most serious dangers."

President Hayes acted quickly and decisively. Issuing an executive proclamation on April 26, 1879, he forcefully enjoined "certain evil-disposed persons" to leave the Indian Territory immediately and abandon any further attempts to occupy land there. Hayes also warned that "any and all such persons who may so offend . . . will be speedily and immediately removed therefrom" by the military of the United States. Detachments evicted the trespassers and troops were posted at points along the lines between the Indian Territory and Texas, Missouri, and Kansas to prevent unauthorized parties from entering. The president, in his third annual message to Congress, explained why he took these steps. "It is my purpose to protect the rights of the Indian inhabitants of that Territory to the full extent of the executive power." Hayes also expressed concern that attempts by whites to squat on Indian land and threaten the Concentration policy would continue. "It would be unwise to ignore the fact that a territory so large and so fertile, with a population so sparse and with so great a wealth of unused resources, will be found more exposed to the repetition of such attempts," he explained. "Under such circumstances, the difficulty of maintaining the Indian Territory in its present state will greatly increase, and the Indian tribes inhabiting it would do well to prepare for such a contingency." This realization, coupled with the tragic effects of sustaining the small reservation approach demonstrated by the Nez Percé and Northern Cheyenne cases, convinced the president that another direction in the federal management of Indians affairs was needed. Hayes's conclusion was reinforced in 1880, when westerners, casting their president's wishes and order aside, again attempted to occupy lands in the Indian Territory. Hayes issued a second presidential proclamation ordering them to desist and remove at once.

Something Old and New

After 1879, emphasis on the relocation of tribes, especially to the Indian Territory, gradually decreased as the government slowly began to modify the long-standing Concentration policy. Instead, it sought the means to bring Indians into the American family, eventually eliminating the necessity for the government to maintain land reserves for Indians and to ceaselessly defend Indians and reservation land from the constant threat of white encroachment. Officials believed that only when Indians were freed of reservations and fully integrated into the American mainstream would their physical safety, material well-being, and legal and property rights be protected. By transforming Indians into productive and self-sufficient members of American society, the greatest benefit would accrue: The nation's Indian question would be solved. Government's active participation in the process was essential. "We can not expect them to improve . . . unless we keep faith with them in respecting the rights they possess," Rutherford Hayes stressed, "and unless, instead of depriving them of their opportunities, we lend them a helping hand."

The policy of Americanization drew upon recommendations proposed over the previous two decades by various reformers, Indian Bureau personnel, and chief executives. It was not so much an iron-clad, unchanging program as an ever-increasing commitment by Washington to seek the acculturation of the Indians and their assimilation into the dominant society. It provided the basis, and became the rationale, of federal Indian management for the next half century; although, as Frederick E. Hoxie pointed out in *A Final Promise: The Campaign to Assimilate the Indians, 1880–1920*, the government's commitment to full acculturation and assimilation waned in the early twentieth century to the point where the goal became providing Indians only the minimal skills necessary to survive in the white man's world.

The policy of Americanization initially rested on two fundamental tenets: one, land reform centering on allotment in severalty and two, a comprehensive government educational program for Indian children. The goals of the first measure were to teach the Indians self-reliance and induce the habit of industry by the holding and working of private property, to direct them toward economic self-sufficiency, and to provide for the ultimate elimination of the reservation system. The purpose of the second was to foster their Americanization by destroying their "Indianness," thus giving Indians the capability of "self-protection in a civilized community." As Hayes stressed in a letter to both houses of Congress in 1881, "the time has come when the policy should be to place the Indians as rapidly as practicable on the same footing with the other permanent inhabitants of our country."

The program received the near universal approval of Indian reform and political action organizations, collectively calling themselves "Friends of Indians," that, with one exception, emerged in the late 1870s and early 1880s. The most important included the Boston Indian Citizenship Committee; the Women's National Indian Association, organized by Philadelphia churchwomen; the Indian Rights Association, founded by Herbert Welsh and Henry B. Pancoast; and the Board of Indian Commissioners, the only one directly affiliated with the federal government, established in 1869 by executive order of President Grant. The Friends of Indians gathered twice yearly to discuss and evaluate initiatives for solving the Indian question under the policy of Americanization. They met in January in Washington for the annual meeting of the Board of Indian Commissioners, and in early fall they came together at the Lake Mohonk Conference in the Catskill Mountains of New York State. The National Indian Defense Association, headed by Dr. Thomas A. Bland, disagreed with the Friends of the Indians. Defending the Indians' right to self-determination, Bland stressed in the reformer Alfred B. Meacham's monthly publication, the *Council Fire*, that he "opposed rather than encouraged governmental action on the theory that Indians should be left alone." His stand drew frequent censure from the Friends of Indians. "Dr. Bland's efforts have been directed toward keeping the Indian as he is, his tribal relations untouched, his reservations intact; and in opposing the sale of his unused lands, upon no matter how equitable conditions, for white settlement," declared Herbert Welsh, leader of the Indian Rights Association.

Private or individual ownership of land was a concept foreign to most tribes, and, until the mid-1870s, except where laws had made special exceptions, Indians held their lands in common. Reformers during the late 1870s, led by individuals such as Senator Henry L. Dawes of Massachusetts who chaired the Senate Indian Affairs Committee, hoped to move Indians in the direction of personal, private property, partly as a pragmatic response to the rapid settlement of the trans-Mississippi West and to the incessant calls from westerners to open the remaining Indian landholdings to white settlement and exploitation. Commissioner Hayt expressed the feeling in January 1879 that "the experience of the Indian Department for the past fifty years goes to show that the government is impotent to protect the Indians . . . from the encroachment of its people." Proponents proclaimed that allotment would also serve as "the most effective civilizing agencies, . . . secure the Indians in their possessions [and] prevent them from becoming forever a race of homeless paupers and vagabonds." Carl Schurz concluded, "I am profoundly convinced that a stubborn maintenance of the system of large Indian reservations must eventually result in the destruction of the red man, however faithfully the Government may endeavor to protect their rights."

To encourage Indians to end tribal associations and take up agriculture, herding, or ranching as a private enterprise, Congress in 1875 passed general legislation that extended the land benefits of the 1862 Homestead Act to Indians willing to surrender tribal status. Few Indians availed themselves, however. Each succeeding year advocates of Indian welfare argued that Indians would be Americanized more quickly if the concept of private property was introduced among them. They stressed that this would remove them from wretched living conditions on reservations, from the "contaminating" influence of tribal affiliation and activities, and from near absolute dependence on the national government for subsistence. Increasingly, they called for legislation permitting allotment in severalty of Indian land. As one agent commented: "As long as Indians lived in [communal] villages they will retain many of their old and injurious habits. . . . I trust that before another year is ended they will generally be located upon individual land or farms. From that date will begin their real and permanent progress." Other Americans, equally supportive of allotment legislation, were little more than potential land-grabbers. They exerted enormous and steady pressure on the government to liquidate most, if not all, of some 155 million acres of reservation land.

Allotment legislation was introduced in the closing session of the Forty-Fifth Congress (1879) and at the beginning of the Forty-Sixth Congress (1880). Those legislators in support of the proposed law agreed with the evaluation of Senator George H. Pendleton of Ohio, that "it must be our part to seek to foster and encourage within [the Indians] this trinity upon which all civilization depends—family, home, and [private ownership of] property." Yet the proposed legislation encountered unexpectedly heavy opposition. Both times it was defeated, in part out of fear that Indians were ill-prepared to hold and maintain private property, and because allotment seemed to stand little chance at the moment of achieving its intended results to advance the Indians' welfare. The minority report issued by the House Committee on Indian Affairs, typifying much of the opposition, stated, "However much we may differ from the humanitarians who are riding this hobby, we are certain that they will agree with us . . . that it does not make a farmer out of an Indian to give him a quarter section of land." Henry M. Teller of Colorado, the staunchest opponent of allotment in the Senate, characterized it as "a bill to despoil the Indians of their land and to make them vagabonds on the face of the earth." Teller predicted, with accuracy, that forty years after the passage of allotment legislation, when the Indians had been alienated by whites from their private allotments, they would "curse the hand that was raised professedly in their defense."

While allotment legislation failed during the Hayes presidency, the movement for it continued during the early 1880s. Hiram Pierce, both James A. Garfield's and Chester A. Arthur's Indian commissioner, pressed for congressional approval; although Henry Teller, now serving as Arthur's Secretary of Interior, strongly opposed it. Likewise, Grover Cleveland's commissioner, John D. C. Atkins, firmly supported allotment proposals. Success finally came on February 8, 1887, when President Cleveland signed the Dawes General Allotment Act into law; legislation that President Theodore Roosevelt in a later message to Congress characterized correctly as "a mighty pulverizing engine to break up the tribal mass." The Dawes Act authorized the president to subdivide the Indians' land into private plots without the consent of the tribes affected. A quarter section, or a 160-acre lot (the traditional plot of a white homestead), was awarded to the head of a family and smaller plots to individual family members. The communal lands that the government designated as surplus (that is, unallocated) were offered for sale to whites. The allottees' lands were held in trust by the federal government for twenty-five years, during which time the Interior Department controlled their economic life.

The allotment system proved an unqualified failure. Senator Henry Dawes's warning was correct: "Severalty must follow, not precede the transition from a wild blanket Indian to one having some aspirations for a better life." Accurate too was the cautious appraisal of Indian Commissioner, John Atkins. Eight months after passage of the Dawes Act he suggested in his annual report: "There is danger that the advocates of land in severalty will expect from the measure too immediate and pronounced success. Character, habits, and antecedents can not be changed by an enactment." Not only did allotment in severalty threaten the cohesiveness of community and challenge gender-based tribal mores about the appropriateness of males being farmers, it violated the Indians' deepest feelings about the place of human beings in nature. Ultimately the legislation also took away from tribes nearly 108 million acres of unallocated land, or seventy percent of the total that was left them at the conclusion of the Indian wars. For the most part, the allotment system failed to transform Indians into self-supporting independent farmers, herders, or ranchers; nor did it eliminate the necessity for federal reservations. The avowed purpose of allotment in severalty was to teach self-reliance and induce habits of industry by the holding and working of private property. By succeeding, the Indians could proudly wear a badge of civilization. Instead allotment hung like a millstone from the necks of most Indians, entrenching even more deeply Indian dependence on the government for subsistence, survival, and protection from land-hungry whites.

Americans widely viewed education, like allotment in severalty, as the panacea for solving the Indian question. It was not a new idea. As early as 1780, the Continental Congress appropriated $5,000, a large sum for that era, for the education of Indian students at Dartmouth College. For decades the national government relied on religious denominations to educate Indians at their missions. From 1819 onward, Congress authorized an annual appropriation for Indian education by missionary groups. By the end of the Indian wars in the 1870s, most Americans believed that the Indian could not continue to exist as an Indian and survive. The Board of Indian Commissioners surmised in 1875, "*education* must be regarded as a fundamental and indispensable factor," while one Indian commissioner remarked, "To educate the Indian in the ways of civilized . . . life is to preserve him from extinction." Survival, however, would come at the steep price of their Indian identity.

Reformers and the Indian Bureau were in general agreement that a complete separation from the aboriginal home environment was important in educating Indian youths in "civilized" ways and skills. Removing children from the influence of their elders and their cultural heritage was judged as critical in breaking the bonds of family, neighborhood, and ethnic identity that white Americans valued so highly when applied to themselves. Supporters of education for Indian youths also hoped that adults on the reservations would be more inclined to remain peaceful and give up their traditional ways if their children were confined in government schools many miles away. Few white Americans would have thought to liken this to the taking of hostages, however.

Although Indian schools had functioned for decades, beginning in 1879 off-reservation vocational boarding schools became an important dimension in federal Indian education. The impetus for this type of school came from the success in educating Indian youths at the Hampton Normal and Agricultural Institute at Hampton, Virginia. President Hayes, in his second annual message of December 1878, called Congress' attention to "the experiment recently inaugurated, in taking fifty Indian children, boys and girls, from different tribes, to [Hampton] . . . where they are to receive an elementary English education and training in agriculture and other useful works, to be returned to their tribes, after the completed course, as interpreters, instructors, and examples." Subsequently, Army Lieutenant Richard H. Pratt (later Captain and finally Brigadier General) established the first off-reservation boarding school for Indians, Carlisle Indian Industrial School.

Situated in old military barracks at Carlisle, Pennsylvania, this school opened in the fall of 1879 and soon boasted a student body of 158 pupils of both sexes, three-fourths of whom were males. The institution's motto, "Kill the Indian and save the man," succinctly summed up its mission. Pratt's two principal goals were to Americanize Indians through the classroom and to demonstrate to the American public that Indians were educable. Pratt elaborated on his educational theories in his volume, *How to Deal with the Indians: The Potency of Environment*. The key to Indian advancement lay in educating the children. "There is little hope of the civilization of the older wild Indians," concluded Commissioner Ezra Hayt, "and the only practical question is how to control and govern him, so that his savage instincts shall be kept from violent outbreak." Commissioner Hiram Price concurred fully: "Educational . . . activities among Indian youth would reclaim the Indian population from barbarism, idolatry and savage life."

Pratt patterned Carlisle, which became the model for subsequent government off-reservation boarding schools, after manual labor institutions. The curriculum included reading, writing, arithmetic, and spelling, but the greatest emphasis was placed on pragmatic training in domestic skills for females and on agricultural and manual arts for males. The Indian pupils also were instructed continually in the precepts of Christianity, American culture, and patriotic citizenship. Such instruction, neither wrong nor harmful in itself, took place at a time when the children's traditional culture was being systematically destroyed and when their relatives residing on the reservation were subjected to scorn and ridicule by missionaries, reformers, and Indian Bureau agents because they had not mastered the new learning. The subjects of history and geography proved the most useful tools in demonstrating to the children their rank on the scale of civilization. Educators hoped that pupils would accept the degradation of their own culture and history as an objective fact, and in turn would be spurred to seek improvement. An examination marked "excellent" was published by one school to demonstrate the institution's pedagogical triumph:

Question: To what race do we all belong?
Answer: The Human race.

Question: How many classes belong to this race?
Answer: There are five large classes belonging to the Human race.

Question: Which are the first?
Answer: The white people are the strongest.

Question: Which are the next?
Answer: The Mongolians or yellows.

Question: The next?
Answer: The Ethiopeans or blacks.

Question: Next?
Answer: The Americans or reds.

Question: Tell me something of the white people.
Answer: The Caucasian is away ahead of all of the other races—
he thought more than any other race, he thought that
somebody must made the earth, and if the white people did not find that out, nobody would never know
it—it is God who made the world.

On another examination one Indian pupil surmised: "The
red people they big savages; they don't know anything." Examination questions also stressed the white historical experience to the exclusion of that of the Indian youths. A third
grade history test asked students to "tell about the voyage of
Columbus and why he wanted to go," as well as "Who were
the Pilgrims and where did they land?" In like manner, a fifth
grade exam questioned, "Why did England tax the colonies?
Tell about the 'Stamp Act'."

The schools the children were required to attend were
strict and authoritarian. They were also, although perhaps not
intentionally, cruel. Rarely allowed to go home to visit their
families, the children were forbidden to speak their native language upon arrival at the boarding schools and were required
to remain silent until they could speak English. "This language,
which is good enough for a white man and black man, ought
to be good enough for a red man," asserted Commissioner
Atkins. "It is also believed that teaching an Indian youth in
his own barbarous dialect is a positive detriment to him. The
first step to be taken to civilization, to teaching the Indian the
mischief . . . of continuing in their barbarous practices, is to
teach the English language." Matriculation typically resulted
in rechristening, as youths forfeited their actual names in favor of "American" ones. The regimen at Carlisle, and other

boarding schools, was steeped in military discipline. Students dressed in cadet uniforms, marched to the classroom and dormitory, and drilled daily in military formations. Youths failing to follow rules were punished with denial of food, or even whippings.

The experiment at Carlisle, little less its putative success, so impressed the national government that the executive branch opened more off-reservation schools and Congress annually increased its appropriation for Indian education. In 1877 the general appropriation by Congress for the education of Indians was $30,000. In 1880 it jumped to $75,000; in 1885 to $992,800; and by 1890 appropriations reached $1,364,368. Eventually the government erected an elaborate three-tiered system of Indian education in the Far West, comprised of reservation day schools, reservation boarding schools, and off-reservation boarding schools like Carlisle. As the number of institutions multiplied, school attendance increased from 3,598 Indian pupils in 1877 to 12,232 in 1890.

The system of Indian education was successful in accomplishing half of its intended aim: it destroyed much of the social cohesiveness and the tribal identification of the Indians. However it did not produce many "White Indians." On the contrary, it bred deeper resentment toward the dominant white society and its culture. It also produced in its wards a keener awareness of the plight of their people and, at least in some, a determination to resist. Some observers pointed out that Indians who attended government schools like Carlisle forgot their training and lessons in "civilization" upon their return to the reservation. Others charged that those who returned were a divisive, rather than enlightening, influence within their tribes and were often shunned by their own people. Historian Francis Paul Prucha has observed that Americanization measures, such as schooling, "did not quickly transform the Indians. Rather, it broke down their heritage and cultural pride without substituting anything in its place, until the Indians became a demoralized people, lost between their historic identity and the white culture they could not accept." Educator

David Wallace Adams concludes that in the aftermath of the era of war "the next campaign was . . . waged in the classroom. The issue at hand was no longer the dispossession of the Indian's land, but rather the possession of his mind, heart, and soul. It was to be a gentle war, but a war just the same." Polingaysi Qoyawayma, rechristened Elizabeth Q. White, attended Sherman Institute at Riverside, California, for four years. Of her experience in the classroom she recalled in her autobiography *No Turning Back*: "As a Hopi, I was misunderstood by the white man; as a convert of the missionaries, I was looked upon with suspicion by the Hopi people. . . . The white man killed the buffalo because the buffalo presented a problem. Indian children are a problem too, but can't be so preemtorily disposed of." Reflecting her own inner confusion and chaos, she concluded with the plaintive assertion, "Don't ask them to peel off their brown skin and become white men."

Americanization: "To Make the World Wiser and Better"

Federal Indian policy from 1879 onward was modified to reflect the belief that government's foremost responsibility was to Americanize the Indians, providing them the wherewithal to assimilate into the mainstream of American life and culture. Only in this manner could the Indians' actual survival be assured. No longer was it sufficient that the Indians simply accept absolute confinement on reservations. They now must forfeit their culture and sacrifice the traditional customs and values that had restored some meaning to their existence. If the Americanization program failed to transform the Indians and solve the Indian question, the Indians would become, as Commissioner Francis A. Walker predicted, "vagabonds in the midst of civilization, which will be festering sores on the communities near which they are located."

Hand in hand with this supposition was the belief that successful acculturation would produce another group of "hyphenated" American citizens. As Polish immigrants in the later nineteenth century became Polish Americans, or Italian immigrants became Italian Americans, so too Indians would be submerged in the American melting pot and come up Indian Americans. Government and civilian planners agreed that sooner or later the unique Indian type would be extinguished. Most Americans were convinced that would not be a bad outcome. Even the more sympathetic believed it would be the inevitable outcome. Everyone concurred, however, that the chief result could only be positive: There would no longer be an Indian question if there were no longer people identifiable as Indians, or people who identified themselves as Indians.

Supporters of Americanization gave little consideration to the possibility that the policy might not be the correct, or fair, or even possible, course. "Savage and civilized life cannot live and prosper on the same ground," Commissioner Hiram Price declared in 1881. "If the Indians are to be civilized and become a happy and prosperous people, which is certainly the object and intention of our Government ... the few must yield to the many." Nor would such distinctions have occurred to the great majority of policymakers and humanitarian reformers, considering their belief system. The program they erected was rooted in a series of deeply held premises and propositions about the nature of the American experience, the lessons of history, and the dominant self-image of American society in the latter third of the nineteenth century.

One premise stressed the desirability of a homogeneous American citizenry. The multiple political, social, and demographic forces propelled by the massive economic expansion of the post–Civil War period severely undermined America's cultural "island communities." Late-nineteenth-century modernization also provoked efforts to impose a heretofore unrealized degree of cultural uniformity upon the republic's social fabric. Increasingly, spokespeople of the dominant culture urged that the United States be blanketed by culturally homogeneous communities, woven into uniformity by common social, educational, and economic institutions. Conformity would be demanded and, if need be, imposed. Successful integration of "cultural aliens" (be they Indians or European and Asian immigrants, for example) would confirm the post–Civil War definition, expectation, and self-image of the United States.

Social evolution was another belief buttressing the Americanization policy. Americans have always had a strong tendency to accept that science provides ultimate truth. Society in turn adjusts to these truths. The attitude of reformers and Indian policymakers found common ground with, and was reinforced by, the research and writings of practitioners in the emerging fields of anthropology and ethnology; foremost among whom was Lewis Henry Morgan of the Smithsonian Institution's Bureau of American Ethnology. Morgan's *The League of the Ho-de-no-sau-nee or Iroquois* (1855) pioneered the use of field observations in the study of Indian tribes. His widely acclaimed *Ancient Society*, published in 1877, buttressed social evolutionary ideas. Henry Adams, the insightful albeit skeptical commentator of the American experience, proclaimed this book to be nothing less than "the foundation of all future works in American historical science." History, to social evolution proponents such as L. H. Morgan and John Wesley Powell, founding director of the Bureau of Ethnology, was not merely the accurate chronicling of people and events of the past. It was a story infused with symbolic meaning. History's foremost purpose was to explain the progress of humankind's ascent on a vertical ladder. According to proponents of social evolution, peoples must pass through three principal stages of cultural development: from savagism, to barbarism, to civilization. (They would have accepted "Americanization" as a synonym for the final developmental stage.) Morgan taught that the degree of civilization, or the extent of social development of all peoples, could be accurately plotted along this continuum.

The scale of civilization was invested with three immutable laws. First, the stage of civilization was superior to the two preceding stages. Second, civilization would always triumph over barbarism and savagism. And third, those people highest on the ladder had a special responsibility to assist the development of those beneath them. This burden, the "white man's burden" using Rudyard Kipling's phrase, stressed the obligation of the white race both to Westernize and Christianize the "darker races" throughout the world. The Lake Mohonk platform of 1895 declared: "Our American civilization is founded upon Christianity. A pagan people can not be fitted for citizenship without learning the principles and acquiring something of the spirit of a Christian people." The burden also was underpinned by paternalism: "We must in a great measure do the necessary thinking for them, and then in the most humane way possible induce them to accept our conclusions," Carl Schurz stated. "This is in most cases much more easily accomplished than might generally be supposed; for, especially in the transition from savage to civilized life, the Indian looks up with natural respect to the superior wisdom of the 'Great Father.' " Reformers acknowledged that the transition would be difficult and often traumatic, but the results would be worth the price paid. The Indians are "in the middle of that swift and treacherous stream which divides civilization from barbarism and which all Indians must cross," asserted Herbert Welsh. "Doubtless its current will carry some away and its quicksands will engulf others, while those who succeed in getting safely over into the promised land will be both stronger and cleaner than they would have been were they not forced to cross it."

Social evolution provided a powerful rationale for why Indians needed immediate assistance, and an equally strong stimulus for reformers to labor diligently to Americanize them and for the government to support their efforts. Indians clearly were relics of an earlier, more primitive, cultural order: "barbarous men" who must be taught to live in a "civilized way," proclaimed reformers. Once they affirmed this premise, reformers shouldered the attendant obligation to provide the means for ascent. Many of them had decried the wars that the United States had recently fought to effect the policy of Concentration. They reluctantly acknowledged them, however, as the harsh but necessary means to fulfill the noble obligation of raising the Indians to a higher level of cultural development. Reservations would be the social laboratories—the "cultural hot-houses"—where Americanization programs could germinate, blossom, and bear fruit under controlled conditions. There, Indians would be provided with the tools for ascent up the scale of civilization. Yet, in the end it was the Indians' choice alone whether they would become an "American beauty rose," in John D. Rockefeller's parabolic expression, or remain a cultural dinosaur. Those who refused the opportunity provided by white society invited extinction. Reflecting the era's faith in another dominant credo, Social Darwinism, Hampton Institute's newspaper the *Southern Workman* explained, "Put [the Indian] under the usual and natural conditions of life; the necessity of labor, law and order, with a good practical education for his children, and we shall see the survival of the fittest."

The policy of Americanization posed a grave threat to the Indians, and they realized it. Once confined within federal reservations under rigid supervision and scrutiny, Indians wrestled mightily with their new situation. Some actively sought to cooperate with the Americans. They believed that their accustomed way of life was gone forever and that their future depended on adaptation to their new role. Others advocated resistance to white society and the government's newest solution to the Indian question, but how? There was little consensus, because there was little in their environment that offered choices. Armed resistance, used to resist earlier "solutions," was out of the question. Flight from the reservation seemed increasingly an unattractive alternative, as white settlers and entrepreneurs transformed their old habitats. Passive resistance, a strategy difficult to implement effectively, held little hope of success among a people who still revered the ethos of a warrior culture. Passivity, in fact, ultimately proved more debilitating than fortifying for those Indians who attempted it, serving only to increase their alienation, discouragement, and dejection.

While a large number of Indians floundered in bewildered uncertainty, perplexed about how to deal with the present or the future, many refused to submit passively to the changes that Americans now tried to impose upon them. Gradually, various responses emerged in an effort to forestall or resist the policy of Americanization. Some resisted the new government system of education, hiding their children from educators and Indian Bureau agents. Others turned to the heavy consumption of alcohol as a means both of tempering the unpleasantness of reservation life and spurning white society. Some, grasping for vestiges of their old life-style, readily joined Wild West exhibitions and itinerant Wild West shows that toured the eastern United States and Europe, demonstrating for excited white audiences their prowess at riding horses and shooting. Still others, in defiance of Indian Bureau regulations and federal statutes, practiced time-honored religious rites such as the Sun Dance, the Snake Dance, or the Katchina ceremony.

Many Indians, clinging to the hope of throwing off white domination and reasserting an identity, resisted by means of new spiritual directions that stressed redemption and regeneration. The Ghost Dance, for example, based on the visions of the Paiute Wovoka, promised that God in the fullness of time would expel the white people and return the earth to the Indians, the living as well as the dead. However, the battle at Wounded Knee in 1890 destroyed people's faith in Wovoka's message and the Ghost Dance. The Peyote cult also emerged in the latter nineteenth century, based on the sacramental use of peyote buttons. At first stressing the hallucinogenic effects of the peyote buttons, the Peyote cult gradually grew to include an ethical code of temperate behavior, honesty and truthfulness, devotion to one's family, and the value of traditional customs and mores. By the early twentieth century, the Peyote cult had become institutionalized as the Native American Church.

United States Indian policy from 1879 through the 1920s had two predominant goals: first, detribalization and the destruction of "Indianism" with its accompanying dress, traditions, religions, philosophies, languages, and social, economic and political systems; and second, continual instruction in American cultural and economic ways and beliefs with the objective of molding them into "White Indians," that is, an ethnic group indistinguishable from any other in the dominant society. The ultimate ambition of the Americanization policy was to legitimate the new cultural experience as a dignified and proper way of life, not merely to coerce the Indians into being practitioners of it. Although Washington modified the policy from time to time, the modification never departed in any significant way from the basic objective: to solve the Indian question; an objective pursued, but never realized, since the founding of the republic, forming an organic whole in the history of United States–Indian relations.

As the nineteenth century drew to a close, tempered optimism prevailed among whites that the vexed question was closer than ever to being solved, even though many Indians consciously, and successfully, resisted the policy of Americanization. As Indian Commissioner Hiram Price noted confidently in 1891, two months after the battle of Wounded Knee:

Since the plow and the sickle have, to a great extent, driven the tomahawk and the scalping knife from the field, thousands of Indians have learned that labor is ennobling and not degrading, and are beginning to see the dawn of a brighter future, where they may stand side by side with those whose aim is to make the world wiser and better.

Indian perception was notably different. Chief Seattle's observation perhaps best portrays a sentiment dramatically different from that of Price:

My people are few. They resemble the scattering trees of a storm-swept plain. . . . There was a time when our people covered the land as the waves of a wind-ruffled sea cover its shell-paved floor, but that time long since passed away with the greatness of tribes that are now but a mournful memory.

Bibliographical Essay

It is hoped that the reader, especially the initiate, will seek out other viewpoints and interpretations of Indian-white relations. The most comprehensive compilations of published titles are *A Bibliographical Guide to the History of Indian-White Relations in the United States* (Chicago, 1977) and *Indian-White Relations in the United States: A Bibliography of Works Published 1975–1980* (Lincoln, 1982), both edited by Francis Paul Prucha. For those who wish to go a step further in their investigation, the National Archives and Records Service holds the essential primary documents pertinent to the history of United States Indian policy. Most are contained in Record Group 75, Records of the Bureau of Indian Affairs, and Record Group 48, Records of the Secretary of the Interior. Helpful directories to the collections in the custody of the National Archives and Records Service are Edward E. Hill's two volumes: *Guide to Records in the National Archives of the United States Relating to American Indians* (Washington, 1981) and *Guide to Records in the National Archives of the United States Relating to Records in the National Archives of the United States* (Washington, 1981).

Since the 1960s a large and expanding literature has emerged about the history of Indian-white relations and the American Indians that presents them as interesting and important people. This attitude, however, has not always prevailed, as two prominent scholars of the American Indians have pointed out. Arrell Morgan Gibson noted that most historians have largely overlooked or ignored evidence that the Indians were more than mere "bit players in the American historical drama." Francis Paul Prucha asserted that "until recent decades Indians did not occupy a very prominent place in writings about American history, and this disinterest and disdain were reflected in high school and college textbooks." David Muzzey, for example, whose textbooks influenced generations of American school children in the early twentieth century, conceded, in his own words, that although the Indians "had some noble qualities ... at bottom they were a treacherous, cruel people." Too frequently writers, until recently, have portrayed the Indians simply as a savage barrier to American pioneer progress, characterizing them as cruel, barbarous, half-civilized, and childlike.

This earlier historiographic pattern has changed dramatically from the 1960s onward, coinciding with, and initially stimulated by, the turbulent events of that decade. Activism bloomed among the American Indians as similar quickenings stirred among other disadvantaged groups in the United States. Increasingly, Indian activists urged the federal government to become more concerned about the difficulties of Indian life. They pointed out bitterly that of all minority groups in the United States, the American Indians were the poorest; three out of five lived below the federally established poverty line. They demanded that something be done, and done quickly, to address the blighted existence of their people, which owed in large measure to federal Indian policy as it developed in the nineteenth century and has continued into the present century. Indians pressed for long-buried rights and demanded that white America fulfill its many unkept promises. The non-Indian world's consciousness was jolted into recognition of these demands by three events: the nineteen-month occupation of Alcatraz Island in San Francisco Bay beginning in the fall of 1969; the takeover of the Bureau of Indian Affairs offices in Washington, D.C., in 1972; and the occupation of Wounded

Knee, South Dakota, by members of the activist American Indian Movement in early 1973.

Wounded Knee received widespread attention from the media and probably even more than the other acts of protest made the American public aware of the Indians and their plight. It also stirred an increasing number of writers and scholars to reinvestigate Indian history and the history of Indian-white relations and offer a new understanding of them. The resultant literary output divides into at least a half dozen groups. The first two groups, judgmental and conspicuously pro-Indian in an effort to awaken the consciences of Americans and redress the past, are Indian activist writing, such as *Custer Died for Your Sins: An Indian Manifesto* (New York, 1969) and *Behind the Trail of Broken Treaties* (New York, 1974) by Vine Deloria, Jr., and the writing of white critics of federal policy and white actions toward Indians, such as Dee Brown's *Bury My Heart at Wounded Knee: An Indian History of the American West* (New York, 1970) and Richard Drinnon's *Facing West: The Metaphysics of Indian-Hating and Empire-Building* (Minneapolis, 1980).

The other four groups sought a less polemical, more impartial treatment of the subject. General histories of Indian-white relations, the third group, typically concentrating on governmental Indian policy as the vehicle for exposition and interpretation, provide an introduction to, and overview of, the subject. Among the most useful are Angie Debo, *A History of the Indians in the United States* (Norman, 1970); Arrell Morgan Gibson, *The American Indians: Prehistory to the Present* (Lexington, Mass., 1980); D'Arcy McNickle, *Native American Tribalism: Indian Survivals and Renewals* (New York, 1973); Francis Paul Prucha, *The Great Father* (2 volumes, Lincoln, 1984); Wilcomb E. Washburn, *The Indian in America* (New York, 1975); and Philip Weeks, ed., *The American Indian Experience: A Profile, 1524 to the Present* (Arlington Heights, Ill., 1988). Two excellent briefer accounts are William T. Hagan, *American Indians* (Chicago, 1979) and Francis Paul Prucha, *The Indian in American Society* (Berkeley, 1985).

The fourth group is tribal histories. While offering detailed accounts of Indian societies and their histories, most concentrate on the postcontact period for tribes and on their relationship with white society. For this reason they are helpful in gaining a greater understanding of Indian-white relations as well as specific tribes. For example, tribal histories shed great light on the details of removal under the policy of Separation and the resettlement of tribes in the southern portion of the Indian Territory. They include Arthur H. DeRosier, Jr., *The Removal of the Choctaw Nation* (Knoxville, 1970); Arrell Morgan Gibson, *The Chickasaws* (Norman, 1971); Grace S. Woodward, *The Cherokees* (Norman, 1963); Edwin C. McReynolds, *The Seminoles* (Norman, 1957); and Angie Debo, *The Rise and Fall of the Choctaw Republic* (Norman, 1934) and *The Road to Disappearance* (Norman, 1941), which is about the Creeks. Colonization of tribes in the northern portion of the Indian Territory as a result of the Separation policy is explained in other tribal histories: Bert Anson, *The Miami Indians* (Norman, 1970); William T. Hagan, *The Sac and Fox Indians* (Norman, 1958); and Arrell Morgan Gibson, *The Kickapoos: Lords of the Middle Border* (Norman, 1963).

Several excellent tribal histories are invaluable in gaining a fuller understanding of the era of the Plains Wars, particularly Donald J. Berthrong, *The Southern Cheyennes* (Norman, 1963); Peter J. Powell, *Sweet Medicine: The Continuing Role of the Sacred Arrows, the Sun Dance, and the Sacred Buffalo Hat in Northern Cheyenne History* (2 volumes, Norman, 1969) and *People of the Sacred Mountain: A History of the Northern Cheyenne Chiefs and Warrior Societies, 1830–1879* (2 volumes, New York, 1981), the latter an especially enlightening study because it provides an Indian view of Indian-white relations and interracial conflict; Mildred Mayhall, *The Kiowas* (Norman, 1962); Roy W. Meyer's *History of the Santee Sioux: United States Indian Policy on Trial* (Lincoln, 1967); Robert M. Utley, *The Last Days of the Sioux Nation* (New Haven, Conn., 1963); Ernest Wallace and E. Adamson Hoebel, *The Comanches: Lords of the South Plains* (Norman, 1952); and

Donald L. Worcester, *The Apaches: Eagles of the Southwest* (Norman, 1979). Two other tribal studies, William T. Hagan's *United States–Comanche Relations: The Reservation Years* (New Haven, Conn., 1976) and Donald J. Berthrong's *The Cheyenne and Arapahoe Ordeal: Reservation and Agency Life in the Indian Territory, 1875–1907* (Norman, 1976), stress conditions for Indians during the reservation period and specific tribal responses to the policy of Americanization.

Biographies, both about Indians and those whites who exerted influence upon relations with Indians, constitute the fifth group. R. David Edmunds's revisionist accounts *Tecumseh and the Quest for Indian Leadership* (Boston, 1984) and *The Shawnee Prophet* (Lincoln, 1983) are important in examining the fate suffered by the northern tribes as the press of white settlement penetrated the Old Northwest. Kenny A. Franks, *Stand Watie and the Agony of the Cherokee Nation* (Memphis, 1979) and Gary E. Moulton, *John Ross, Cherokee Chief* (Athens, Ga., 1978) provide interpretations of the struggle within Cherokee society, both in Georgia and after removal to Oklahoma, to chart that tribe's national course.

Important aspects of the efforts of the Plains Indian tribes to resist the policy of Concentration are developed in other biographies like James C. Olson, *Red Cloud and the Sioux Problem* (Lincoln, 1965) and Angie Debo, *Geronimo the Man, His Time, His Place* (Norman, 1976). William H. Armstrong's *Warrior in Two Camps: Ely S. Parker, Union General and Seneca Chief* (Syracuse, 1978) assesses another side to the era of the Plains Wars by detailing the role played by Ulysses S. Grant's friend and first commissioner of Indian Affairs.

Informative biographical essays of the commissioners of Indian Affairs and their role in shaping and executing federal Indian policy appear in Robert M. Kvasnicka and Herman J. Viola, eds., *The Commissioners of Indian Affairs, 1824–1977* (Lincoln, 1979). Biographies of principal American military personnel in the Plains Wars are plentiful. Offering a vantage point different from that of the Indian biographies for understanding the wars to implement and enforce the policy of Concentration, they also frequently serve as a defense of federal Indian policy. Robert G. Athearn's *William Tecumseh Sherman and the Settlement of the West* (Norman, 1956) describes the role played by one of the dominant military figures in that era. Volumes about other important U.S. commanders include Virginia W. Johnson, *The Unregimented General: A Biography of Nelson A. Miles* (Boston, 1962); John W. Bailey, *Pacifying the Plains: General Alfred Terry and the Decline of the Sioux, 1866–1890* (Westport, Conn., 1979); and John A. Carpenter, *Sword and Olive Branch: Oliver Otis Howard* (Pittsburg, 1964).

Period and episodic studies make up the sixth group. Indian policy in the Jeffersonian era, underpinned by its intellectual rationalizations, is treated in Bernard W. Sheehan, *Seeds of Extinction: Jeffersonian Philanthropy and the American Indians* (Chapel Hill, 1973) and Reginald Horsman, *Expansion and American Indian Policy, 1783–1812* (East Lansing, 1967); while important studies about the origins and implementation of the policy of Separation include Reginald Horsman, *The Origins of Indian Removal, 1815–1824* (East Lansing, 1970) and Ronald M. Satz, *American Indian Policy in the Jacksonian Era* (Lincoln, 1975). Examinations of American expansion into the trans-Mississippi West during the 1840s and 1850s and changing federal Indian policy leading to the policy of Concentration are few. The best account is Robert A. Trennert, Jr., *Alternatives to Extinction: Federal Indian Policy and the Beginnings of the Reservation System, 1846–51* (Philadelphia, 1975). Robert M. Utley's *The Indian Frontier of the American West, 1846–1890* (Albuquerque, 1984) is an excellent period piece about United States–Indian relations during the second half of the nineteenth century.

Much recent scholarly attention has been directed toward the post–Civil War period, especially Indian reform efforts and the Americanization policy. Important works include Robert W. Mardock, *The Reformers and the Indian* (Columbia, Mo., 1971); Henry E. Fritz, *The Movement for Indian Assimilation, 1860–1890* (Philadelphia, 1963); Loring B. Priest, *Uncle Sam's Stepchildren: The Reformation of United States Indian Policy,*

1865–1887 (New York, 1969); Francis Paul Prucha, *American Indian Policy in Crisis: Christian Reformers and the Indian, 1865–1900* (Norman, 1976); and Frederick E. Hoxie, *A Final Promise: The Campaign to Assimilate the Indians, 1880–1920* (Lincoln, 1984).

Episodic studies are bountiful. Many focus on the more dramatic martial events in Indian-white relations, of late especially in the West during the nineteenth century. The Santee Sioux uprising and its aftermath has been most fully explored in Kenneth Carley, *The Sioux Uprising of 1862* (St. Paul, 1961); and C. M. Oehler, *The Great Sioux Uprising* (New York, 1959). Stan Hoig's *The Sand Creek Massacre* (Norman, 1961) is a good survey of events in Colorado and the assault on the Southern Cheyennes at Sand Creek by John Chivington's militia. Dorothy M. Johnson, *The Bloody Bozeman: The Perilous Trail to Montana's Gold* (New York, 1971), explores the American conflict with the Oglala Red Cloud over the issue of the Bozeman Trail.

Examinations of the Red River War, the last major conflict on the southern plains, are contained in James L. Haley, *The Buffalo War: The History of the Red River Indian Uprising of 1874* (New York, 1976), and Stan Hoig, *The Battle of the Washita: The Sheridan-Custer Indian Campaign of 1867–69* (Garden City, N.Y., 1976). The concluding conflict of the Plains Wars has drawn considerable literary attention. Events surrounding the Great Sioux War are treated in Donald Jackson, *Custer's Gold: The United States Cavalry Expedition of 1874* (New Haven, Conn., 1966); J. W. Vaughn, *The Reynolds Campaign on the Powder River* (Norman, 1961); and John S. Gray, *Centennial Campaign: The Sioux War of 1876* (Fort Collins, Colo., 1976).

These six groups dominate the literature of Indian-white relations, but new approaches in methodology have appeared in recent years, too. They include institutional studies such as Paul Stuart, *The Indian Office: Growth and Development of an American Institution, 1865–1900* (Ann Arbor, 1979); land policy studies such as Leonard A. Carlson's *Indians, Bureaucrats, and Land* (Westport, Conn., 1981), which explores the Dawes Act and its effects on Indians; and ecological and environmental studies such as Gary C. Goodwin's *Cherokees in Transition: A Study of Changing Culture and Environment Prior to 1775* (Chicago, 1977), William Cronon's *Changes in the Land: Indians, Colonists, and the Ecology of New England* (New York, 1983), and Christopher Vecsey and Robert W. Venables, eds., *American Indian Environments: Ecological Issues in Native American History* (Syracuse, 1980).

INDEX

*Farewell, My Nation: The American Indian
and the United States, 1820–1890* was copy-
edited and proofread by Claudia Lamm
Wood. Production editor was Lucy Herz. The
text was typeset by Impressions, Inc., and
printed and bound by Edwards Brothers, Inc.

The cover and text were designed by Roger
Eggers.